IN SEARCH OF DREAMS

SUNY Series in Dream Studies
Robert L. Van de Castle, Editor

IN SEARCH OF DREAMS

RESULTS OF
EXPERIMENTAL DREAM RESEARCH

Inge Strauch and Barbara Meier

Foreword by David Foulkes

STATE UNIVERSITY OF NEW YORK PRESS

Published by
State University of New York Press, Albany

© 1996 State University of New York

All rights reserved

Printed in the United States of America

First published in German as Den Träumen auf der Spur:
Ergebnisse der experimentellen Traumforschung
© 1992 Verlag Hans Huber, Bern

For information, address State University of New York Press,
State University Plaza, Albany, N.Y. 12246

Production by Diane Ganeles
Marketing by Theresa Abad Swierzowski

Library of Congress Cataloging-in-Publication Data

Strauch, Inge.
    [Träumen auf der Spur. English]
    In search of dreams : results of experimental dream research /
Inge Strauch and Barbara Meier.
        p.   cm. — (SUNY series in dream studies)
    Includes bibliographical references and index.
    ISBN 0-7914-2759-5 (alk. paper). — ISBN 0-7914-2760-9 (pbk. :
alk. paper)
    1. Dreams. 2. Dream interpretation. I. Meier, Barbara.
II. Title. III. Series.
BF1091.S7713 1996
154.6'3—dc20   95-8151
                                                                      CIP

10 9 8 7 6 5 4 3 2 1

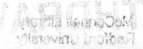

Contents

Foreword

As the reader of this small but substantial book, you are in for a rare treat: a scientifically sound yet thoroughly comprehensible and enjoyable account of what laboratory study has revealed about dreams and dreaming. There can be very few questions that you ever have asked about human dreamlife that are not addressed, and, evidence permitting, answered clearly, in the pages that follow. As you read along, you also will find yourself asking new questions, and thinking about dreams and dreaming in ways that otherwise might not have occurred to you. At the end, you should have as clear a picture as now exists of both the accomplishments and the continuing challenges of dream science.

The phrase 'dream science' may sound oxymoronic. But the authors nicely describe the psychophysiological discoveries some forty years ago that have revolutionized dream psychology in our time. In the same year, 1953, that the report of the discovery of REM sleep was first published, a psychologist reviewing dream research in the first half of the twentieth century admitted, in effect, that such research had not resolved any important issues about dreaming and was at a standstill. As this book will show, much has been learned about dreams and dreaming since 1953. This has been the case not so much because physiology provided answers where psychology couldn't, but because the recording procedures of the psychophysiological dream laboratory gave dream psychologists, for the first time, a way to study human dreamlife systematically and representatively. The authors are quite clear in their commitment to this new methodology, and, in their own research, have exploited it widely and well.

Much of the research which the authors describe and explain is from their own laboratory in Zürich (where I recently had the great pleasure of collaborating with them). Through the years, successive generations of students have conducted thesis research at this laboratory in numbers that would both astonish and enervate any American academic. And yet the impression is not that of a joyless research 'factory', but of genuine collaboration and mutual enjoyment in the pursuit of truth. The result of all of this effort is the large databank of representatively sampled and systematically analyzed dreams on which the authors base most of their discussion.

But this does not mean that the book is, in any sense, a parochial one. On the one hand, when the theoretical or empirical contributions of others are relevant, they are appropriately mentioned. On the other hand, one of the quiet pleasures of this book for North American dream researchers will lie in the degree to which Zürich observations fall neatly in line with their own.

Another pleasure of the book, this one more for the general reader than the North American researcher, lies in its whole-hearted commitment to the basic description of dreaming. The characterization of dream phenomenology has played a relatively minor role in our dream research. We are in such a hurry to 'manipulate' some aspect of dreaming that we fail to note the baseline properties of that aspect; we are so deeply enmeshed in a theory about some particular aspect of dreaming that we don't locate that aspect in its whole dream context. This is part of a larger picture in which our psychological science seems to have become alienated from its wellspring in simple human curiosity, valuing ingenuity and complexity rather than the sort of basic description that most directly addresses the sources of our curiosity. The authors of this book have put matters in a proper perspective: before performing fancy 'manipulations' or weaving elaborate theory, they want first to investigate exactly what it is that dreaming is. With systematic analyses of information from their databank, they then proceed to do this about as well as anyone ever has.

Another distinctive way in which this book meshes nicely with basic human curiosity is its admirable blending of the general and the particular. Some dream books are scarcely more than collections of individual dreams, and few of us are likely to be that interested in someone else's dreams. Other dream books are so generalized that individual dreams hardly ever make an appearance. This book's authors have chosen the happy middle path: important generalizations are almost invariably illustrated by particular dream reports.

Even in the modern dream research community, which likes to see itself as much more scientific than its questionnaire-wielding or deep-interpreting predecessors, there is much theoretical dispute over the meaning or importance of particular observations. Dream books often seem to be written more to make some ideological point than to convey to the reader the current state of the evidence. I think that you will find that this book is a refreshing exception to this generalization. The authors have no visible axes to grind, no particular enemies to refute, and no positions to defend regardless of the evidence. I commend them on adhering to data rather than presupposition, and on giving you what is the best all-around current introduction to dream psychology. If I had to recommend a single book to a friend who expressed an interest in dreaming, or if I had to choose just one book to teach dreaming to beginning students, this would be the one.

DAVID FOULKES

Preface
and Acknowledgments

This book addresses readers who, in addition to their own dream experience, would like to know more about the world of dreams generally. We offer insight into methods and results of dream research and attempt a comprehensive presentation of the ways in which our dreams surface. We describe, in detail, the creative means that enable dreams to transform specific themes, how dream content is revealed, where its building blocks originate, and how dreams are embedded within the course of sleep and of the waking experience.

Our findings are based on the evaluation of dreams we elicited within a sleep laboratory, utilizing standardized conditions. Dreamers were mainly young adults who spent several nights in the lab, were awakened from their sleep several times, and asked about their dreams.

We deal with different aspects of the dream experience by using primarily the results of our own studies. We cannot provide complete accounts of the many studies undertaken by dream researchers during the past thirty-five years; but we have selected several studies to trace the development of dream research and to illustrate the extent of dream investigations.

Our research approach is concerned with the nature of dreams and with the way in which the dream experience may be characterized generally. Within this framework, any purely personal meaning that a dream may yield must fade into the background, as this would enter a realm of dream experiences that can only be presented individually and which, at any rate, eludes the experimental approach.

As the case material presented in the body of this work indicates, our research took place in Switzerland, specifically in the city of Zürich. The dreams that form the basis of our evaluations in this book were mainly collected as part of studies undertaken in obtaining academic theses. Depending on the aims of these dream studies, additional information was obtained or special coding techniques were applied, which were then incorporated into our presentations.

We are indebted to Renata Ackermann, Myriam Borioli, Regula Brändli, Jean-Martin Büttner, Micha Gross, Sonia Hofer, Richard Korbel, Ulrike Kunz, Ariane Loepfe, Mario Marques, Ursula Niederer, Thomas Sacher, Roberto Saredi, Michael Spitz, Stephan Stauffer, Beat Steiger, Fränzi Straumann and Doris Waldvogel, who conscientiously looked after the dreamers in our sleep laboratory. Over the years, all of them contributed to the collection of the large numbers of dreams that helped to build up our Dream Databank.

We most particularly thank Lotte Böhringer for her attentive and helpful survey of this manuscript.

Finally, we wish to express our gratitude to Martin Ebon (New York), who took time from his own schedule as an author to undertake a patient and meticulous translation of this book.

1

An Approach
to the Subject of Dreams

There has been a great deal of speculation about the dream, and much has been said and written. The subject of dreams remains inexhaustible, because the variety of dreams is unlimited; it is stimulating, because we do not know how dreams originate, and it is ultimately provocative, because there has, so far, been no answer to the question of why we dream. Beyond this, dreams are particularly fascinating because they take us into a world of experiences, where, seemingly separated from our waking lives, we lead a second existence. In dreams, we create our own world, during which we encounter experiences that appear as real as when we are awake.

Dreams are purely personal experiences, and the dreamer alone is witness to the dream. Even when, while dreaming, we relate to an environment, we only seem to share our experience with other people. It is only when we look back on our dream, and report it on awakening, that we are able to integrate the dream into the waking world. And while dreams belong entirely into our private sphere, they are nevertheless related to the community, because all people dream, and our dreams deal with people and their world.

Many common ideas concerning the nature of dreams are influenced by everyday experiences. In our individual experience, we are singularly impressed by the unusual and striking features of dreams that startle us in daily lives and thereby manage to hold our interest.

What Features Make Dreams Particularly Interesting?

Dreams continue to surprise us. We are unable to anticipate them, can't tell when they will happen, or what their topics are likely to be. Even though the dreamer is the only one who invents the dream, he or she is nevertheless merely an unconscious, unknowing creator, not able to select the dream's theme, and equally incapable of recalling it by sheer willpower. As the dream eludes conscious control, and occurs apparently without our input, many people find it difficult to imagine that they actually are the originators of their dreams.

Dreams tend to amaze us when their contents and progress are out of tune with our waking existence: people and objects appear whom, to the best of our knowledge, we have never encountered; we talk to individuals whom we have not seen in years; we find ourselves in unknown locations, move around without limits as to time and space; or act in a manner we would find alien in our waking lives. When we speak of the bizarre in dreams, we refer to those features that deviate from our experience and behavior while awake.

Dreams also make a lasting impression when their events take a dramatic course and when our emotions are strongly involved. Dreams may engage us in adventurous happenings, with rapidly changing situations, placing us at the center of events that lead to a dramatic climax. Dreams may be accompanied by intensive pleasure and feelings of happiness; alternately, they may become so threatening that we awake in a state of anxiety, with all the symptoms of physical excitement.

By far the most striking elements of a dream is our personal feeling of reality. Only when we are awake do we recognize the dream as a sleep fantasy. Detlev von Uslar described this unique feature of the dream phenomenon extensively in his book *Der Traum als Welt* (1964). He considers the dream initially as an existence of its own, as the dreamer's actual world. Only on awakening does the transition take place, the conversion which turns the sleep experience into a dream, into an 'unreal' world. This second viewpoint coincides with the origin of the English word 'dream' and its German equivalent, 'Traum,' both based on the Germanic 'draugma,' or 'phantom,' possibly evolved from the Indo-European term 'dreugh,' which stood for 'deception.'

Finally, many people are fascinated by dreams because they can integrate their meanings into waking life. Dreams may be understood and interpreted as testimony of actual life situations, as efforts to come to terms with the past, and as an expression of hopes and fears regarding the future. Dream interpretation offers insight into areas of being that are not necessarily conscious and accessible when we are awake.

Defining a Dream

Dreams are daily phenomena and everyone has an idea of what a dream is. The question of how to circumscribe dreams, however, is not easy to answer. A definition of the dream is only simple and clear-cut when we are satisfied with the observation that we are dealing with an experience that occurs during sleep. This definition refers to the physiological state in which we dream, but it does not testify to the structure and nature of dreams.

It is much more difficult to define the dream based on content and quality, because dreamlike phenomena exist outside the sleep condition. The daydream, for instance, is a waking experience that is qualitatively related to the dream. Just as images during the waking state may be dreamlike, thoughtlike events occur during sleep that do not display the dreamlike features usually expected from a dream.

The following examples should provide an initial view of the qualitative variety of dreams. A 23-year-old female student recorded all three reports in a dream diary, upon awakening in the morning, over a period of four days.

"There's a border control in the middle of City Hall Square, on the way to the Railroad Station. A customs officer stands there, people go past him, and he checks them now and then. I hear from people around me that border checks have recently become quite lax, and that it is fairly easy to do a bit of smuggling. I approach the officer and ask him how often he searches people. He answers that he usually checks every fifth person. I figure that, under these circumstances, smuggling remains a pretty risky business."

"I walk along the Rhine river bank, together with several other people. We want to get to the town of Breisach. It is still far, one can only see the landscape by the river and, far away, a village. The river bank is wet. There seems to have been some flooding. I walk ahead of the others. I hear my friend Rita as she cries out. The embankment behind her has collapsed and she nearly skidded down the slope. She turns back, looks down laughing, but bends too far forward and now really goes into a skid. I walk back, too, laugh at her as she sits helplessly in the mud. But, before I know it, my feet give way and I go, smack down, right next to her."

"Some kind of crime has been committed, related to me. Everything seems to work out all right, but the chain of proof is still incomplete. A big sheep dog, my trusted companion, leads me through a dark forest. It is a steep uphill and I make only slow progress. We are looking for fresh traces of the perpetrator. The dog, triumphantly, discovers a small egg that is somehow connected to the case. I praise him and we slink ahead. I see a shadowy figure that crosses my path and disappears to the right. All of a sudden, another one pops up. In the light of a burst of fire I recognize a sailor in blue. I drop to the ground, pretend to have been mortally wounded and hold my breath. I know that the sailor speaks only French and I try desperately to find the right words. Once again, the fire flashes brightly, and I am terribly frightened."

The first dream appears quite mundane and realistic. While its theme is a 'border situation,' it is not particularly dramatic and presents no striking oddities. The dreamer behaves appropriately at the border point and thinks reasonably. It could have been the kind of event that might actually take place, although a customs officer would, in reality, not be quite as forthcoming in talking about his work. It could just as well have been an incident that the student imagined while awake, as she toyed with the idea of smuggling. However, additional information reveals the dream's setting to be unusual: the square in which the dream took place was in the center of the town where the dreamer lived, where there could be no customs control. In this case, the dream contains one bizarre feature, the location of its setting.

The second dream is somewhat more imaginative than the first example. Still, could not the mishap involving a friend during a walk, after the rain, have taken place while awake? On the one hand, it might seem possible; on the other hand, it is rather odd how quickly the embankment collapses during the dream. The accident was forecast by the wetness of the river bank, but the dream characters are quite unprepared for it. Once again, additional information indicates an unusual element within the dream. The dreamer's friend Rita, who was the first to skid down the slope, had actually gone to school with her, but they had not met in years and lived in different places. In this case, the dream merged elements that were unrelated in either space and time.

The third dream fits the dream category most easily, as it contains specific features that are usually associated with dreams. Its theme is a mysterious crime, which the dreamer seeks to track down, accompanied by her gifted dog. Strange things happen during this adventurous search. Her encounter with the shadow and the threatening sailor give events a dramatic turn. Finally, an anxiety-filled climax is reached: the dreamer fears an attack on herself, which she can only avoid by pretending to be dead. The dream is startling in its mythological nature, which extends beyond mere parallel reflection of a life situation, presenting as it does the symbolistic recreation of an existential situation that expresses self-discovery.

These examples provide a first impression of the multifaceted images and thoughts that may appear during sleep. These dreams share a staging of settings and events which, at the time they took place, were regarded as real by the dreamer. Although the three dreams were recalled by the same person over a short period of time, they differ greatly as to the degrees of their dreamlike qualities and the drama of their events. They illustrate how difficult it is to arrive at a definition that encompasses the total qualitative variety of dreams.

The American dream researcher Calvin Hall, who collected and classified the dreams of several hundred people, sought in his book *The Meaning of Dreams* to present a cautious definition of the structure and content features of the dream experience by establishing their 'greatest common denominator':

> "A dream is a succession of images, predominantly visual in quality, which are experienced during sleep. A dream commonly has one or more scenes, several characters in addition to the dreamer, and a sequence of actions and interactions usually involving the dreamer. It resembles a motion picture or dramatic production in which the dreamer is both a participant and an observer." (1953, p. 2–3)

Hall did not, at this point, refer to the origin and meaning of the dream, but attempted a general reflection of the ways in which dreams make their appearance, as related to structure and content categories. Such a descriptive definition has the advantage of being subject to immediate verification of appropriate phenomena. We may examine whether Hall's dream criteria are necessary or even sufficient to identify dreams comprehensively.

"Avenues" to the Dream

Two questions, "Where do dreams come from?" and "What is the meaning of dreams?", have been pursued over centuries, and new answers have constantly been put forward. All these dream theories were related to prevailing philosophical and psychological concepts of the human condition and to links between body and mind. Contradictory views regarding the origin and meaning of dreams were, for example, polarized in such beliefs as the dreams' physiological causes ("Dreams come from digestion") or their psychological bases ("Dreams are a mirror of the soul"), or by imbuing them either with significance ("Dreams reflect unconscious motives") or meaninglessness ("Dreams are like dust").

As contradictory hypotheses regarding the origin and meaning of dreams always existed simultaneously, changes in attitudes toward the dream do not fit neatly into different periods of cultural history. Even Aristotle questioned the prominent belief of his time that dreams were messages from gods and demons when he stated that they might just as well be "motions of the senses." A comparable contrast is still evident today. According to the neurophysiologists Allan Hobson and Robert McCarley (1977), dreams are caused by the random activity of certain nerve cells within the brain stem. Conversely, representatives of parapsychology, who regard the appearance of telepathic and prophetic dreams as established, favor the concept that certain dreams have an extrasensory origin.

Ever since Sigmund Freud demonstrated, in *The Interpretation of Dreams* (1900), that the dream should be viewed as a meaningful psychological phenomenon, based on an unconscious latent wish, the origin and psychological significance of dreams have been the subject of numerous theories and methods of interpretation. Since then, a variety of dream theories have continued to center on the psychological content of dreams, although they propose a different understanding of its significance. Thus, Medard Boss (1953) considers dreams as representations of existential life situations, Thomas French (1954) assigns them the function of coping with current psychological conflicts, and C. G. Jung (1928) sees dreams as anticipating the individuation process.

Dream theories and the practice of dream interpretation occupy a prominent position in the long history of dream psychology. Therefore, it was the origin and meaning that have largely stimulated speculations concerning the dream. Conversely, an approach to the dream that would reveal how dreams 'really' are has enjoyed less attention. Such an examination of the dream is not least required because many views have long been based on the dream's particularly striking features but not on its general elements. If dreams are consistently considered as bizarre, dramatic and emotionally-oriented, one needs to know whether the exceptional in the dream also represents the typical.

While selected dream examples illustrate specific aspects of the dream experience, they do not permit conclusive findings concerning the nature of dreams. Only extensive, systematic examinations enable us to determine what is exceptional and what is typical regarding dreams and to clarify whether dreams present a much wider panorama of experiential characteristics and forms of expression than is generally assumed.

If we want to establish clearly what dreams actually are we need to define their appearance, independently of their interpretable content. It is logical and appropriate for basic dream research to follow Hall's descriptive definition of the dream. We regard this as the best presupposition, one designed to establish specific hypotheses concerning the origin and function of the dream.

Historical Development of Dream Research

Although a psychology of dreams has existed for centuries, the history of actual dream research is relatively short. The moment of its birth is difficult to fix, depending on how broadly or narrowly research is defined.

Systematic observation of dreams began with the work of individual dream psychologists during the second half of the nineteenth century. For example, the French scientist Alfred Maury observed his own dreams carefully and, in addition, sought to influence them through external stimuli (Maury 1865). His contemporary and fellow-countryman, Marquis d'Hervey de Saint-Denys, published a book in 1867, based on his own dreams, collected over a period of five years and recorded in twenty-two notebooks, complete with illustrations. He was particularly interested in establishing to what degree dream events may be controlled and whether dreams contain creative solutions of problems.

The American psychologist Mary Whiton Calkins occupies an important position in the history of dream research, as she was the first to not only observe dreams, but to systematically evaluate 375 dreams which she and her partner recorded on awakening. She categorized dream contents, for example, which groups of people appeared in dreams and in what setting the dreams occurred. She captured the appearance of a dream by decoding sensory perceptions, and she sought to reach the sources of dreams by establishing their links to life situations. Her study, published in 1893, presented these stock-takings in the form of carefully annotated tables.

Experimental psychology, well established at the beginning of the century, experienced a rapid advance. However, compared to numerous published studies dealing with the waking experience, dream research utilizing a broad empirical basis was a rarity. The few dream studies that were undertaken remained largely based on self-observations, though they utilized extensive dream material designed to deal with the phenomenology of dream events in a differentiated manner. Thus, the German psychologists Friedrich Hacker (1911) and Paul Köhler (1912) analyzed the image and thought activities in hundreds of dreams, recorded in their diaries, with great scientific precision, but their results were not developed in any subsequent studies.

The dream as a research theme was not neglected because of any lack of interest on the part of psychologists, but because researchers lacked appropriate methods to reliably grasp events that occurred during sleep. Dreams seemed to elude every experimental technique and failed to meet experimental requirements: dream events could not be observed in an organized manner, were only recalled haphazardly, could not be provoked systematically, and occurred erratically. As a result, experimental variations could not be planned in advance and phenomena had to be recorded retroactively.

Any examination of the dream was, therefore, subject to severe limitations. All questions of dream psychology, whether concerned with the phenomenology or significance of what was dreamed, depended on spontaneously, mostly sporadically remembered dreams. All of the vast dream literature in the non-experimental realm was inevitably based on selected dreams that offered no assurance that they represented the whole gamut of experience or that they were actually experienced during the sleeping state. This restriction had, however, no impact on the practice of dream interpretation. The casuistic approach toward the dream, aimed at interpretation, is not designed to objectivize the dream experience; it utilizes dream contents entirely as codes, designed to reveal unconscious dynamic processes.

Up until the 1950s, empirical dream research found itself in a highly uneasy position. On the one hand, there were numerous techniques and standards enabling psychotherapists to interpret their patients' dreams; on the other hand, little was known about the very basics of dreams as such. Many simple, but decisive questions concerning dream events could not be answered with certainty. One was not even sure whether everyone has dreams: some people were able to talk about their dreams each morning, while quite a few insisted that they had never had a dream.

There was much speculation about the frequency and timing of dreams during sleep, areas in which individual claims were particularly at odds. Many people thought they remembered to have dreamed all night long. Others expressed the view that their dreams took place only as they fell asleep, and still others concluded from their experiences that it was the transition from sleep to awakening which encouraged their dreams. Although opinions concerning the timing of dreams during sleep covered all possibilities, the sleeping periods closest to the waking state were regarded most favorably—either, because phenomena could be most easily observed at this time, or because it seemed plausible that dreams are related to the waking state.

It was, however, thought that the length of dreams could be fixed quite readily. Many people who awake in the morning and then fall asleep again, remember a long dream after they wake up again, only to discover that they had, in fact, slept only a few minutes. These observations support a viewpoint, maintained for decades in dream literature, that complicated continuities of dream events could be condensed into a very brief timespan, and that the dream should therefore be regarded as a phenomenon that occurs within a few seconds.

Even more controversial and stubborn in its domination of dream literature was the opinion that the dream is prompted by an external signal, an outside stimulus. Key witness for this view was Alfred Maury's often-cited guillotine dream (1865), which seemed to show convincingly that a bedpost that fell on Maury's neck caused, in fragments of seconds, a detailed and dramatic dream of the French Revolution, climaxing in Maury's execution. The impressive quality of this dream silenced all counter-arguments, including the fact that Maury did not record this dream until ten years later.

The questions of whether everyone dreams, how often they dream, just when dreams occur and how long they last, could not be answered with certainty, as long as there was no criterium independent of self-observation that somehow indicated mental experiences during sleep. The bases of dreaming could only be specifically examined once better documented knowledge of the physiology of sleep became available. And these, in turn, could only be achieved when appropriate methods of measuring were at hand.

One historic dream example anticipated the period of psychophysiological dream research. In 1910, Paul Köhler recorded the following dream:

> "I am lying on a sofa, at an unknown place. I was awakened by a gentleman I know. He stands before me and says: 'You just had a dream lasting 35 minutes.' I answer quickly, surprised: 'How come? How did you find out?' The gentleman: 'That's really a very simple matter!' I, quickly: 'Thanks a lot! Simple matter! Until now, we've known next to nothing about the length of dreams.' The gentleman interrupts me: 'I tell you, a friend of mine has settled the matter brilliantly and has written to me that it is very simple!'" (1912, p. 461–462)

Köhler cites this case as proof that a dreamer is fully capable of criticizing a false statement cogently. Today we would judge this dream differently, noting that the dreamer mistakenly questions a known fact. As it happens, Köhler's absurd dream was fulfilled in 1953. Since then, we are aware that dreams can, indeed, last 35 minutes and that the gentleman who "settled the matter brilliantly" is the American Eugene Aserinsky.

Aserinsky, a doctoral student of the well-known sleep researcher Nathaniel Kleitman of the University of Chicago, recorded the eye movements of sleeping subjects, in order to study cortex activity during sleep. While engaged in these experiments, he made the unexpected discovery that, aside from slow, gliding eye movements—which actually were his only target—rapid, jerky and conjugate eye movements took place, remarkably similar to vision actions while awake. Both scientists assumed that such rapid eye movements might be related to dream events and decided to test this hypothesis with awakening experiments. Ten sleepers, whose eyes made jerky movements, were awakened a total of 27 times. They remembered vivid dreams in 20 instances, while 23 control awakenings from phases of eye rest yielded dream reports in only four cases. Thus, a first 'objective' feature became evident that seemed to chart the process of dreaming, and a decisive impetus for systematic psychophysiological dream experiments emerged (Aserinsky & Kleitman 1953).

Actually, Aserinsky and Kleitman were not the first to link rapid eye movements with dream activity. In a study of falling-asleep phenomena, published in 1892, George Trumbull Ladd, professor of philosophy at Yale University, voiced the supposition that people move their eyes as rapidly during vivid dreams as they do when they perceive their environment while awake. Many years later, the American psychologist Edmund Jacobson (1938), today often cited because of his relaxation technique, was prompted by occasional observations to draw attention to the same phenomenon. He even suggested that, to prove his point, sleepers should be awakened during eye movements and asked about their dreams. The presentiments of the two authors were, however, overlooked and only the independent discovery of rapid eye movements by Aserinsky and Kleitman led to their resurrection from the literature.

At least two elements were responsible for the fact that the renewed discovery of rapid eye movement during sleep, at this time, led to intensive follow-up experiments, as well as to a revitalization of experimental dream research. First of all, the Chicago University team itself, aided by the physician-psychologist William Dement, took the initiative to elaborate its surprising results through additional experiments. Furthermore, extensive knowledge concerning the physiology of the sleeping state was available by then, ready to be linked to these new insights.

Sleep research, although just as neglected as dream research, nevertheless entered a new period three decades earlier. This development started 1924 in Jena, Germany, when the psychiatrist Hans Berger succeeded in recording fluctuations in the electrical potentials of the human brain. In 1931, Berger for the first time demonstrated changes in the electroencephalogram (EEG) during the sleep state. Subsequent systematic studies soon showed that sleep is not a uniform condition, but that several different stages, which manifest during the course of sleep, alternate as part of a cyclical process.

The methods and findings of sleep research finally enabled experimenters to link the physiology of sleep with the psychology of the dream experience. For one thing, it was of decisive importance now to be able to determine whether a dream report had been preceded by a sleeping state. Then, too, it became possible to find out whether different features of the sleep state were indications of a dream's specific aspects of experience.

In recent decades, empirical psychological dream research has expanded into psychophysiological dream research. At present, not only are psychological aspects of the dream under scrutiny, but it has become possible to study bodily processes as they occur during this experience. Psychological aspects of the dream continue to be approached by traditional as well as new methods. Therefore it is not that the original questions concerning the dream have changed decisively, but that methods of inquiry and evaluation of the dream experience have become more abundant.

2

Methods of Dream Sampling

During past decades, methods of dream sampling have become increasingly varied. Outside observation has supplemented self-observation, case studies of individual dreams were extended by systematic dream collecting, and standardized dream recording was added to spontaneously remembered dreams.

One significant qualification must, however, be noted at the outset: no single method in dream research is capable of directly capturing dream content and of observing the progress of a dream event. Every method of dream study merely permits us to approach the dream event indirectly and retroactively. The dream, itself an internal phenomenon, is accessible only to the dreamer. And only the dreamer is capable of providing information, when later calling upon memory introspectively.

Still, the dream experience is not always accessible to the dreamer, as dreams do not appear on demand; upon awakening, they often either escape from memory altogether, or, as is frequently the case, are difficult to describe. Dreams are private experiences that do not permit outside observers; the dreamer is the only witness of the dream event. If we want to give others insight into our dreams, we must first give them communicable shape. This essential transformation of the dream has the result that any dream report is limited to what may be captured in words or, for example, in drawings.

If we decide not to keep dreams to ourselves, as purely personal experiences that may be impressive, enriching or even frightening, but to retain a dream in order to ponder over it or evaluate it, then we have to translate it into language and to record it in some manner.

Collecting Spontaneously Remembered Dreams

Dream research began at a time when individual scholars started to systematically observe and record their own dreams. Alfred Maury and d'Hervey de Saint-Denys maintained such dream diaries, as early as during the past century, providing interesting insights and testimonials concerning the nature of the dream.

Dream diaries may be organized in greatly different ways. Decisive factors are time and manner of protocol maintenance. First of all, much depends on just when we record a dream. We might do it whenever we awake, or we can wait until we get up in the morning and then record any nightly dreams we still remember. Or, we may not become aware of a dream until later in the day, and record it at that time. Obviously, recording a dream immediately usually provides more detail, as it is closer to the actual experience than a later report. The more time elapses, the more details are likely to fade and dream memories tend to mix with waking thoughts.

The manner of protocol maintenance dictates the precision and comprehension with which a dream is transmitted. If we merely note highlights in a few catch phrases, we might grasp a dream's basic theme, but gain only limited evidence of the representation and the overall design of the dream. If, however, we succeed in describing all valid details, we will later be able to analyze content, structure and progress of the dream event a good deal more thoroughly. If, in addition, our dream report includes subjective impressions—if, for example, we estimate how vivid and how emotionally significant a dream experience was—then we capture qualities that do not always enter into a dream report spontaneously. In addition, we may record explanations and ideas concerning dream situations and their waking context.

Even early dream researchers were aware that dream records require carefully defined conditions. Mary Calkins, for example, described her procedure as follows:

> "To record each night, immediately after waking from a dream, every remembered feature of it. For this purpose, paper, pencil, candle and matches were placed close at hand. Early on the next day, with rare exceptions, these abbreviated notes were re-read, copied in full and enlarged by comments, by description of all attendant circumstances, and by the indication in all possible cases of the connection of the dream with the waking life." (1893, p. 311)

In our day, the light on a night table may replace a candle and matches, but Mary Calkins' instructions could well remain as a basis for the maintenance of contemporary dream diaries. We are now, of course, able to record spontaneous dreams more easily. We no longer need to write them down on awakening, but can record them directly on tape. This eases the procedure a great deal, as telling a dream, in contrast to writing it down, requires a lowered degree of wakefulness and less strict motor coordination. An oral record does, however, frequently differ from a dream that is recorded in writing. A dream transmitted by spoken words, being closer to the actual dreaming event, directly reflects the process of remembering. It may, therefore, contain scattered thoughts, repetitions and less coherence than a dream recorded in writing, which tends to reflect a good deal more preparation and structure.

Dream researchers are, of course, not only interested in the appearance of the dream but also in the interrelation of dreams with sleep and the waking state. As a result, researchers have, in addition to careful dream records, frequently gained supplementary information that relates to the context of the dream. Paul Köhler, for example, used to record his daily activities in his dream dairy, he noted the conditions under which he fell asleep, the depth of sleep on awakening, and whether he had experienced any stimuli that might have influenced his dream.

The collection of such spontaneous dreams in diaries remains, to this day, a frequent practice. It has special advantages: dream recollection occurs in a setting familiar to the experimental subject, permitting collection of comprehensive dream material over a longer period, and without extensive involvement. Yet, this method has its limitations: data collection is not controlled, because only the dreamer knows how carefully he or she has followed instructions. Beyond that, one should keep in mind that spontaneous dream memories represent only a limited selection of dream experiences. After all, the sleeping person does not awake after every dream; possibly, spontaneous awakening occurs only when the dream is particularly vivid and dramatic.

Eliciting Dreams by Awakening

Using the method of waking the subject enables us to supplement spontaneous dream recollection. When causing awakening from sleep, we tend to 'provoke' dream memory. In such instances we do not limit ourselves to letting sleepers awake by themselves. This waking method was used, early on, by individual dream researchers, who sought to collect as many dreams as possible, or because they wanted to ascertain whether dreams are actually remembered when a sleeping person does not awake spontaneously. As it was not possible, at that time, to measure sleep physiologically, researchers had to limit themselves to observing a sleeper's behavior or to trust the subject's judgment as to whether a dream had, in fact, been experienced during sleep.

Waking a subject from a dream requires specific aids. These might be mechanical waking devices, designed to provide waking signals at a specific time, or persons are assigned to undertake the actual waking-up. Alfred Maury may have been the first dream researcher to engage such an 'experimenter.' Maury used to place someone next to his bed who observed him while asleep, and who stimulated him prior to awakening, such as using perfume.

For reasons of economy, awakenings lacking an accompanying control of the sleep condition are still in use today. Consequently, sleepers are being awakened at home, by telephone, and questioned about their dreams. The awakening technique did not, however, achieve its outstanding role until it became possible to control the physiological conditions that precede awakening.

Dreams Collected in the Laboratory

In order to monitor the progress of waking and sleeping in the laboratory, we register different physiological processes throughout the night. Sleep cannot be regarded as a uniform condition, but as the consistent succession of different sleep levels. Such sleep observation enables us to undertake dream awakenings with precision. These pinpointed awakenings permit, on the one hand, a dream report to follow the sleep stage immediately, and, on the other hand, to link a dream to a specific physiological condition.

What methods and insights of sleep research are required in order to elicit dreams experimentally? The standard method of defining sleep stages consists of a continuous recording of brain waves by electroencephalogram (EEG), eye movement by electrooculogram (EOG), and muscle tension at the chin by electromyogram (EMG). Of course, additional body activities may be measured, such as frequency of respiration, heart beats, and body temperature.

Nightly variations in brain activity are reflected in changing EEG frequencies and amplitudes. The density of successive waves permits the reading of potential changes, while the amplitude of deflections provides a measure of electric power. Brain activity changes constantly during sleep; but, on the basis of predominant EEG patterns, sleep researchers agreed to mark the code of a specific sleep stage in segments of 30 seconds, including eye movement and muscle tension. Rules governing these practices have been standardized, internationally accepted and published in a manual issued by the U.S. Public Health Service (Rechtschaffen & Kales 1968).

In addition to waking, five separate sleep stages have been determined. Figure 1 shows the notable characteristics of the waking state and the first four stages of sleep, as they appear on the sections of a recording.

During the waking state, the EEG shows rapid frequencies of lower voltage, alternating with regular sine-type oscillations; the discoverer of the EEG, Hans Berger, gave these phenomena the name Alpha rhythms. Alpha waves appear particularly when a person is relaxed, withdrawn from the outside world; in contrast, more rapid fre-

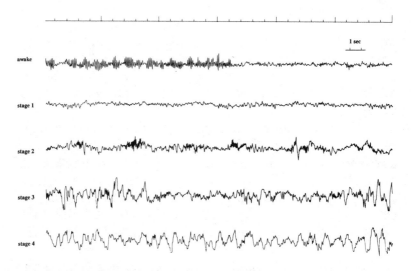

FIGURE 1. EEG Patterns during Waking and Non-REM Sleep Stages. Each thirty-second epoch characterizes a stage. During relaxed waking stage, regular Alpha waves are notable; during Stage 2, sleep spindles and K complexes appear. Brain wave activity decreases as sleep deepens.

quencies, known as Beta rhythms, are characteristic of an intense and alert waking state.

EEG stages 1 to 4, numbered to correspond to a continuity following the onset of sleep, reveal a wave pattern of progressively deeper sleep, as reflected in a slowing-down of frequency and increased amplitudes.

Stage 1 is characterized by a cessation of Alpha rhythms, while waves of lesser voltage dominate, of which single smaller and lower swings begin to be discernible.

Stage 2 shows higher voltages and single but strikingly vivid patterns emerge. The sharp spike in the illustration is known as a K-complex; because of their characteristic form, the tight, short-term patterns are called sleep spindles.

Within Stage 3, an increase of slower, higher and regular waves can be specified. These so-called Delta waves are the dominant features in Stage 4. Stages 3 and 4 are regarded as periods of deep sleep, illustrated by the fact that, during these stages, sleepers are particularly difficult to wake.

The fifth stage of sleep is presented separately in Figure 2, because, in addition to the EEG, eye movement and

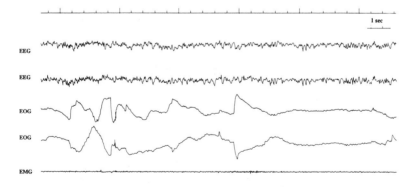

FIGURE 2. Typical Features of REM Sleep. EEG shows similarities with sleep Stage 1. The channels designed to record eye movement (EOG) are counter-switched: convergent deflections correspond to leftward movements, divergent swings to rightward. Muscle tension (EMG) has reached a very low level.

muscle tension are significant for its description. Although, during this stage, the EEG shows a flat basic pattern, and thus appears similar to Stage 1, two notable features indicate a difference between the two stages. During the fifth stage, sudden jolts of rapid eye movements occur, while muscle tension disappears. As such Rapid Eye Movements led to the discovery of this particular sleep phase, the initials of the descriptive term prompted it to become known as REM sleep. First of all, the REM phase is characterized by quick movements of the eyes, which appear periodically but not consistently; in addition, it may be accompanied by a higher pulse rate and increased breath frequency. Because of this overall increased body activity, the REM period is also frequently regarded as 'active' sleep. REM sleep is differentiated from other sleep phases, characterized by greater relaxation of the organism, and grouped into the category of Non-REM sleep (NREM).

Various physiological processes that occur during sleep, leading to classification of different stages, are characterized by still another interesting feature: their orderly cyclical progression. One typical progression, recorded during an undisturbed night, is pictured in Figure 3. It shows the eval-

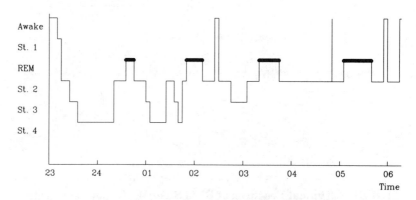

FIGURE 3. Sleep Profile of an Undisturbed Night. NREM stages 2 to 4 and the REM stages, marked in black, alternate in cycles of about 1 1/2 hours. Deep sleep (stages 3 and 4) appears only during the initial half of the night. In the morning, REM phases become extended.

uation of the laboratory night of a young adult female. During the first hour of sleep the subject passed, in descending sequence, from sleep Stage 1 to 4. After forty minutes in deep sleep, she returned to Stage 2, succeeded by a first brief REM phase. After about one-and-a-half hours, this REM phase completed the first sleep cycle. Later, three additional sleep cycles followed, each with a rhythm of one-and-a-half to two hours.

Observing the sleep profile, it is of additional significance that deep sleep stages are limited to early hours. The sleep profile flattens during the second half of the sleep period, and REM phases alternate only with sleep Stage 2. Variations that occur during separate nights are not reflected in the illustration, but it shows the regularity in sleep stage successions, the cyclical occurrence of REM sleep and the percentages individual sleep stages occupy within the total sleep period. Cyclical development of sleep stages provides the most important basis for fixing the moment at which a sleeper should be awakened, in order to be asked about his or her dreams.

We shall outline, step by step, just how a laboratory night of experimental dream elicitation is organized; it adheres to a standardized procedure, established in our dream laboratory over a period of several years (Gass, Gerne, Loepfe, Meier, Rothenfluh & Strauch 1983). Dreamers who are motivated to spend several nights in our dream laboratory are generally recruited by advertisement. We usually look for solid sleepers who, in everyday life, remember their dreams frequently. We select solid sleepers because we have found that they adapt more easily to the unfamiliar sleep environment and to the experimental setting. We prefer those who remember dreams well, because they have access to their dreams in everyday existence, causing us to assume that they will remember their dreams, frequently and in detail, in the laboratory setting as well. We depend on the self-assessment of the experimental subjects, but we may also prompt them to keep a dream diary for about a week, which enables us to gauge the frequency of their spontaneous dream recall.

During an initial interview, we familiarize the experimental subjects with the framework of the study and brief them on the experimental technique. We outline our evaluation methods and explain the waking procedure. Once the appointment for an experiment has been fixed, we ask the subject at what time she or he goes to bed and gets up; we allow for this personal pattern within the experimental schedule. In acknowledgment of their cooperation, subjects receive a small reward, 30 Swiss francs per night, at the conclusion of the experimental series.

The initial interview has the additional value of observing any anxieties that may be related to the laboratory setting, enabling us to reduce them with factual information. Apprehension may be related to the expectation that the sleepers will be subjected to electric currents or that they must remain motionless, in order to permit recording and evaluation. But erroneous expectations need also be corrected, such as the belief that dream content may be revealed by brain waves, or that their dreams will be psychologically interpreted.

Figure 4 shows an experimental subject, ready for the dream experiment. The subject had arrived at the laboratory a full hour before her usual bedtime. Once she had changed for the night, she was prepared for the physiological recordings. The experimenter first attached electrodes to the subject's head. These are discs of gold, connected to a thin cable. To permit EEG recording, they are glued to several spots of the scalp; for the EOG, they are connected to the corner of the eyes; and for the EMG, below the chin. The cables are then plaited together.

The subject will sleep in a separate room that does not exhibit any particular laboratory characteristics, but tends to resemble the setting of a plain rooming house. The electrodes are plugged into a box above the head.

The cables permit the subject sufficient leeway to settle into a preferred sleep position in her bed, and she is able to move her body freely during the night. One microphone hangs above the bed, and a second one is attached to her

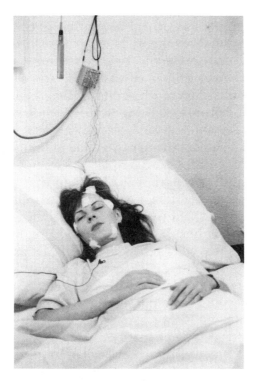

FIGURE 4. A Dream Subject in the Sleep Laboratory. Electrodes, fastened to subject's forehead and face, are linked by cable with a connecting box, permitting ample movement. Two microphones facilitate full recording of dream reports.

pajamas; they convey her dream reports. A reverse speaker is linked to the experimenter, whom the subject can alert at any time, simply by punching a key.

An adjacent control room contains a polygraph, designed to continuously monitor the different physiological measurements, to amplify and to record them on paper. These recordings are observed by the experimenter, in order to decide on appropriate waking times. When we established our standard procedure, we decided to wake our subjects, as a rule, four times a night, and always during periods of REM sleep. To start with, we wake them five minutes after the onset of the second REM phase; the second waking takes place ten minutes after the beginning of the third REM phase. Additional awakenings occur fifteen minutes into the fourth REM phase and twenty minutes into the fifth REM phase. We wait longer with each succeeding period, because the duration of REM phases lengthens during the night. We do not interrupt the first REM phase, because it often is not continuous and because we want to enable the experimental subject to enjoy a period of undisturbed deep sleep, prior to the first awakening.

As we fix the length of REM sleep that precedes the awakenings ahead of time, we create comparable conditions, but have to accept that we interrupt the phases before their natural terminations. It would, at any rate, be difficult to wake subjects just before the end of a REM phase, as it does not signal its own ending. Frequently there is sudden body movement, followed by a different sleep stage. Should that happen, we would have missed the opportunity of waking the subject during REM sleep.

It is, of course, not essential to wake a sleeper only during REM sleep. Dreams are not limited to these periods. But experience has shown that sleepers awakened during REM sleep remember their dreams more easily and frequently than those awakened during other sleep stages; we naturally prefer periods that yield more data.

Figure 5 shows a typical laboratory night of four REM awakenings. It is apparent that a cyclical sleep structure was maintained during the night, although the experimental subject was awakened four times and then reported her dreams. As she quickly fell asleep each time, she managed to sleep 6 1/2 out of the 7 1/2 hours she spent in bed.

Not every night passes under such ideal conditions. Even good sleepers have difficult nights, at times having trouble falling asleep and experiencing restless sleep. In such cases we may be limited to awakening the subject only three times per night, because the cyclical succession is disrupted or REM phases are delayed. The experimenter is usually able to achieve awakening during a REM phase. Only rarely does one miss a whole REM phase. On the other

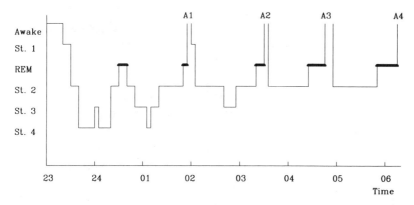

FIGURE 5. Typical Laboratory Night with 4 REM Awakenings.
Sleeper was not awakened during first REM phase, only beginning with
second REM phase. Awakenings (A) and questions concerning dreams did
not interfere with the cyclical succession of sleep stages.

hand, maintaining the scheduled REM duration is not that
easy, as REM phases do not always proceed with regularity.
They might be shortened during morning hours, or chopped
up, interrupted by other sleep stages. In such cases it is difficult to fix the beginning of a phase, or its length, with
accuracy.

As soon as the polygraphic recording indicates that
proper conditions have been established, the experimenter
awakens the sleeper through the speaker. The subject,
called by her first name, is asked: "What was going through
your mind before I called you?" Dreamers are never interrupted while they report a dream. Only if they seem to be
falling asleep, which the EEG record would indicate, or
pause for any length of time, we encourage them by repeat-
ing the last words. When it appears that the dreamer's
report has come to an end, the experimenter makes sure by
asking: "Was there anything else?" Only when the subject
has related everything that can be elicited at that point,
does the experimenter ask: "How did you feel during the
dream?" In addition, emotional intensity is rated on a scale
of 1 to 5. This procedure is maintained at each awakening,
and all interactions are recorded on tape.

The rather impersonal manner of awakening, through the reverse speaker, has the advantage that dreamers remain alone in their room, able to concentrate on their dreams, and not distracted by the physical presence of an experimenter. This method also protects the interviewer from the temptation of commenting on the dream report, or to reflect in any non-verbal manner possible elements of surprise or disappointment. Our opening question deliberately avoids any reference to a dream as such. We are, after all, interested in eliciting whatever images and thoughts may have preceded the waking stage, and not just in what the subjects regard as a dream. We ask about emotional reactions during the night, as emotions are not usually related spontaneously, and because dream feelings tend to fade quite rapidly from memory.

We wait until morning to gather additional information on the dream reports. After the subject gets up, we present her with the dreams of the night and give the following instructions: "I will now play your dreams back to you. Afterwards, I'll ask you about some things that aren't clear to me. While you're listening, please keep in mind whether there is anything in this dream that really happened to you, or that concerns you in any way."

The morning interview completes the dream report. We are thus able to clarify which dream images and dream locations are known to the subject, what her relations to them are, and which dream elements originate in her life situation. Questions are designed to supplement the report, enabling us to categorize dream elements during our final evaluation, and to place them into appropriate classifications. We do not inquire into associations with or related impressions of the dream, as this might happen in a psychotherapeutic setting; in our experimental setting, we are not dealing with dream interpretation.

Extensive physiological and psychological data emerge from each experimental night. Polygraph records of a single night of eight hours cover about 300 meters of recording paper, plus several tape recordings of dreams. The experimenter also keeps a protocol of planned and unexpected events during the night. Among these data are the moment lights were turned off, the beginning of REM phases, and times of awakenings. We also record when the subject called on us, possibly to go to the toilet, or whether we encountered technical handicaps, such as a blocked recording pen. In order to preserve anonymity during later evaluations, protocol sheets and tape cassettes are identified by code, rather than with the subject's name.

The experimenter transcribes the tape recordings later. Although dream reports frequently contain repetitions or incomplete sentences, everything is to be transcribed literally. Even pauses and non-linguistic expressions, such as laughter, moaning, or a humming sound, are recorded. Names and locations are identified merely by their first letter, in order to safeguard anonymity in later evaluations. Our dream elicitations in Switzerland encounter a singular problem, as most of our subjects report their dreams in the country's unique language, Swiss German. Because Swiss German is not a written language and therefore difficult to transliterate and read, we decided to transpose these dreams into standard written German. We do, however, retain colloquial sentence structures and expressions that could only be paraphrased or are subject to different interpretations. Data from the protocol sheets and tape recordings are ultimately computerized and stored in a 'Dream Databank.'

This standardized process of dream elicitation has stood the test of time, covering a series of projects undertaken in our dream laboratory. More than 100 subjects were examined during more than 300 laboratory nights. As our dream awakenings proved to be successful, we were able to deposit nearly 1,000 reports in our dream databank up until the present time. Several students, engaged in graduate studies, were employed as experimenters. They were prepared for their tasks, during one semester, by attending a technical course. Although different experimenters were engaged in our projects, studying a variety of specific hypotheses, standardized elicitation nevertheless enabled us to achieve an overall evaluation of dreams.

Rules of this standard method represent a basic structure. The technique is subject to expansion and change in all links of procedure: additional physiological activities might be recorded; awakenings could take place at different times, and in accordance with other criteria; and dream elicitation might be supplemented by additional questioning and ratings.

We employ supplementary physiological functions when we suspect that they provide a more direct connection to the dream experience than do the standard physiological sleep measurements. Elevated pulse and respiration rates during REM sleep could, for example, offer a better indication of anxiety dreams than a record of rapid eye movements.

We include awakenings from other sleep stages when we want to know what dreams arise during the total sleep period, and how dreams during different stages compare with each other. To compare REM dreams and Stage 2 dreams, for example, we have to change the awakening pattern, so that both stages run parallel in terms of duration and time of night.

Waking time must be fixed not only on the basis of the length of a sleep period; waking criteria may also depend on specific features within a sleep stage. As eye movements during REM sleep do not appear continuously, we are able to wake subjects after lively eye activity and during periods of eye rest. Comparison of reports under these conditions may show whether dream impressions during more active eye movement are more intensive, and are more neutral during eye rest.

Questioning may be expanded when we concentrate on specific features of the dreams, elements the dreamer may ignore or that are lost during reporting. As a rule, dream reports tend to favor actual events over concurrent reflections. Dreamers are inclined to report what happens in a dream, but put less emphasis on how intensive or detailed their dream impressions are. Translating a dream experience into words often leads to neglect of details. For instance, we received differentiated accounts of sensory impressions when we questioned our subjects more closely, at the end of a nightly dream report, as to what they had seen, heard, smelt or felt. Without these additional questions, these dream reports would have been more simplified.

All these procedural elements are designed to achieve a comprehensive account of dreams, including an understanding of their context. Specific hypotheses suggest whether and how we should make changes in the psychological or physiological features of our experiments.

Experimental Impact on Dreams

Dreams develop against a background of manifold experiences, which encompass the past, contemporary life situations and the anticipated future. When we question our subjects about the sources of their dream experiences, we encounter a very wide spread of individual testimonies. However, when we influence a dream experimentally, we have the advantage of knowing at least one of the conditions that may have had an impact on the dream.

Experimental stimulation of the dream is a method designed to track a dream's formation. To achieve this, dreams are systematically influenced: we may vary conditions of the pre-sleep situation or provide different signals during sleep itself.

At the outset, we create pre-sleep conditions in the laboratory that enable us to gauge whether and how they are included and absorbed into the dream. We may, for example, present the subject with either a neutral or an anxiety-inducing film. Should the pre-sleep situation influence the dream, we may expect that, during succeeding nights, the fear-inducing film will, in contrast to the neutral film, cause dreams that reflect directly or indirectly the absorbed anxiety. The experimenter may also offer different 'dream commands': one night, the command may be, "Face a lion in the desert!"; and, the following night, "Steal a car!" Later on, we can study whether these instructions found entry into a dream and, if so, what their elaboration was.

While we have unlimited possibilities for varying presleep situations, stimulation during sleep itself faces considerable restrictions. While asleep, the subject's attention is removed from the outside world. In order to select signals that will, nevertheless, influence a dream's progress, we must make sure that they do not wake the sleeping subject. We have, for example, chosen sounds that remain below a waking level. We then scanned the dream reports to see whether they contained hints that indicated reception of these signals, and what incorporations they might have undergone.

Stimulus presentation during sleep is subject to a special problem: we can't be sure whether a sleeper has, in fact, received and recognized a given signal. In contrast to influences given during the pre-sleep period, dream researchers cannot use complex stimuli, such as meaningful sentences during sleep. Instead, they employ sounds, sudden lights, dripping water or smells, assuming that, while dreaming, the sleeper is better able to deal with 'simple' signals.

The varied methods of dream elicitation have helped to expand and deepen our knowledge of dream events. When tackling specific questions, we have to gauge the advantages or disadvantages offered by the choice of a specific procedure. We collect spontaneously remembered dreams when we are interested in samples from many people over a long period of time, thereby taking into account that spontaneously remembered dreams represent only a small segment of the total dream experience. We prefer elicitation of dreams in the laboratory under controlled conditions, when we want to gain immediate access to several dreams during a single night. This means, however, that we can study only a limited number of subjects over a limited number of nights.

3

Methods of Dream Evaluation

Once a dream has been successfully seized, a fairly time-consuming period of evaluation begins. We have accumulated a number of dream reports whose condition of collection is known. Reading through these dreams, we are impressed by their unlimited variations in content and events. Dreams are so exceedingly diverse that neither their common characteristics nor their differences emerge from a quick examination. We are, therefore, forced to decode their complexity. To do this, we need to categorize or quantify dreams and to place them within a structured framework.

Evaluation of dreams requires different criteria, be they mere calculations, content analyses or intuitive appraisals. Methods differ as to what aspects of dream experience they encompass, just how differentiated they are, and how specific any rules of application have been formulated.

Generally, dreams may be evaluated in terms of form or content characteristics. Dream research encompasses many attempts at quantification. In 1979, Carolyn Winget and Milton Kramer published a compilation of 132 scales of dream evaluation; by then, they had been utilized in 375 dream studies.

The large number of available scales indicates how rarely dream researchers have related their methods of evaluation to each other. Such limitations are not, however, unique to dream studies; they can be found throughout research. Leaving these considerations aside, the unlimited variety of dream phenomena has prompted researchers to create ever-new categories and dimensions.

Evaluating Formal Dream Characteristics

Extent and structure of dreams are formal characteristics. We define both these aspects differently and accordingly translate them into evaluation instructions.

Dream length may be expressed either through the number of words or lines of text. We may also calculate the number of thematic units. This can be done, for example, by subdividing a dream report on the basis of successive events and situations.

When dealing with written dream reports that are focused on the dream events, we can simply count words. But when facing transcripts of oral dream reports, we may be forced to go through a weeding-out process before any calculation takes place. We eliminate remarks that address the recipient of the dream, as these merely concern the interactive situation that existed when the dream was elicited. In addition, we erase passages that do not provide fresh information but simply reflect the narrator's efforts to translate a previously experienced dream into words.

Whether such editing of the dream text is required depends on the situation that existed when the dream was elicited. A dream that is reported immediately and orally upon awakening often presents difficulties in word selection; oral reports are, on the whole, more spontaneous and less well organized than a dream that is recorded in writing. Such reports often contain interactive remarks, directed at the experimenter and designed to provide more precise information.

Two cases might serve to illustrate the utilization of different measures of length. Both dreams originated with a 31-year-old female; she recorded her first dream at home, in writing, and conveyed her second dream, immediately upon awakening from her third REM phase, onto a recording tape.

Home Dream:

"It was a beautiful day. I found myself in the midst of a green and flowering meadow. A magnificent forest of varied vege-

tation lay not too far beyond; I clearly recognized birches, fir trees and, specifically, four oak trees. I had to get to this forest at all cost, but could not quite *manage to move,*   [A1]
as something was the matter with my feet. When I looked down on my feet, I discovered to my dismay that, instead of shoes, I wore box-shaped baking tins. I stood on cakes which, with every step, rose higher and higher. The cakes were of an attractive golden-brown color. Soon I was *running*   [A2]
on tall stilts, looking toward the forest, had to maintain my balance, but finally *toppled off*   [A3]
my baking tin stilts."

Laboratory Dream:

"[The beginning was quite odd: somebody came, I think], somebody *came and said*:   [A1]
'We are leaving on a trip' [but I don't know who it was]
and then
I *said*:   [A2]
'That's not true, I can't go on a trip, that's impossible.'
Then he *said*:   [A3]
'Yes, yes. That's okay. Everybody is coming, the kids and everything.' And then we filled a lot of cartons (not a single suitcase, but all kinds of paper cartons). And then Michael *filled*   [A4]
his carton full of shoes (all kinds of shoes), summer shoes, winter shoes, with ski shoes on top. Brigitte,
she *took* only stockings *along.*   [A5]
One whole carton full of folded-up (stockings). And my husband, he *took* all kinds of baby things *along,*   [A6]
all kinds of diapers, a whole carton full of (diapers). And I had all kinds of notes, and somebody *kept saying,*   [A7]
'She reads from notes, she reads from notes,' (somebody kept saying). And then [that certainly originates with the neighbors]
I *took*   [A8]
a whole carton full of notes."

If we simply count all the words, the first report amounts to 129 words, and the second one to 167 words. But the longer, second report shrinks, step by step, in length, depending on what we count as belonging to the dream text. To start with, we exclude all interactive remarks, which appear in the text inside brackets. These are comments ["The beginning was quite odd"], explanations ["I don't know who it was"], associations or ideas ["that certainly originates with the neighbors"]. This initial weeding-out shortens the dream to 145 words. In addition, we remove linguistic repetitions and negations which, in the text, appear in parentheses. This additional editing process reduces the dream to 126 words. It now closely resembles the first dream report, which we did not have to clarify, as it was wholly devoted to the narration of the dream.

If we measure dream length by actions [A] that are printed in italics, we are able to distinguish between the two dream reports more accurately than by mere word count. The first dream contains only three actions, while the second dream totals eight. We have to apply specific rules in order to extract actions from dreams. We restricted ourselves to individuals' motor activities, rather than utilizing verbs that describe either intentions ("I had to get to . . .") or observations ("I discovered to my dismay . . .") We scored new actions when they involved different people ("Michael filled . . ." and "Brigitte took only . . ."), or when, in someone's action, they were clearly separated ("Soon I was running . . . but finally toppled"). On the basis of these criteria, there is higher action density in the second dream: a greater number of individuals make their appearances, and they do different things; by comparison, the first dream is limited to the Dream Self, the narrator, and a description of the dream's setting occupies more space.

We are also able to deduce features of form from structure and progress of the dream, both of which determine its pattern. In contrast to a word count, such formal features are not independent of dream content. They are, however, to be regarded as formal criteria, abstracting from content, in order to reveal basic principles of dream construction.

When we use the metaphor 'drama' to describe a dream, we attempt to monitor the dream's structure of events from beginning to end. A dream may, indeed, proceed like a classical drama, developing with logical continuity, from an initial phase through accelerating events, reaching a climax and arriving at a solution; or, like a modern stage play, it may proceed in an associative manner, characterized by undefined location, time and participants, as well as by changes in constellations and perspectives.

The following examples illustrate how dreams differ in dramatic construction and happening. The supermarket dream was recorded on tape by a 28-year-old man, at home, in the morning:

> "I had gone shopping at a big supermarket. I was pushing a shopping cart around, and threw a few items into it. Next, I went to the check-out counter and wanted to pay. And I suddenly discovered that I did not have any money with me. Of course, I was terribly embarrassed. I didn't know what to do. Just then, a co-worker came along, and she volunteered that she would quickly stop over at my home and bring the money. And that's what she did. I simply waited right there; she brought the money, and I was able to pay."

The dream starts with a routine shopping scene at a supermarket, which turns into an embarrassing situation, as the dreamer discovers that he cannot pay. In this disagreeable situation, the appearance of a helpful co-worker leads to a pleasant solution. The dream has a simple, dramatic structure, reflected in a straightforward, self-contained succession of events, although lacking any particularly intensive highlights.

A dream dealing with an extraordinary wedding was reported upon awakening, on tape at home, by a 27-year-old man:

"My mother had died. There was the funeral, and everyone was quite depressed. And after the wake, we all went home. And about two weeks later, I met a woman in the street. She asked me for an address. I had never seen her before. And then we fell in love, and decided to get married three weeks later. I didn't see her again until the day of the wedding. When I got to the registry office, she was there, with all her papers. She had my mother's name, and, although I had known her for three weeks, I only now saw her face. She looked like my mother when she was 25 years old. We got married and went to church, had a big party, and went home. My co-workers did the usual thing: barricading the home from the outside. We started to work on it, but, as we opened the door, we did not find ourselves inside a house but in a forest. We had, in fact, not lived in a real house but just a false front. Beyond were woods and rivers. And I looked around, baffled, and I never met that woman again."

This dream may be seen as a drama in four acts. The first act is his mother's funeral, which provides an opening and sets the scene for a choice of partners in the second act. The third act provides the observer with heightened drama: only at the registry office does the dreamer recognize that he will be marrying his young mother, whose identity has apparently been hidden from him prior to the marriage ceremony. Still, despite this discovery, the wedding proceeds. During the final act, events develop further twists that lead to a surprise ending. Once they break through the barricades, the couple finds that there is no cozy home behind the door, but the uncertainty of open country in which the female partner is lost.

This dream presents a coherent narrative structure, wherein eventful and differentiated periods are logically related in time. It becomes particularly difficult to consider features of form separately from those of content, because the symbolic dream content provides a special dramatic touch.

The next dream, recorded by a 25-year-old female at home, following a spontaneous nightly awakening, deals with an interrupted telephone conversation:

"Either Helga or Renate, I think it was Renate, called me on the telephone. We were staying at a sort of home for girls. Our call was interrupted. First she called me, and then I called back. The call had to be transferred, but this proved difficult, because the call had to be routed through an ice cream parlor. The place had to be called first, and they had to relay it. Suddenly we found ourselves in the street. I saw the owner of the ice cream parlor run past, and we had to wait for the telephone call to be transferred. At one point it seemed as if I was making the call, then as if he called, then as if the ice cream store was on my side, but next, as if it were really across. It did finally work out all right. But as soon as we had spoken a few words there was another interruption, this time from an American military unit. Now the whole thing became totally confused, the calls mixed up, with cables and networks torn apart. In any case, I didn't know, once again, whether I could reach Helga or Renate."

A threat of uncertainty permeates the whole dream: Who wants to contact whom and why, and what is the actual setting of all these events? The situation switches abruptly from the home for girls to the street; it remains unclear just how the setting is arranged topographically, and where the dreamer actually finds herself. The telephone connection, which links the dream personalities, malfunctions from the start, and finally collapses altogether. This dream does not follow a classical drama pattern but exemplifies an associative structure. It is characterized by persistent uncertainty concerning the dream figures' motivations, by their unrealized intentions, by changes in time and space, and by a discontinuity in the progress of events.

Different features of form that may determine a dream's characteristics refer not only to the extent of the dream experience; they also reveal the principles that mold the dream. When we rely on formal features in order to determine a dream's progress, we also discover just how closely form and content are related and how difficult it is to separate them: formal and content-qualitative attributes supplement each other.

Determining Content and
Qualitative Dream Attributes

Content and quality in dreams are closely related. A dream's content always states something about its quality; dream quality, in turn, is based on content. Methodical procedure does provide different guidelines on how to determine content-qualitative attributes. We may place individual dream contents within different categories, or rate the dream as a whole in qualitative dimensions.

Categorization of dream contents may be undertaken on different levels. It depends on degrees of abstraction, and on the specific nature of a category, whether we are able to derive it directly from the dream, or arrive at our conclusions indirectly. A content category which, for example, differentiates only between female and male, or between known and unknown individuals, represents a simple classification of dream figures. If we wish, however, to determine the number of authority figures in a dream, we need to define whether only older male individuals fit into this category, or whether our definition covers the authoritarian attitude of younger or female dream figures as well.

In 1966, dream researchers Calvin Hall and Robert Van de Castle published a classification system of dream content that has enjoyed broad application, as documented in a recent book by dream researcher Bill Domhoff (1993). Their content analysis defines the dream world in terms of where a dream takes place, what objects are present, which dream characters appear, which activities and interactions take place, what emotions are expressed within the dream, whether persistently pursued events do or do not lead to success, and whether events cause fortune or misfortune.

The two researchers subdivided these major categories into further classes and subclasses. Each dream figure, for example, is coded as to whether it appears alone or with a group, what its sex and age are, and what status it occupies. Thus, some 19 codes are available, showing dream characters' relations to the dreamer; whether they are father, mother, son, relative, acquaintance, stranger or person in public life. Social interactions are initially determined as to whether they involve aggressive, friendly or sexual activities. Within these subdivisions, additional levels of expression are scored; for example aggressive interactions may comprise covert, verbal or outright physical violence.

The following dream, recorded by a 36-year-old woman in her diary, may serve to illustrate bases of the coding procedure established by Hall and Van de Castle:

> "I am riding a white horse through the Bahnhofstrasse, by way of a narrow road to the Münster Square. I enter a restaurant that appears quite medieval. Hans puts up a Leica camera, it topples over, and his mother stands up, greets me, and I say something polite. Next I stand below my garden and talk to Mrs. G. Suddenly, four men appear, all dressed in light yellow: two fat ones, a thin one, and one tall and very good-looking man, who turns around once more and asks me whether we will come down to the carnival. I answer quite haughtily: 'We had planned on that since this morning.' He jumps up, runs to catch up with the others, keeps turning around and waves with his guitar. I am delighted with this."

This example permits the following description: The dream takes place in three locations, two out in the open and one inside a closed room, with all settings familiar to the dreamer. The dream features seven items: street, square and garden are coded as regions; the restaurant as a place of entertainment; the Leica camera and guitar as leisure objects; and, separately, clothing.

In addition to the dreamer, one animal and seven adults make their appearances. Of the five men, only Hans is known to the dreamer; the rest are strangers. On the other hand, the two women are classified as acquaintances.

The Dream Self and the other dream characters engage in a total of sixteen activities—all in the categories of motor activities, movements and conversation. Beyond this, activities are assigned to participating individuals. Thus, "I talk to Mrs.

G." is translated into "Dream Self directs verbal activity to a known female adult." With regard to social interactions, we encounter four friendly activities, with two forms of expression. "Greeting," "saying something polite" and "waving" project friendliness, verbally or by gesture, at a second person. A more specific and active form of erotically cordial attention is the request to "come down to the carnival." We encounter aggressive interaction in only one instance: we classify "replying haughtily" as verbal aggression. The codes of social interaction also include which person is actually participating.

The only classifiable emotion is the dreamer's pleasure at the end of the dream. Success or failure are not coded in this dream, because intentions are not specifically formulated and the result of events remains open. Events occurring without the assistance of dream characters, whether good fortune or misfortune, are not present in this dream.

Hall and Van de Castle transfer all coded dream elements onto a scoring sheet and base their additional evaluation mainly on whether, or how frequently, specific categories appear, and how they relate to each other. In this evaluation, they do not consider a dream's progress or the positional value of dream elements in their sequence. Thus, their classification system permits, primarily, an inventory of dream contents, a segmentation of the range of experience within the dream world.

The range of experience within the dream world may also be described differently: dreams are not decoded in terms of single content categories, but according to situations, themes and motives.

A dream scenario describes the overall setting in which a dream takes place. The dream can be located in different areas of daily life. It may, for example, deal with professional matters or domestic activities; it may mirror leisure time activities or deal with a fantasy world, quite unrelated to realistic life situations.

Dream themes characterize a dream on the basis of dominant contents and progressions of events. Thus, for example, themes of 'Persecution' or 'Separation' may be expressed in dreams in a variety of fashions.

While dream situations and dream themes encompass contents, dream motives reveal underlying dream dynamics, needs and drives, as well as their satisfaction and realization. Dream researchers have adopted motive lists from the psychology of personality. For use in the Thematic Apperception Test, for example, where subjects invent stories prompted by pictures, evaluation criteria were utilized that permitted analyses of such apparent motives as 'Achievement,' 'Affiliation,' 'Dominance' and 'Succorance.'

The following dream example outlines an evaluation of dream motives:

> "I was waterskiing on a lake. At first I was in a big boat, together with other people. I could do the steering myself. At one point I decided that I'd like to manage the boat by myself. By then I had my own sailboat. But now I was no longer waterskiing but able to move on the water, standing up, as if I had my own sails. Was quite flexible and, above all, able to move independently from the other boat. Although I had learned this only just now, it felt very good. A feeling of strength and freedom."

> (Female, 24 years-old, 2nd night, 5th REM phase)

The situation in this dream belongs into the leisure category, and we may label the dream theme 'Clear Sailing.' The motives of this dream are freedom and self-determination, enabling the dreamer to realize her feelings, as she steers her own boat. Once achieved, this independence evolves into a grandiose fantasy, as the dreamer suddenly develops the incredible ability to move on the water as if she were flying. We would need to utilize associations in order to ascertain what kind of value this enhanced desire for independence occupies in the dreamer's life.

A structural approach to the analysis of interactions in dreams was developed in Zürich by Ulrich Moser and his research team (Moser, Pfeifer, Schneider & von Zeppelin, 1980). As a first step, they segment a dream text into individual dream situations. Each situation yields interactive links between figures who appear in it. If the Dream Self is present, but not directly involved in a specific activity, an Observer-Spectator Connection (O) is codified, such as "My brothers threw stones." If the Dream Self stands alone on the stage set, this position is noted as a Setting Connection (S): "I stayed alone in the apartment." If the Dream Self is joined by others, but has no relations to these other dream figures, this position is recorded as a Zero Connection (Z): "I stood in the street, among people."

Every dream figure involved in a situation may also be identified as either initiator (active) or recipient (passive) of an activity. Where one-sided involvement (U) is concerned, an activity originates exclusively with one dream character: "I found a letter," "Someone stops me in the street." Where there is mutual involvement (M), activity is reciprocal: "We talk to each other." Where there is parallel connection (P), it runs in the same direction: "My husband and I were mowing the lawn."

Beyond this, activities are evaluated as to their quality. There is a difference between Approach (ap): "She helped me" and Avoidance (av): "He turned away from me", and Disturbance (ds): "The policeman stopped us".

For the following dream we classified the interactive connections of each situation, as well as the participation of the Dream Self. We eliminated repetitions, pauses, explanations and ideas from the text.

"My girlfriend and I rode our bicycles through a specific street to the next village	[P / Dream Self active]
And then, about halfways, we encountered her sister, who says we should stop,	[U,ds / Dream Self passive]
as she lost the stone of her piece of jewelry	[O,U,av / Dream Self uninvolved]

and we should help her find it. That's what we did.	[P,ap / Dream Self active]
And I did find it.	[U / Dream Self active]
I asked her where she got the stone. She said that she didn't know. She found it at home.	[M / Dream Self active]
Now, by coincidence, one of her brothers appeared	[U,ap / Dream Self passive]
and said, yes, they were his.	[U / Dream self passive]
He had received them as a gift, at a particular shop."	[O,U,ap / Dream Self uninvolved]

(Female, 23 years-old, 2nd night, 3rd REM phase)

We assigned nine interaction codes to this dream. The dream is rich in connection types and their different combinations. It contains one-sided, parallel and mutual interactions, as well as activities of approaches, avoidance and disturbance. Even participation of the Dream Self is manifold. We discover active as well as passive participation, and situations which feature the Dream Self only as observer. While the dreamer appears both active and passive in several situations, it is notable that she appears as the sole executrix of an activity only once.

In contrast to pure content classification, or motive determination, this interaction analysis derives to a greater extent from specific dream contents. A single example cannot fully illustrate to what degree the codification of interactions can extend beyond mere descriptive summary. Identical or different structures of dreams may be recorded when, for example, dreams from a subject's various life segments are examined, or when we compare the dreams of different groups. Interaction analysis is, therefore, capable of expanding the stock-taking concerning the questions of which principles or laws govern the structure of the dream process.

The dream researcher David Foulkes has analyzed the cognitive structure of dreams in even greater detail. In his *Grammar of Dreams* (1978), he presented a sophisticated procedure, designed to codify manifest dream contents, as well as related associations, that lead to latent dream thoughts. Foulkes sought to show that the translation of latent dream thoughts into manifest dream contents adheres to grammatical rules. He divides each dream text into separate sentences. Each sentence expresses a relation in which two substantives, a grammatical subject and object, are linked by a verb. There are four interactive and three associative forms of relations. Interactions are subdivided into 'Moving Toward' (TOWARD), 'Moving From' (FROM), 'Moving Against' (AGAINST) and 'Creating' (CREATING). 'Moving Toward' defines interactions in which the subject notices, approaches or supports an object. 'Moving From' is codified as the subject withdraws from, loses or neglects an object. 'Moving Against' encompasses sentences where the subject encounters the object in a hostile manner, criticizes or attacks it. Finally, 'Creating' covers activities whereby the subject thinks of something, achieves or develops it.

Every interactive sentence calls for codification of the Dream Self as either subject or object; it may be assumed that all relations that find expression in a dream may be traced to the dreamer's motives. Where the Dream Self is absent from interactive sentences, it needs to be inserted at an appropriate point. Take, for example, the dream sentence: "The woman helped the grandfather and the boy climb the stairs." In this case, the 'Ego' can be substituted for the woman, assuming the dreamer is a female. Should, on the other hand, the dream sentence come from a young man, dream context and associations determine whether the Self is represented by grandfather or boy.

'Associative' sentences represent togetherness or identification with the object, wherein subject and object play the same role, or where the object acts as an aid, in order to strengthen a relationship. In addition to the form or relationship, all dream figures are divided into eight classes, independent of whether they are either subject or object within a given sentence: father figures, mother figures, siblings, spouses, female or male peers, children, and the Ego. Items and locations, on the other hand, are not differentiated, but grouped together in the category 'Symbolic.'

We have selected, from one of our dream examples, only the aspect of interactive sentences, in order to illustrate the complex codification procedure, and to show into which structural features a dream text becomes transformed. Interactive sentences are particularly interesting, because Foulkes assumes that latent dream motives are hidden within them.

"A beautiful house inside a forest. Quite an isolated place, actually; not really furnished, just a bit. There were several mailboxes inside this house, and *I should really have collected the mail* from one of them.   [TOWARD]
That day, too, I should have collected the mail, but *I forgot the key.*   [FROM]
Then a visitor came,   [TOWARD]
whom I did not want to admit.   [AGAINST]
And *he said: 'Now you'll go for a walk with me.'*   [TOWARD]
And I said: 'Certainly not.'   [AGAINST]
Then *we walked downstairs,*   [FROM]
when *I saw that he had a giant dog*   [TOWARD]
by his side, a boxer dog, a very big, exceedingly playful animal.
Suddenly it was totally dark and *I lost a shoe.*   [FROM]
Those were sandals, open-toed sandals, and behind us were many people, girls and men,
and I said: [TOWARD]
'I have lost my shoe.'   [FROM]
One of them yelled: 'Here.'   [TOWARD]

And so *I get it back*	[TOWARD]
and *put it on.*	[TOWARD]
But it wasn't the right one. I went a few	
steps, but *then I held it up*	[TOWARD]
and *said:*	[TOWARD]
'That isn't the one, *I have to have another*	[TOWARD]
one,' and I simply *put it down.*"	[FROM]

(Female, 47 years-old, 3rd night, 4th REM phase)

This dream contains interactions that most frequently express approaches, while activities involving separation and aggression are quite rare. However, the mere frequency of various forms of interactions does not, by itself, prove much, as long as it is not supplemented by the additional interaction of participating dream figures and objects. This dream shows an approach by the dreamer eight times, but only three times by others. She is also the one who manifests actions that signify rejection and separation. Further structural analyses, which would include the dreamer's associations, might possibly clarify whether the rejection which the Dream Self expresses toward the male individual is based on an interaction pattern that originates within the dreamer's life story in any meaningful way.

Compared to the content analysis of Hall and Van de Castle, particularly suited to elicit appearances common to many dreams, Moser's and Foulkes' approaches are targeted more to illustrate the structure that underlies individual dreams. Both methods provide an opening toward the process of dream generation; Foulkes' system of codification particularly emphasizes the analysis of individual motive structures.

Dreams do not only convey contents, but leave an overall impression behind that may be captured through the evaluation of its qualitative dimensions. This window on the dream, which supplements categorization of dream contents, is often selected because it conveys the ambience of dreams, whether they are perhaps felt as realistic or fantastic, dramatic or mundane, vivid or bland, lively or tough.

Dream research can look back on a long tradition of systematic collection of judgments based on impressions. Such dream evaluations are based on instructions that contain more or less detailed descriptions of a given category, while providing a gauge as well. The example of 'dramatic quality' illustrates such differing possibilities of evaluation.

We may present a judge with a dream and ask simply: "How dramatic is this dream?" This enables him or her to decide what 'dramatic' really means. Here, however, we face the problem that the evaluator may have an opinion of what is dramatic that varies from a commonly accepted view; he or she may regard whatever is dramatic in a negative sense and consider it as equal to greatly exaggerated or disturbed. In order to avoid this, we might add an additional definition to our instructions, such as: "Dramatic indicates how eventful, vivid and emotionally gripping the dream is." Another possibility is the definition, at the start, of different dramatic aspects, which can then be judged separately and jointly evaluated later on.

Standards applied to evaluations differ in their respective approaches. They might be divided into individually labeled levels or into successive grades of intensity. 'Dramatic quality' could be estimated as 'high,' 'medium' or 'low,' or as ranging in value from 1 ('little') to 10 ('much'). Our choice of a gauge depends on how appropriate it is, after all, to establish different levels of 'dramatic quality' and how significant these different expressions really are.

Overall qualitative evaluations of dreams are frequently employed in dream research, in order to assess, for example, inventive imagery, dreamlike quality, realism, or to judge how emotionally-oriented, bizarre or uncontrolled dreams are. Overall evaluations of dreams are not to be regarded as a mere stocktaking of dream contents; rather, they lead to a typological approach to dreams, to the establishment of different classes of dreams. Such categorizations permit, for example, an initial view of differences between dreams that have their origin in specific sleep stages or that are reported by people who find themselves in different life situations.

Reliability of Dream Evaluation

Individual methods of dream evaluation differ as to how firmly and reliably they may be utilized. Just how exacting a method is depends on how simple or complex it is, how many rules of application it demands and how clearly these have been formulated. Dream research shares these problems with all disciplines that are concerned with the evaluation of personal experiences, be they the remarks of a patient during psychotherapy, narratives recorded during psychological test situations, or reports dealing with fantasies during the waking state.

We check the reliability of dream evaluation by subjecting identical dream material to several ratings. This enables us to verify whether different evaluators arrive at uniform conclusions. If ratings are complex, judges are usually trained by evaluating a selection of earlier dreams before facing their actual task.

Whenever features can be directly derived from a dream text, dream research often employs outside judges. This makes it possible to subject the dreams of different people to the same criteria. There are, however, facets of dream experiences that do not always find expression in a dream report. If that is the case, it can be advantageous to utilize the dreamer himself or herself as evaluator; it is the dreamer, after all, who has the most direct access to all aspects of the dream experience.

The following dream, which returns the dreamer to his school, shows the problems which, for example, arise from outside and self-evaluation of dream emotions:

"I was talking to a woman, and I was a grammar school pupil. It was a class room, where the female teacher sat in the center, and the pupils formed a circle around her. And then test results were handed out, which turned out to be horribly bad. Somehow I wound up with a six [*Note: In this school system six is the highest grade*], but did not know it, and had to go to the blackboard, in order to clean the board. While I was busy cleaning, I heard that I had received a six. And the others had tears in their eyes. And there was a girl who gave me a kiss and went away."

(Male, 25 years-old, 2nd night, 4th REM phase)

If we judge this dream as outsiders, we can start by isolating the emotions that were expressed directly within the dream, whether related to the dreamer or to other dream persons. Using this criterium, we encounter no emotions. As a second step we codify emotions that are directly and clearly expressed in events. Two emotions may be found in this dream: 'Distress' on the part of the other pupils ("turned out horribly bad . . . tears in their eyes") and 'Pleasure' on the part of the dreamer (". . . who gave me a kiss"). Although codification of 'Distress' is suggested by the dream context, we cannot be certain, when using the 'Pleasure' codification, whether the kiss did not release different emotions as well. If we try another approach, designed to elicit emotions that are indirectly hidden within the dream situations, it might be possible to place a 'Fear' code at the point of the dream where the dreamer is unaware of how the test came out. We might use a 'Shame' code when he has to clean the blackboard, and, once again, 'Pleasure,' when he discovers his good grade—and, finally, 'Surprise,' with the kiss. Using indirect codification, we place ourselves inside the dream situation and seek to assume what kind of emotions it could have aroused. We are, of course, guided by our own personal attitudes and experiences, and must also assume that dream emotions are comparable to situations during the waking state.

Obviously, agreement among outside judges is more frequent when a limited range of emotions are overtly expressed in a dream report. Still, even when outside evaluators agree on an indirect determination of emotions, their conclusions do not necessarily coincide with those of the dreamer. We were, therefore not surprised to find that emotions noted by the dreamer differed markedly from those of the outside judges. When asked: "How did you feel during this dream?", he answered: "Depressed, somehow, and puzzled that I am a pupil." Although the outside evaluators ascribed different emotions to separate dream situations, the dreamer himself expressed only an integrated mood of distress and surprise, reflecting his experience of the dream as a whole.

Differences between self-evaluation and outside appraisal of emotions, as illustrated by this dream, tend to suggest that dream emotions should only be judged by the dreamers themselves. One must, nevertheless, keep in mind that the dreamer, too, has a specific point of view. He or she is likely to report only emotions that were particularly vivid or had a pronounced after-effect. The dreamer is also likely to report only emotions that need not be rejected, and which the dreamer feels free to admit to the experimenter. When we deal with the emotional content of dreams, as reflected in symbolized episodes, even outside evaluations may lead to appropriate conclusions.

Different methods of dream evaluation are not mutually exclusive; rather, they represent efforts at clarification that supplement each other, whenever a multiplicity of dream phenomena is assigned to viewpoints that vary appropriately. Ultimately, the aim of research determines whether we select formal or content-and-qualitative dream characteristics, whether we categorize the dream in detail or judge it from an overall viewpoint, and whether we assign the evaluation of a dream to outsiders or to the dreamer.

4

Recalling Dreams

Memory, the link between dreaming and waking, provides the only means of tracing dreams. But dream recall is willful and unpredictable. Because it follows its own rules, dreams are a familiar experience for many people, a rare event for others, and for some a totally unapproachable phenomenon.

Dream researchers have long wondered why some people cannot remember their dreams at all, while others are able to report a dream each and every morning. Up to now, researchers have been unable to fully explain just what causes these differences.

A representative survey among the population of Switzerland illustrates what answers we receive when we ask people simply how often they dream (Borbély 1984).

Figure 6 shows that those questioned fall into approximately three categories: people who remember frequently; others, who remember their dreams now and then; and finally, a third category that is rarely or never aware of its dreams. These types of dream memory are not restricted to the Swiss population, but, as a result of surveys undertaken in several countries, could be found with comparable frequency elsewhere. We may, therefore, assume that there are people for whom dreams are a daily event, while others find this area of experience totally closed.

Remembering or forgetting dreams may, in addition, be subject to variations over a period time—as shown in our longitudinal study of sleep behavior which, among other topics,

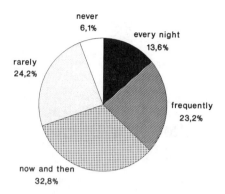

FIGURE 6. Frequency of Spontaneous Dream Recall. A representative survey of 1,000 inhabitants of Switzerland. Percentages of answers to the question "How often do you dream?" (Borbély, 1984).

revealed the frequency of dream recall. We began this project in 1975, when we first queried a group of students, then from 10 to 12 years old, and later repeated our inquiry seven times, at two-year intervals. Figure 7 shows how the frequency of dream recall changed during the second and third life decades of the 92 people who consistently answered this question.

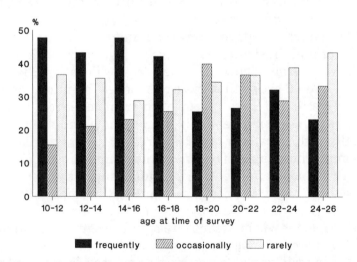

FIGURE 7. Frequency of Dream Recall during Second and Third Life Decades. Over a period of fourteen years, 92 students were asked, every two years, how frequently they recalled dreams spontaneously.

Dream recall in youth was clearly more frequent than in young adulthood. During the initial four inquiries more than forty percent of the youths remembered several dreams a week, placing frequent recall in first place. By the eighteenth year, however, the ratio changed: at this point, rare or occasional dream recall gained in prominence, and frequent memory had to yield its primacy.

Improved dream memory during the second decade of life might have reflected the young people's increased self-awareness, prompting them to pay more attention to their dreams as factors in their process of individuation. In contrast, dreams during subsequent young adulthood lost some of their importance, because the demands of daily life came to overshadow them.

Dream memory followed this pattern generally, but its changes did not affect everyone the same way. Figure 8 shows consistency as well as variability of dream recall. We have separated the individual patterns of the 92 persons

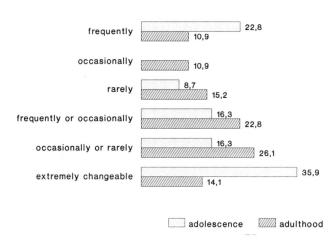

FIGURE 8. Variability of Dream Recall during Second and Third Life Decades. Individual types of dream recall among youths and young adults. Four times, during their second and third life decades, the same 92 people estimated dream recalls. The categories 'frequently,' 'occasionally' or 'rarely' represent individuals who were consistent in this description. Other types describe various changing frequencies.

into three consistent and three variable types, divided between youth and adulthood.

During the first four inquiries, nearly every third student made the same reply, claiming consistently that he or she remembered dreams frequently or rarely. Teenage subjects reported varied results much more frequently during this period, in particular extreme changes in dream memory. Among young adults, too, only about one third of those questioned reported their dream memory as stable; but frequent, occasional and rare dream memories were reported with equal frequency. The most significant change from youth was evident in that the now adult subjects showed a marked lessening of extreme variations in memory. Apparently, access to dreams had settled into a relatively routine pattern and varied only to a lesser degree.

Accounts of dream memory do not, of course, provide reliable information concerning the actual appearance of dreams. Earlier surveys were often based on the assumption that dream memories were equivalent to dreams as such, whereas our present approach distinguishes strictly between the process of dream recall and the appearance of dreams.

Even Freud deduced from his observations that people dream more than they can remember, because dreams leave only elusive imprints on memory and are easily forgotten:

> "It is a proverbial fact that dreams melt away in the morning. They can, of course, be remembered; for we only know dreams from our memory of them after we are awake. But we very often have a feeling that we have only remembered a dream in part and that there was more of it during the night; we can observe, too, how the recollection of a dream, which was still lively in the morning, will melt away, except for a few small fragments, in the course of the day; we often know we have dreamt, without knowing what we have dreamt; and we are so familiar with the fact of dreams being liable to be forgotten, that we see no absurdity in the possibility of someone having had

a dream in the night and of his not being aware in the morning, either of what he has dreamt or even the fact that he has dreamt at all. On the other hand, it sometimes happens that dreams show an extraordinary persistence in the memory. I have analysed dreams in my patients which occurred twenty-five and more years earlier; and I can remember a dream of my own separated by at least thirty-seven years from to-day and yet as fresh as ever in my memory" (1900/1964, p. 43).

Since then, Freud's concepts have been confirmed by numerous dream experiments, whereby people were able to report their dreams more frequently during systematic awakenings than in everyday situations. But even an awakening in a laboratory setting does not permit us to anticipate with certainty that it will actually yield a fresh dream for our data bank.

In order to achieve optimal conditions for the recollection of dreams, dream research has dealt intensely with the interesting topic of dream recall. This has shown that there is no simple explanation for degrees of fluctuation in dream memory, inasmuch as multi-leveled physiological and psychological elements encourage as well as hamper our access to the dream.

Physiological Elements of Dream Recall

Dream recollection depends, first of all, on the sleep stage from which the sleeper awakens. Although dreams are reported from all sleep phases, not all stages of sleep are equally favorable to the collection of a dream. Sleepers remember a dream most easily when we awaken a subject in the sleep laboratory directly from REM sleep. Under these conditions we are able to obtain between eight and nine dream reports from ten awakenings. Fewer dreams emerge, however, when we awake a sleeper from Sleep Stages 2 to 4, where only about every second awakening yields a dream memory.

REM sleep thus should be regarded as a particularly promising condition for dream memory. In our sleep laboratory approximately nine out of ten REM awakenings yielded dreams among good spontaneous dream recallers. Although the number of unsuccessful awakenings was, on the whole, not very high, it demonstrates nevertheless that awakening from REM sleep does not guarantee a dream memory in every instance. Even under experimental conditions, individual variations are of great significance. While many subjects were able to relate a dream over several nights, following each REM awakening, there were others whose memory failed now and then, while some could only report a dream after two out of three awakenings.

What is the sleep profile of someone who, in everyday life, does not remember any dreams at all? The assumption that such non-recallers have a different sleep structure could not be confirmed. This question was examined soon after discovery of REM sleep, when it was ascertained that cyclical REM phases of comparable length also appear with those who do not recall their dreams.

Still, how do people, who cannot report dreams from everyday life, act when awakened from their REM phase in the sleep laboratory? We selected ten subjects who maintained that, at home, they spontaneously remembered at most one dream per month, and asked them initially to keep a dream diary for one week. We then woke them from their REM phases over four nights, and asked them about their dreams. After the laboratory nights had ended, they maintained their dream diaries for another week.

These poor recallers were able, on the average, to report a dream after two out of three REM awakenings. We further subdivided these unsuccessful awakenings: there are 'non-rememberings,' where the subjects are conscious of having dreamt, although the content eludes them. We call these 'white dreams' and separate them from non-remembering cases where subjects maintain that, prior to awakening, nothing had passed through their minds. About half of the 'non-rememberings' consisted of such white dreams.

Figure 9 indicates the frequency of dream memory, as recorded in the diary and in the REM awakenings. For each person, results are conveyed separately, as the degree of fluctuation in dream memory presented a significant feature under both conditions.

Although all the subjects we selected described themselves as recalling dreams only rarely, the mere request to pay particular attention to dreams at home, and to record them, caused a differentiation of this group and led to dreams by more than half of them. Once in the laboratory, dream recall for this group increased still further. One subject, who had not recorded a single dream in his diary, remembered two dreams in the lab. The majority of subjects actually turned into good dream recallers, and not only those who had previously recorded more dreams in their diaries but others, as well, who had only experienced a significant increase in dream memory after REM awakenings. Nevertheless, three subjects have to be separated from this group, because even under favorable conditions

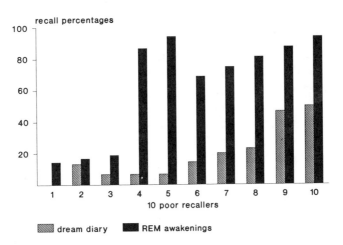

FIGURE 9. Dream Recall: Individual Differences. Varying levels of dream recall in dream diary and sleep laboratory, following REM awakenings of ten individuals who had categorized themselves as recalling dreams only rarely.

they were able to remember dreams only rarely.

These results make it clear that the sleep stage cannot, of itself, be considered as a condition sufficient for dream memory. As the division of sleep stages is governed by outstanding features, with short-range fluctuations in activity less notable, some researchers have explored a further area, seeking to anticipate dream memory more readily through the use of refined EEG analyses. Several studies, including those with rare recallers in our own research, suggested that dream recall succeeded more frequently when, prior to awakening, the EEG had indicated a short-range increase in activity (Meier Faber 1988). Although, accordingly, the extent of activation can have a significant impact on dream memory, it has not yet been possible to define precisely and to anticipate exactly how, and for how long, the EEG has to be activated, if access to a dream is to be possible in each case.

Other signs of changes, such as the phasic appearance of eye movement during REM sleep, also failed to contribute to a solution of the dream memory puzzle. During several experiments, sleepers were awakened after rapid eye movements or periods of eye rest, but awakenings that instantly followed eye movements did not always result in improved dream memory.

When we remember a dream, we are thinking back from the waking state to an experience that occurred during a different state of consciousness. A dream is only remembered once the transition from sleep to the waking state has taken place. Obviously, this transition from one state of consciousness to another is easiest if the dream state is closest to the waking state. REM sleep, with its distinct activity features, is closer to the waking state than is deep sleep, from which it is more difficult to wake a sleeper. REM sleep dreams are, therefore, easier to recall: dreams from a near-waking phase are more directly accessible.

Two Zürich researchers, Martha Koukkou and Dietrich Lehmann, have designed a psychophysiological model of dreaming that links the EEG's fluctuating functional states with information processing during sleep (Koukkou & Lehmann 1983). They assume that various EEG states are associated with specific cognitive strategies and categories of memory storage. They regard the slow waves of sleep as a functional state that is linked to the thought strategies of childhood. The revival of new or old memory material fluctuates in accordance with stronger or weaker activated physiological states. They maintain that only adjacent storage areas are capable of exchanging information, and that, therefore, it is easier to remember a dream from an activated, near-waking functional state than from deeper sleep.

Research into physiological constituents of dream recall has provided clear-cut proof that we dream more than we remember spontaneously, and that specific sleep phases permit easier access to dreams. Although dream recall as a whole increases inside the dream laboratory, there still remain differences between individuals, although these are not as marked as during spontaneous dream recall.

What do these results tell us about dream memory in everyday existence? We are apparently most readily able to remember a dream when we awake from an activated REM phase. Examining a typical nightly sleep profile, we realize that REM phases gain in value with longer sleep periods. We might assume that we should recall a dream, as we awake from REM sleep, every two or three days. But, with most people, dreams do not appear quite that frequently or regularly. And not every awakening from REM sleep in the laboratory results in a dream report. This sleep state and its closeness to the waking state cannot, therefore, of itself be the decisive factor in dream memory. In addition, we have to account for the personality of the dreamer, the dream context, and the very nature of the dream; these psychological elements have an impact on the likelihood that the sleep experience will, almost literally, see the light of day.

Psychological Elements of Dream Memory

As there are people who never remember their dreams, we must ask ourselves whether they differ in thought, memory and emotional experience from those who have ready access to their dreams. Are those who do not remember dreams rational thinkers in their waking hours, in tune with reality, while people who remember dreams are emotionally-oriented and given to lively fantasy? Or, to be still more pointed and even judgmental: are non-rememberers forced to repress their internal images, and are frequent recallers engulfed by their imagination?

Dream research has a long tradition of tracing different expressions of dream memory to personality characteristics. Numerous studies have attempted to discover whether good and poor dream recallers differ in basic characteristics and capabilities. The results of these studies proved, however, to be uneven and contradictory. Different aspects of personality were utilized and related to dream memory. Studies sought to establish, for example, whether good dream rememberers were particularly intelligent, given to anxieties or more adapt at expressing their emotions, and whether people who forget their dreams are distinguished by ego strength and tend to repress emotions during their waking existence. As soon as a study confirmed one of these correlations, another study arrived at opposite conclusions.

There were fewer contradictions concerning relations between dream memory and single aspects of thought and imaging. Those who remembered dreams also demonstrated a vivid fantasy activity in the waking state, as well as a capacity for dealing easily with visuo-spatial patterns of imaging. It should be emphasized, however, that until now no overarching personality pattern has been established that would closely and reliably correlate with the variability of dream memory.

We, too, singled out a specific aspect of dream memory, acting on the assumption that dreams—because of their unique nature—might be more difficult to remember than everyday experiences that occur within a firm and familiar framework of experience. Do people who do not report dreams fail to do so, because they find it difficult to accept this special form of experience and to turn it into communicative language?

We sought to establish whether non-recallers are capable of relating dream material appropriately. To do this, we asked them to remember alien dreams. We first selected dreams of others, which independent judges had categorized as either difficult or easy to remember. We then asked those who remembered dreams only rarely to relate these dreams in the same setting in which they had to report their own dreams. During one night we woke our subjects during the REM phases and asked them about their dreams in the usual manner. During another night we again woke them from the REM phases, but quickly played a tape of another subject's dream, asking them to place themselves into the dream setting, and then to re-tell it. If, at that point, they remembered a dream of their own, they merely mentioned it in a key phrase or catchword, and reported it afterwards.

The non-recallers in this study were quite capable of appropriately relating the external conditions and qualitative content of others' dream reports. This result permits the conclusion that non-recallers are not generally handicapped in the comprehension and rendering of dream material. This has no bearing, however, on the question of whether non-recallers dream differently from good recallers and therefore have less access to their dreams.

There was, then, no confirmation of the somewhat unlikely assumption that those who did not remember their dreams displayed basically different waking behavior than people who remembered well. More successful were efforts that related dream memory to the motivations and attitudes of the subjects and that placed greater emphasis on situational elements.

Several studies suggested that people who remember dreams well are more likely to believe in the relevance of dreams and like to deal with them, while non-recallers are more inclined to regard dreams as meaningless and are indifferent toward their own dream experiences. We noted among a group of young adults that nearly all those who manifested frequent dream recall reacted positively to dreams, while every second subject who remembered dreams only rarely regarded them with indifference or actually rejected them. Whether this marked absence of interest is the result of lacking dream experiences, or of a predilection that restricts dream memory, remains an open question.

During lectures on dream topics we have frequently observed how interest in dreams influences the memory of dreams. We began, for example, one semester with a questionnaire on the frequency of spontaneous dream memory, followed by a second set of questions at the end of the study period. Concern with the subject of dreams led one group of students to increased dream memory. However, greater interest in dreams does not, by itself, guarantee results; there were students who, despite all efforts, did not produce an increased number of dreams.

Attitude toward dreams also offers a possible explanation for sex and age differences observed during several studies. Women often display better dream memory than men, and dream memory fades with age. Accordingly, women would remember their dreams more frequently because they ascribe more relevance to them, and the lowered interest of older people might prompt their lessened recall.

Motivation toward dreams need not, in fact, be an invariable personality trait, but might fluctuate in accordance with specific life situations. The number of dreams could well increase under the stimulus of changes in living conditions, during crises that prompt concentration on psychological developments, but also during leisure times, such as vacations, which simply offer more time for dreaming. Dream memory may also vary from day to day, because we do not always pay the same amount of attention to our internal processes.

Distraction from dream experience can, quite clearly, be affected by the manner of the awakening situation. If we wake up in the morning, get up immediately and face the demands of the day, access to dreams is more easily hampered than when we stay in bed for a while and give ourselves some time for recollection. These hints sound obvious, but are not always effective. On the one hand, recollection does not necessarily lead to realization of a dream and, on the other hand, there are dreams that virtually force themselves into our waking consciousness, regardless of the manner of awakening.

We are often under the impression, in everyday life, that dreams with particularly vivid images and dramatic events are quite easily accessible. But as access to non-remembered dreams is closed, we are unfortunately unable to determine what the unremembered dreams are like and how they differ from remembered dreams. We are forced to select an indirect approach, examining remembered dreams to see how easy or difficult it was to grasp them, or to examine whether a once-remembered dream may be recalled later on.

Two examples illustrate differences in the process of remembering. Both dreams were reported by a 25-year-old female student during the second night, after we had awakened her from the second and fourth REM phases.

"[20 seconds pause] Hmm, I was combing my hair and was talking to somebody, but I don't know who. Oh yes, yes [10 seconds pause] yes, yes, it was like the situation of getting ready for a night in the sleep lab. And, well, I had to get myself ready. And at that moment I was at a place, with a view . . . like an overlook terrace above a lake, I think it actually was Lake Zürich. And [5 seconds pause] now I was with somebody, talking to somebody [5 seconds pause], whether women or men are better suited, are somehow better suited to act as experimental subjects or not. Hmm, yes there is, I have the feeling there is more, or that there is more to this, but I have trouble remembering. [15 seconds pause]. Yes, I don't know any more."

"[Sighs] I was at the Bern railroad station, and wanted to take the train to Zürich, and I was wondering whether I should take the bicycle along. On the one hand, I thought it might be a good thing to have, to get around in the city, but I hesitated, too, because I was somehow afraid of the traffic. And then it came down to the last possible moment for taking the bicycle on that particular train. And I finally decided about the bicycle, decided to take it along. And I walked through the underpass and up to the platform, came up the opposite side; at the very end was the mail car. That's what I saw. And as I got there, the train just started to move. But I was somehow almost able to throw the bicycle on the train. And just then you woke me up and I didn't have time to look how I could get on the train. I think I am just standing at the railroad station, without bicycle."

The first example emphasizes the dreamer's effort to seize a dream that she finds difficult to grasp. The long pauses of reflection and her efforts to comprehend the dream situation mirror a difficult memory process. The dream was perhaps also difficult to recall, because of its associative structure and because locality of events and dream figures remained vague.

The second dream was more easily accessible. The dreamer gives the impression that she is still well within the dream. She relates events without hesitation and clearly remembers what thoughts went through her mind. This dream also presents a clearer structure and a continuity of events, which may have facilitated recollection.

If we assume that recollection of a dream also depends on its structure, then the subject remembered her second dream more easily because it represented a finite and vivid experience. Of course, this presumes that both dreams were really dreamed exactly as they were told and that the differences did not develop during the process of recollection.

By having dreams related twice, we undertook a special study of what types of dreams turn out to be particularly well remembered. We awakened 24 subjects from their nightly REM phases, recorded their dreams, and later, after they got up in the morning, asked them to report the dreams of the previous night for a second time.

Two-thirds of a total of 114 dreams were spontaneously remembered by the subjects during their second recall. With the help of a catchword the segment of twice-remembered dreams increased by an additional 20 percent, while 12 percent of the dreams that had been reported during the night could not be recalled in the morning at all.

It is actually surprising that not every one of the subjects' dreams was remembered in the morning, considering that it had entered waking consciousness once before. What distinguished the dreams that were remembered twice, unaided, from those that were totally forgotten? First of all, known processes that control our memory were at work, such as position effects: dreams were more frequently remembered from the second half of sleep, where the elapsed time between the first and second memory is shorter, but there was also better dual recall of a night's first dream, which starts a series of dreams. A longer waking period, following awakening, was also linked to improved re-remembering, apparently because the dream could imprint itself more firmly within waking consciousness. In addition, long and dramatically intensive dreams were more accessible in the morning than dream episodes that were short and lacking in tension.

Differences in the type of dream might also have significance for spontaneous dream recall, that represents only one segment of the total dream experience. In everyday life mainly particularly vivid and impressive dreams are remembered. By comparison, laboratory awakenings also open the door to dream experiences that are not marked by outstanding characteristics.

Qualities of Dream Memory

Whenever a dream is reported twice, even a first reading shows that a previously related dream is told differently the second time around. Comparison of the first and second reports may, therefore, reveal which dream features are more readily recalled and which are more likely to be forgotten.

One example illustrates how a morning's second dream memory differed from the dream report of the preceding night. One 32-year-old woman reported a dream during the second experimental night that dealt with 'bottles on a journey'. Her report came after the first of four REM awakenings, and was rereported in the morning without the aid of a catchword.

"I was seeing a train with wheels like Bulldog wheels, tractor wheels. And in the train sat a lot of bottles, real bottles. And all around were basket bottles. They were quite differently dressed, I mean really dressed, it seemed to me as if they were dressed, some in a dark basket, others in light ones, others with bast, lengthwise, others braided across, really quite differently. And they all talked to each other. And this train continued to move right on. The wheels were oddly loose, as if they weren't fastened, and everything shook a little. And it kept going uphill, downhill-uphill, not on a really level roadbed. And it kept moving on, and on, and on. And suddenly this thing grew something like wings, and, whoops, up in the air. And that's all there was."

"Oh yes, the one with the bottles. That was some kind of train, and this train was totally filled up, just with bottles. And the bottles were like dressed, some dark, some light, and some had basket weave around them, they were like wine bottles, litre bottles. And they acted as if they were talking to each other, they kept nodding, and I don't know any more."

The second version, in the morning, presented the dream event substantially condensed and shortened. Because of the elapsed time, the report sounds less immediate. Repetitions of dream elements are eliminated, and the number of gaps is significant. Details of the bottles' dress are lacking ("with bast, lengthwise . . . across"). Details of loose wheels and of the whole train ride, with its fantastic conclusion, are lost. Simplification, and particularly abbreviation, make the whole train ride seem colorless and lacking in drama. The second report also provides new information. The bottles are described more precisely as "wine bottles, litre bottles." There is only one striking change: originally, the bottles were said to have "talked to each other," but in the morning, adjustment to waking thought brought the correction that "they acted as if they were talking to each other, they kept nodding."

We used a sample of twenty-one dreams, which provided both night and morning versions, to utilize David Foulkes' coding method to determine whether morning memories and night reports differ basically in their cognitive structure. We asked ourselves whether, for example, unknown dream figures appear less frequently in twice-remembered dreams than in initial reports, or whether dream persons change roles and social interactions.

On the whole, this evaluation did not yield any significant differences in the distribution of dream figures or in their positions as subjects or objects. But night reports contained a greater emphasis on verbs which, in one way or another, expressed active relations. As the dream example illustrated, many night reports appear as direct and 'active' experiences, while the morning narratives are often less immediate and a good deal more organized. Greater distance from the dream experience appears to induce reformulation, which prompts the second report to adhere more closely to standards that govern our waking thoughts. Freud introduced the concept of secondary elaboration to describe such processes of reformulation.

When we group all dreams together, our results tend to suggest that night reports and morning memories do not basically differ in cognitive structure. Whatever was forgotten during a morning report is clearly not different, structurally, than anything that was added to the original version. However, when we study individual dreams, we note that morning reports contain numerous changes and eliminations that may be categorized in the codes of

dream figures and types of relations. They differ, nevertheless, so markedly from dream to dream and subject to
subject that a summary of all dreams tends to submerge
them once again.

A further study with 20 subjects dealt with qualitative
changes between the first and second dream reports. Out of
100 REM dreams, originally reported during the night, our
subjects spontaneously remembered 80 dreams the following morning. We first divided these 80 pairs of dreams into
experience units. Next, we compared the two reports by
scanning the morning report for items that had either
remained the same, were missing, had been added or
appeared in different guise. Only 22 percent out of a total of
876 units from the first version appeared with the same
content the following morning. The same percentages were
totally missing from the morning report, but 55 units had
been newly added. The remaining dream segments were
changed in some way, with simplifications in first place, followed by elaborations and transformations. There were also
quite a few experience units that had undergone several
changes.

We also encoded experience units by content, in order
to determine what dream contents were missing, had been
newly added or changed. Changes between the first and
second dream reports occurred in all content categories. For
example, compared to activities, neither dream figures nor
objects were more likely to be forgotten, newly introduced or
enriched.

When interpreting these results, we have to keep in
mind that such changes are partly determined by the same
standards that govern waking behavior. Furthermore, we
cannot be sure, whether a morning report refers to the
actual dream or is confounded by the initial narration of
the dream.

One dream, dealing with an indiscreet experimenter,
was reported by a 25-year-old student during his first laboratory night, initially after awakening from his second REM
phase and, for a second time, the following morning:

"Ah yes, exactly, I had a talk with your colleague, but she looked quite differently, much younger, like someone I went to school with, perhaps a 13-year-old girl. And I was dreaming of this dream setting, this test setting. Yes, actually it was a very cool room, with a blinding light. And she sat at a table, and before her, yes, I believe at some kind of table, and with my diary opened before her. And she kept leafing through this diary in a rather listless manner. And I kept watching her and wondering at the time whether I should consider this laid-back. Then we talked about whether she was actually capable of reading. And she said, 'Well, yes, sometimes I'm able, sometimes not.' And I wondered, yes, should I tell her now that I really don't care for this, that I don't think it's a great idea, what she is doing there. (How did you feel during this dream?) I think a bit unsure, as I could not tell whether I should react to her or not."

"Well, the first one I told you about took place in a test setting and a room, cold light. And a younger woman, outwardly looking like someone with whom I went to school when I was 13 years old, is leafing through my diary. And I, I am annoyed."

At first glance, it is once again remarkable how much shorter, compared to the night memory, the morning version is. But the condensation did not only prompt a tighter presentation of the dream event, but information is also lost and transformed. During the night report the dream character had been identified as the other experimenter, who looked like one of the dreamer's former fellow students. In the second report she is only a fellow student and the identification with the experimenter was dropped. Furthermore, and interestingly, by morning all interactions between the dreamer and the other person had disappeared. At this point the dreamer remained silent, while the woman kept snooping through his diary.

Tracing the motives behind these changes, we observe that the original version of the dream events quite openly expresses the dreamer's critical attitude toward the experiment. The experimenter is downgraded: at one point she resembles a school girl, at another she displays a listless manner and is indiscreet, and finally she is not even able to read properly. True, lack of privacy protection remains a central issue during the second version, but the theme is concentrated less clearly on the experimental setting, is strikingly removed, with the laboratory setting transformed into an undetermined environment. This may have enabled the dreamer to admit his negative feeling of annoyance more readily.

In this case we have, to begin with, emphasized the qualitative changes that emerged from the first to the second report. We have focused less on similarities, which are not as evident, simply because the morning version was substantially abbreviated. The relationship between the two reports is nevertheless obvious, because the central theme— of a test setting that is disagreeable and presents an invasion of privacy—is maintained, and because we are able to assign the transformed experience units of the second report to the nightly dream.

The research unit at Bologna headed by Marino Bosinelli has examined changes between first and second dream memories in several studies; they, too, used Foulkes' scoring system (Bosinelli, Cicogna & Cavallero 1983). This research group made the interesting attempt of ascribing specific changes in dream figures and relationships to psychological defense mechanisms. When, in one sentence, one dream figure was substituted for another, they spoke of a change as a 'Displacement': "I quarreled with my father," turned into "I talked to my brother." One example of 'Denial' was said to be "My mother was there, too," which became "My mother did not come." An interactive relationship was weakened by 'Neutralization': instead of "I kissed the flower girl," the phrase became "I was together with a flower girl."

Their dream material included such interesting psychological transformations only rarely, being limited to 1.8 percent of all sentences. This result indicates that defense mechanisms which, according to Freud, are of decisive importance in the creation of dreams, play only a minor role in the process of recollection.

The question arises whether such deviations between first and second dream recall may contribute to our understanding of what impact the nature of dreams may have on the memory process. Our results show, first of all, that remembered dreams are not firmly anchored in detail; a dream, once remembered, is usually presented in a changed manner when recounted a second time. This incompleteness of dream memory does not only consist of any lack of unimportant dream elements and the retention of remarkable features. Although intensive, dramatic and vivid dreams stand a better chance of imprinting themselves on our memories, some quite significant dream elements may be either forgotten or undergo transformations that gain meaning only when placed against the background of a dreamer's life situation.

Complexity of Dream Memory

How relevant are the different approaches and results in regard to dream recall? Dream laboratory awakenings have clearly documented that we dream more than we remember. With this in mind, even someone who remembers well, who is able to recall a dream each morning, is basically a poor dream recaller; even he or she has managed to hold on to only a small segment of nightly dream experience.

Results of dream memory studies do not answer the question of whether we dream always or only periodically, as we can only deal with dreams that have entered and established themselves within our waking consciousness. We cannot, therefore, ultimately decide whether lack of a dream memory means that we did not dream at all or whether our access to the dream was blocked. 'White dreams' do, however, indicate that memory blockage may often play a significant role. One category of delayed recollection are dreams we recall suddenly, later in the day, when we encounter something that abruptly brings them to mind.

As we have noted, dream memory depends on numerous factors. Memory is aided when we have a positive attitude toward dreams and it is hampered when we are indifferent to it. Dreams enter our waking consciousness more easily when we are in an activated physiological condition and when we are not awakened from deep sleep. Focusing dream recollection in the morning is more likely to favor dream memory than an awakening situation that distracts us from the dream. And, finally, dream quality is a contributing factor, as vivid dreams are more likely to be remembered than 'unobtrusive' dreams.

Yet, all the elements we have collected refer only to generally encouraging or inhibiting conditions of dream memory; they do not enable us to anticipate, in individual cases and with certainty, whether a dream will actually manifest itself. Judging the various elements is extremely difficult, as they differ in impact and may mutually neutralize each other. A dream may be so impressive that it anchors itself firmly in memory, even though there is no attentiveness during the waking situation. In this case, the nature of the dream is stronger than any distraction during the waking situation. An awakening from activated sleep may, on the other hand, cause the recall of less impressive dreams. In this case, the vividness of a dream is less important, because awakening is taking place under optimal psychophysiological conditions.

Dream researchers David Koulack and Donald Goodenough presented in 1976 a model of dream recall that incorporated physiological activation, the salience of a dream, conditions of awakening, as well as the psychodynamic mechanism of repression. They described the process by which a dream is anchored in memory and elicited at a later date. They maintain that a dream can only be stored in memory if it is followed by a brief awakening of which the dreamer need not be aware at all. Once a dream is stored, eliciting it depends on its affective quality. This means, on the one hand, that emotionally neutral dreams may simply be forgotten, because they are not striking enough to compete with waking thought. On the other hand, dreams that arouse intensive feelings may not always be remembered, because they threaten the dreamer and prompt a process of repression. The concept that dreams are not remembered because they are repressed was already central to Freud's theory of dreams. According to Koulack and Goodenough, dreams in the middle range of emotional intensity are the most easily remembered, as they arouse sufficient attention but do not provoke a defense.

This approach is theoretically interesting, because it relates psychological and physiological elements that influence dream memory. However, it eludes direct empirical testing as we do not know whether unremembered dreams are, in fact, of lesser or greater emotional intensity.

Even if we knew all the conditions that make dream memory either more or less difficult, we would still not be able to answer the question of whether it is unnecessary or essential to remember dreams at all. Whatever meaning the remembering of dreams might have, would basically depend on the function we ascribe to dreams. If we view dreams as representation of psychological situations and as problem-solving efforts, it might be valuable to remember them. If, however, we regard them as the coincidental products of nightly-activated memory content, it would seem less important to transfer them to the waking state.

The meaning which dream memory has for the individual is determined by his or her experiences with dreams and with the value level bestowed on dreams by society. Dream recall, on the one hand, may be encouraged and strengthened when dreams represent an enriching element, when we are able to share them, and when they provide fresh insights. Dream memories may, on the other hand, be regarded as less desirable when dreams are experienced as causing apprehension, when no one responds to them, and, when we are unable to make sense of them.

5

The Language of Dreams

Dreams create a world we experience with our senses and which we, as dreamers, embrace with our thoughts and feelings. The dream experience includes perceptions, thoughts and feelings, encompassing all dimensions familiar to us from the waking state. Nevertheless, the dream is also capable of exercising its creative powers in an unusual way, taking elements from our memory pool, transforming them, and combining them into new images that strike us as alien and bizarre.

Perceptions in Dreams

Dreams appear to be real and to be situated in a seemingly external world and that is why the sensory quality of dreams occupies a prominent position in our experience. Dream researchers have been particularly concerned with perceptions in dreams. Back in 1893, Mary Calkins published in her paper a table of the frequency with which different sensory perceptions appear in dreams. Her two dream series showed vision and hearing to be the most prominent sensory impressions, while touch and smell were employed only rarely, and there was no reference to a sense of taste.

This frequency range at which senses participated in dreams was confirmed in later examinations, based on a broader data base. Visual impressions appeared in dreams with few exceptions, and auditory phenomena were encountered in roughly two out of three dreams. However, touch, smell and taste were found in dream experiences only rarely. When we keep hearing that dreams speak in visual images, then this description, while quite accurate, does not do justice to the range of perceptions that manifest in dreams, as all senses are capable of being involved.

We studied the frequency and quality of dream experiences by asking dreamers to describe in detail how they perceived their dream, what they had thought or felt. In this experiment we awakened five subjects from REM sleep only once or twice per night, as we intended to interview them in depth during the night, once they had concluded their dream report. The dreamers were asked to define the kind of representation with particular precision. If, for example, the dream report contained the sentence, "I washed the dishes and my father dried them," the dreamer should describe exactly how this scene was experienced. It might involve purely visual dream elements, which the dreamer could portray more closely: did the dreamer perhaps wash blue earthenware cups, and had the father worn a grey suit? We would register an auditory element if the dreamer had heard the dishes rattling, and a kinetic sense would be added if the dreamer had felt hot water. Sensory impressions might be less vivid if the dreamer had seen the father only indistinctly or was simply aware that he was drying the dishes. Thus, a weakly differentiated visual impression would have been combined with a cognitive element.

A dreamer who recalls how he or she experienced a dream, transfers attention from its actual content to his or her own experiences during the dream. Close questioning, which follows immediately upon the dream, therefore yields a great deal more information concerning the dream experience than an initial dream report. Our dreamers had seen something in every dream and heard something in most dreams. Furthermore, they also recalled that they felt and thought something in many of the dreams. Impressions of smell or taste were, however, only rarely reported during such intensive inquiry.

Even as we note the nature of perceptions that occur during a dream, we have not yet answered the question of how consistently sensory impressions influence the dream experience, how they are differentiated and, above all, what importance they have, compared to thoughts and feelings.

The upper circular chart of Figure 10 indicates the positions which sensory perceptions, thoughts and feelings

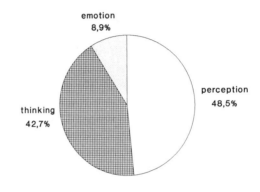

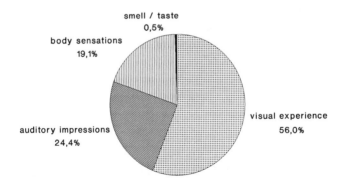

FIGURE 10. Perceptions, Thought and Emotions in Dreams. Top illustration shows the percentages of 778 codes and their mode of representation. Lower illustration subdivides sensory impressions according to different modalities.

occupied in our dream study. A total of 778 codes were assigned to the dreamers' descriptions. Most of the dream impressions were sensory perceptions, but nearly as many were conveyed as thoughts, knowledge and memories. Feelings occupied a much smaller part of the dream experience. Intensive inquiry proved that dreams are not simply made up of perceptions. Dreams frequently contain admixtures of thought processes and are, on and off, accompanied by emotions.

The lower circular chart shows sensory perceptions, divided by their modalities. Visual impressions clearly occupy first place, followed by auditory perceptions and bodily sensations. As in previous studies, smell and taste were noted only rarely.

Dreamers were able to differentiate visual and bodily perceptions easily, but as a rule described auditory phenomena with less precision. There exists a parallel to the waking state, which enables us to communicate visual experiences particularly well and in detail, if only because we have a good deal of practice in doing so and our language offers a multiplicity of expressions.

Some dream segments illustrate how various modalities in dream perceptions may be expressed.

"We were at the theater, and I didn't like it. Then I want to go home and I have two tickets for the checkroom. And I tell the checkroom attendant, it is the military overcoat, petrol-green in color."

(Female, 29 years-old)

When questioned later, the dreamer described her visual impressions in greater detail. The checkroom, equipped with a cash register, looked like a store counter. The tickets were small, totally crumpled, yellowish green, and had been torn off a roll. The dreamer had seen the woman behind the checkroom counter so clearly that she would easily recognize her. The woman was elderly, bony, with wavy white hair that had a bluish tint, and she wore conspicuous Dior glasses. Interestingly, the petrol-green military overcoat in the dream had not been a visual image; the dreamer merely knew that she had to pick it up.

> "I am on the road, in a car, and I get to a big intersection, in fact it is a traffic circle. And a car in front of me explodes, a truck, which blocks the road. Now I have to wait and I am on the side, over on the shoulder. And Roger comes along and does some controlling."
>
> (Male, 24 years-old)

In this dream, visual impressions gained a particular quality from the colors reported afterwards. The truck was sheer white, the explosion created lightning yellow and Roger wore a dark blue suit, a white shirt and a tie that was diagonally striped in either red-and-black or red-and-blue. The colors in this dream are in no way extraordinary, and that is probably why the dreamer did not specifically mention them in his dream report.

> "I was in a crowded football stadium. And a black player is placed into the team. He runs onto the playing field, faster and faster, straight up to the ball, and shoots a goal. Actually, I don't see that he hits the goal, I hear the crowd yelling."
>
> (Male, 24 years-old)

This dream scene contained two visual perceptions: the running and the kicking of the ball, which were simultaneously auditorily presented. The dreamer added to his auditory impressions as follows: "The man enters the field. I don't hear a thing. He starts to run, and I hear him running. The grass seems to be wet, and I hear him kind of pounding. But everything sounds rather subdued. And when he kicks the ball, you can hear the impact quite well. And, as I hear the crowd afterwards, it is not a fierce cry, more like a murmur."

There is a good deal of talk in dreams, but it is not always clear whether it is an auditory phenomenon. Dreamers often find it difficult to decide whether they actually heard the words, or whether they just knew somehow that there had been talk.

> "I am leaving an airport and find myself on an immensely wide street. And a woman comes along, a stewardess. And she tells me she will try to book a ticket from New York for me. It would, however, cost 1200 Swiss Francs. And I say, yes, please try that."
>
> (Female, 24 years-old)

The report suggests that the whole conversation between stewardess and dreamer should be categorized as auditory perception. But the woman who reported the dream claimed that, while she did hear the stewardess call out, the voice quality was extremely poor, and she never heard herself speak at all.

> "You just woke me and stepped inside. And I said: 'May I go back to sleep?' You answered: 'Yes, until *Castle Rodriganda*.' And I said: 'No, I am just now in *The Senator from Lake Titicaca*, which is also a novel by Karl May.'"
>
> (Female, 29 years-old)

This dream segment contains an actual conversation. The dreamer still felt afterwards that she could hear the sound of her own words. She clearly recalled the whining sound of her voice and the rhythmic sound of the second, fictitious book title of a popular German author. She was not sure, however, whether she had actually heard the words spoken by the laboratory experimenter.

> "I am standing in front of a big wardrobe and have to hang up my grey summer dress neatly. It sits on a hanger and has wide straps. I have to push down, because it is crowded inside the wardrobe, and when I put it on the hanger, it gets all wrinkled. And I smooth it down, to straighten it."
>
> (Female, 29 years-old)

During this dream scene, the dreamer felt the smooth cotton material against her hand and noticed that it was tight to push it among the dresses. As she recalled it, she remembered an additional bodily perception, having felt just how awkward it was to bend down in order to straighten the dress.

The American sleep researcher Allan Rechtschaffen, together with a co-worker, studied the specific visual quality of dream images in a totally different way (Rechtschaffen & Buchignani 1983). They began by using the photograph of a young woman sitting on a sofa in her living room, creating 129 variations of it by changing color tone, brightness, sharpness and focus. Judges then categorized each picture in accordance with the degree to which individual versions differed from 'normal' waking perception. Awakened from REM sleep, laboratory subjects were asked to select the picture that most closely matched the quality of their last dream scene. In this study, dream images largely corresponded to waking perceptions concerning brightness and sharpness, but on the average showed fewer intense colors and focused on the foreground, against a blurred background.

The task of judging dream impressions by subtle degrees assumes that the dream is clearly remembered. When dream images are less vividly described, it remains in doubt whether the visual dream experience possessed a particular quality initially, or whether an originally clear impression had faded during the recall process. Blurred and unclear dream images need not necessarily be the result of the poor recall, as the dream might use them as means of symbolically presenting a psychological situation.

Sensory impressions are the preferred tools of expression in dream experiences. Just as in the waking stage, copious abundance of visual dimensions is uppermost. Still, one cannot compare dreams with silent films, as dreams form an experience that employs all senses.

Thinking in Dreams

Thought processes during dreams, which encompass all dream elements that do not manifest in sensory or emotional qualities, should be regarded as an essential part of the dream, as dreamers do not just observe an event, but react to it. As Figure 10 showed, thoughts in dreams are not a rarity. Dreamers are not only involved in dream events but reflect on them, make assumptions or remind themselves of something.

Although dream researchers have not entirely ignored dream thinking, they tended to neglect it. They did not consider it as significant as the dream's ability to translate internal psychological processes into sensory experiences and events, thereby creating a world that provides symbolic images of a dreamer's thoughts.

Thinking during a dream is a means of creation, not to be confused with a dreamer's thoughts while he or she remembers the dream. During reporting, additional elements may enter, such as comments, speculation and ideas, which did not originate with the original dream but that evaluate it from a waking perspective.

Three samples from our dream databank illustrate thought processes that originated during the dream and which demonstrate how thought and perception are subject to manifold linkages within the dream.

> "I was at a market. And there was a wooden stand, Felix's stand. I don't see Felix, but there simply is a painted sign, which says 'Felix'. And I wonder what he may have sold, and what he had built it for. And I realized that he had already sold the things he'd had for sale, and that's why the stand was available."
>
> (Female, 24 years-old, 4th night, 6th REM phase)

This dream sequence offers a clear and informative dream image. We understand not only that we are dealing with a wooden sales stand, but also who its owner is. These visual images provoke speculation on the part of the dreamer, which lead her to believe that the stand is available. The visual image is enhanced by the dreamer's thoughts, which not only appear comprehensible but contain an explanation of the dream situation as well.

> "I just talked to my father on the telephone and discussed a television show we had seen. And he also told me he had been in Zürich and insisted on meeting me at a particular bar. And I said: 'Great, I'll go and see where it is.' And then I just remembered during the dream that we had been there before, and told him so, and he was quite surprised. And I said to him: 'That's the place where we drank a whisky together.'"
>
> (Male, 27 years-old, 2nd night, 3rd REM phase)

The event of this dream takes the form of a conversation, with auditory elements most prominent. Recollection of the memory of an earlier joint experience is logically embedded within the conversation between father and son. The dreamer's recollection does not run parallel to the conversation, but is prompted by the father's wish, incorporated into the son's reply and, in turn, provokes a reaction and additional memories. In this instance, dream thought has a decisive impact on dream events.

> "I noticed someplace that 'La Dentellière' is coming to a movie house and I wondered whether the film had been dubbed into German, but discovered that it hadn't. I talked to somebody about whether or not I should go and see it. While thinking about that, I traveled in a bus full of Americans. And I knew somehow that these were mainly people whose husbands had been in the army and who, for some reason, had remained in Switzerland. And I wondered whether I should sit next to one of the women, but then I thought, no, I better sit by myself, and so I picked a single seat."
>
> (Female, 24 years-old, 3rd night, 4th REM phase)

Within this dream, the dreamer first has thoughts, evoked by a dream image, that do not actually merge with subsequent events. She sees a movie advertisement and wonders about the film's language. But it remains unclear whether the question of dubbing has any significance for the conversation that follows. We find thoughts in this dream also in the form of knowledge that is not, as in the father-son conversation, based on memory, but is quite simply available to the dreamer. She knows that the people on the bus are Americans in a specific life situation, although the dream setting does not convey this information. And the dreamer finally arrives at a consideration that anticipates dream action and prompts her to make up her mind. She wonders where she should sit, comes to a decision, and acts on it.

These examples show that thoughts not only accompany dream events but may enrich and influence them meaningfully. Thoughts should be viewed as elements in the creation of dreams, as much part of the dream as are sensory dream experiences. Thinking in dreams is nevertheless characterized by a degree of simplicity and by a lack of lasting impact. We did not encounter dreams wherein subjects tackled complex relations or reflected on questions logically and consistently from all points of view. Our dreamers did not puzzle at length over a problem; their thoughts were scattered across largely action-oriented dream events that were neither continuously weighed, nor guided by reflection.

In recent years, a particular dream pattern has become popular under the label of so-called lucid dreams. Lucid dreams deal with experiences whereby the Dream Self is aware of the dream and is capable of influencing dream events. The hope that dreams might be controlled in this manner has excited many people who regard it as a means of expanding consciousness and gaining command of unconscious powers.

Still a dream about dreaming need not signal an altered state of consciousness. As all types of waking experiences are capable of influencing dreams, including knowing about dreaming, it is not at all surprising that dreamers sometimes dream that they are in the midst of a dream. This observation has already been noted in early dream literature. Such lucid experiences are, however, rare in spontaneous everyday dreams, and we have found no clearly lucid dream among our experimentally elicited dreams. It has, however, been reported that some people with auto-suggestive aims are often able to learn how to bring such experiences about more frequently.

In 1978, Allan Rechtschaffen wrote an article that emphasized the 'single-minded' nature of dreams. He observed that images and thoughts in dream experiences do not, as a rule, run parallel, that usually only one theme is present, not concurrent with other thoughts. When, for example, we are engaged in a dream event or observe a dream scene, we do not think about something totally different at the same time, as often happens while awake.

The single-minded nature of the dream experience is particularly notable in lack of self-reflection regarding the dream condition: we are usually unaware that we happen to be dreaming, while, during the day, we are generally conscious of being awake. Dreams may also be considered as single-minded, because the dreamer is more likely, than while awake, to accept a dream event naively and unhesitatingly, only rarely calling it into question. Such reduced self-reflection is related to the fact that the dreamer is unaware of his or her 'historicity' and does not evaluate the immediate dream event against a background of earlier experience or of expectations directed toward the future.

Emotions in Dreams

Dreams represent a vivid reality, which not only captures the dreamers' thoughts, but also absorbs them emotionally. Dream emotions signify internal participation, enabling the dreamer to round out the dream event and to imbue it with the character of a coherent experience.

Emotions are a particularly impressive feature of the dream experience; their intensity and quality may reverberate well into the day. But are all dreams accompanied by emotions? Do dreams mirror the total panorama of our emotions, or is the dream's emotional range more limited? Are unpleasant feelings or happy experiences more prominent? Are dream emotions particularly intense, or do they have the same shadings as waking emotions?

We selected 500 REM dreams from our Dream Databank, in order to study the frequency, quality and intensity of emotions (Strauch & Meier 1989). The dreams originated with 44 subjects who spent a total of 161 nights in the sleep laboratory. We did not ascertain these emotions from the dream texts, but evaluated the dreamers' answers to our question of how they felt during the dream and how intensive their feelings had been. Decisive for this procedure was the finding that dream texts do not reliably manifest the dreamer's emotions. We therefore considered and categorized only the dreamers' freely described emotions. We began by distinguishing between specific emotions, such as anger, pleasure, shame, and general mood levels, such as "I felt comfortable" or "I wasn't really well." In addition, we evaluated all the statements according to their positive, negative or neutral qualities.

Several of our examples illustrate how diverse the emotional experiences of dreams can be:

> "I was on the street, together with a colleague, on my way home. And Anita and her brother and another colleague decided to play a trick on us. They caught up with us, and sent two people ahead whom we did not know. And they were supposed to use some excuse to sell us tickets. We were suckers and bought the tickets. And then they turned up and laughed at us a little because we were so naive and let just anybody with the phoniest excuse sell us something in the street. And, somehow, there were camels on those cards. Then they took us along in their car. We were driving on the highway and suddenly there was an

animal transport that had a breakdown. And all the animals, sheep, horses and even a pig, left the truck and came on the highway. We passed all this, and I looked back, wondering what might happen, with all these animals on the highway."

(Female, 29 years-old, 5th night, 5th REM phase)

Asked how she had felt during this dream, the dreamer answered, "Well, comfortable. It was, somehow, a positive kind of feeling." This dream was dominated by a basically positive mood and did not cause any marked emotions, although, from a waking point of view, such feelings could have been assumed. The dreamer did not feel ashamed, although she had been tricked and laughed at, and the potentially dangerous situation of animals roaming the highway was not, in her experience, linked to fear.

"My husband and I were at a boarding school. Accidentally, we ran into the son of a couple who are friends of ours. He showed us the school and told us what one of his routine day was like. We were just about to say good-bye."

(Female, 29 years-old, 1st night, 5th REM phase)

In this case, the dreamer said after her report: "I know that I was pleased to meet the son, because I had not seen him in years. And somehow that excited me, gave me the feeling of pleasure that I just happened to run into him." The dream report had not immediately conveyed the specific feeling of pleasure. It could have been a routine encounter, unaccompanied by any special emotion.

"We were riding in a streetcar together. Somehow, we were on the wrong train, but it had been the first one to come along. And then it happened that whenever we got to a stop and another streetcar came along, we quickly jumped on it and traveled on that one. But it, too, traveled in the same direction, as if it had just overtaken us. It was simply important that we get onto the other train, important to you, but not for me. It seemed as if these streetcars provided insight into the journey of life. It was quite difficult to do this all the time, because sometimes a train came from the opposite direction. One had to be careful not to get run over by a streetcar. We did all this many times, and the last time we did it, you said: 'I think this time we can't make a switch.' Then I said: 'Sure, sure, come along, we can make it.'"

(Female, 31 years-old, 4th night, 2nd REM phase)

Her answer to the question about emotions was: "It seems odd, but I felt untouched, although the trains nearly ran over us at times, and you stood right between them. Everything seemed remote." Although a lot happens in this dream, and the dreamer finds herself with the experimenter on a fairly varied trip, she remains untouched and does not experience specific emotions or different moods. The dream event appears analogous to the experimental situation: the constant switches to different streetcars symbolize awakenings, with their frequent changes from waking to sleeping, and emotional involvement may be lacking because responsibility remains with the experimenter.

"My brother and I were traveling someplace without a car. Some people passed who offered us their cars. First an American car, and we didn't want it, and next another two, three cars, which we also didn't want. At some point, we took a lemon-yellow VW Golf. We were driving around in it, at the Railroad Square, trying to turn back. To do that, we had to drive across a steep, icy pile of snow. I kept thinking, we'll never make it without getting into a spin. But we did get on top, and down the other side. I thought, oh boy, that is more than ten percent incline, and my brother said, if I have at least four centimeter distance to brake, that'll be enough. Then we drove away."

(Female, 31 years-old, 3rd night, 4th REM phase)

The dreamer described the emotional experience of this dream as follows: "While we were going downhill, I felt that it was quite steep, and I pushed my feet forward. But it was not fear, rather an uneasy feeling, although my brother sat next to me, and one should not be afraid when he is driving." In this case, and perhaps in a defensive mode, the dreamer makes a clear distinction between her general unease and an actual feeling of fear.

> "My mother and sister had to go to the dentist. And a girlfriend and I drove with them. And then we walked back and said we would meet later at a bar. It was daylight, but suddenly it was night once more. And we were sitting in this bar, where there were only low-life types, like drug addicts. And one of them came to threaten me with a needle, as if he were going to shoot me up. And I sat down to wait for my friend, who had gone to get something to drink. And another one comes and starts to choke me, for no reason at all, and I didn't know him."

> (Female, 22 years-old, 3rd night, 6th REM phase)

The dreamer experienced intensive fears when threatened by the addict and during the choking scene, and we can easily understand her feelings on the basis of the dream events.

> "An experiment was underway and there was a tent, quite big. And, more as a gag, I wanted to see what was inside the tent. And there was some kind of central station, like in the laboratory, from which one could partly see and hear what was going on. And I somehow lifted it up, and suddenly I found myself down there, like alone inside a house. And I could not get out, and started banging. I was utterly frightened, and kept on shouting."

> (Female, 27 years-old, 2nd night, 2nd REM phase)

Intense emotions of being threatened and of claustrophobic feelings are anchored directly within this dream. The dreamer is trapped, locked-in, reacts in panic, seeks to free herself and cries for help. One cause of the fear in this dream is undoubtedly the laboratory situation, which arouses the dreamer's curiosity, but turns into a trap.

As the circular chart in Figure 11 indicates, emotions are not a consistent feature of the dream experience. Not every dream is emotionally-oriented, but about three out of ten dreams were experienced as neutral. Specific emotions were part of about every second dream, and nearly every fourth dream was accompanied by generalized mood states. Dreams experienced as neutral did not differ from emotionally-oriented dreams, as to abundance of content. Any lack of emotion cannot, therefore, be explained as due to fragmented recall. Emotional participation in dreams apparently has as many levels as we experience while awake.

Even though individual dreams did not display several emotions, we found that our dream collection contained the full range of specific emotions we encounter while awake. Their range is illustrated in Figure 12. Although all emotions manifest in dreams, they do not appear with the same frequency. While joy, anger, and fear accompany about every tenth dream, such subtler emotions of contempt, guilt and disgust are comparatively rare. It seems surprising, at first, that a feeling of pleasure appears up front, as dreams are commonly associated with negative emotions. But when we categorize specific emotions according to quality, negative emotions appear twice as often as do positive ones; the

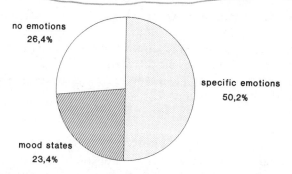

FIGURE 11. Incidence of Emotions in Dreams. Frequency of emotions and mood states in five hundred REM dreams. Evaluation of replies to the question, "How did you feel during the dream?"

prominence of pleasure should, therefore, be carefully qualified. Still, we must not conclude that dreams are overwhelmingly subject to negative experiences, as this belief is only supported by specific emotions. In dreams that contain only one general mood state, a reverse image appeared. In such cases, positive feelings were most prominent, to a point of being 2 1/2 times more frequent than negative feelings.

The circular chart of Figure 13 illustrates the emotional qualities of dreams. It indicates a balanced ratio of

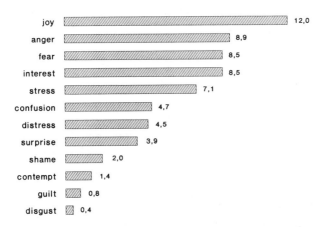

FIGURE 12. Repertoire of Specific Dream Emotions. Percentages of different emotions during five hundred REM dreams.

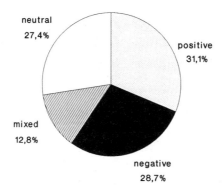

FIGURE 13. Qualities of Dream Emotion. Percentages of positive, negative and neutral emotional tone in five hundred REM dreams.

positive, negative and neutral dream ambience. Dreams, then, are not predominantly influenced by fears, dismay or stress, but frequently display wellbeing and pleasant experiences. Disagreeable experiences do, however, find more frequent expression in specific emotions, whereas positive experiences are more likely to be expressed by general moods.

Whether or not specific emotions or mood states are described, the emotionality dominating a dream is likely to be single-leveled, as dreamers usually reported only one emotion at a time. Also quite small was the part played by conflicting emotional qualities. Dreams only rarely reflected changing mood colorations, but were either located within a positive, negative or neutral ambience. Limited variety of emotional feelings is an indication that emotional experiences in such dreams encourage a unified pattern.

In our dream sample, the intensity with which dream emotions were experienced tended to move within a middle range. Extremely strong or extremely weak intensities were experienced less frequently. The intensity of specific emotions and mood states was evenly distributed. Specific emotions were not, therefore, associated with a stronger emotional involvement than the general mood states.

In daily life, dream emotions are particularly impressive and lasting when they do not coincide with waking experiences, because they are either lacking entirely or do not fit a given situation. For instance, dream literature keeps emphasizing that horrible things happen in dreams while the dreamer remains untouched, or that a threatening situation is met with inappropriate hilarity.

David Foulkes was the first to study with his collaborators empirically, how appropriate dream emotions are when viewed from a waking perspective (Foulkes, Sullivan, Kerr & Brown 1988). He first awakened his subjects from REM sleep and asked them about their dreams and emotions while dreaming. Afterwards, they were asked to explain how they would have felt about these dream experiences if they had occurred while awake, and whether these reactions coincided with their dream emotions. For the most part, subjects registered the same emotional reactions that they would have had while awake and facing a similar situation. In second place came dreams that lacked emotional involvement, although the same experience would have caused emotions while awake. Dream emotions that did not correspond to waking reactions were extremely rare.

The interesting observation that many dreams did not cause emotional reactions stands in contrast to a conception that emotions are crucial to the dream experience. Emotions may well act as an important channel of expression, but do not have a continuous impact on the dream experience and do not necessarily form part of these events.

The Bizarre in Dreams

Whenever there are references to the bizarre character of dreams, it is understood that dream contents and the process of dream events appear unusual or impossible. This characterization does, however, always originate from the viewpoint of a waking world. While dreams are happening, dream reality is dominant, and dreams are rarely regarded as bizarre. Only when we compare the recalled dream with our waking experience do we assign bizarre qualities to it.

Dream researchers are agreed that dreams may offer bizarre features. Viewpoints differ only as to whether bizarre elements represent dominant or sporadic dream features, and to what degree the bizarre should be incorporated into a definition of the dream. Sleep and dream researcher Allan Hobson regards the bizarre as "the most distinctive feature of dream mentation" (1988). By contrast, sleep researcher Frederick Snyder arrives at the following conclusion:

"We found that by far the largest portion of the reports were entirely credible as descriptions of waking events, and not at all bizarre as descriptions of the reality we all know in waking life. There were many reports which did display these very dreamlike features of bizarreness and incredibleness, but the really surprising thing to us was just how uncommon these were." (1970, p. 146)

Henriette Haas, a member of our group, developed a scale designed to gauge features of the bizarre in form and content (Haas, Guitar-Amsterdamer & Strauch 1988). Bizarre in form are reports that are extraordinary in structure and progress, because individual words, sentences or paragraphs are incomplete, scattered or erratic. Bizarre in content are elements and events which, from an everyday perspective, are unusual, because they are distorted or improbable, violate social or cultural standards or run counter to the laws of physics.

Utilizing this scale, we examined elements of the bizarre in 117 REM dreams. The dreams originated with thirteen subjects, each of whom recalled three dreams during three nights. We noted how often bizarreness in form occurred and how bizarre aspects were distributed among the categories of settings, characters, objects, actions, speech, perceptions, thoughts and emotions. To start with, we underlined those passages in each dream report that contained any bizarre elements, either in form or content, and then decided on the category to which they belonged.

The circular chart of Figure 14 shows how often bizarre elements occurred in these dreams. We notice immediately that certainly not all dreams displayed strange features, as we did not find any bizarre elements in every fourth dream. Relatively most frequent were dreams with only single bizarre elements, loosely scattered among dream events. Not quite every third dream incorporated somewhat stronger bizarre features, but only a few dreams contained manifold unusual appearances.

The circular chart of Figure 15 shows how bizarreness in form and content is distributed among dreams. It seems appropriate to separate the two categories, as form and content aspects of the bizarre appeared together in only every

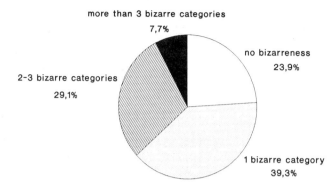

FIGURE 14. Degrees of the Bizarre in Dreams. Frequency of bizarre feature categories, as coded in 117 REM dreams.

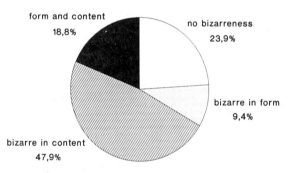

FIGURE 15. Categories of the Bizarre in Dreams. Distribution of the bizarre in form and in content, in 117 REM dreams.

fifth dream. Bizarre contents far outweighed bizarreness in form; approximately every other dream showed unusual content, while less than ten percent of dreams were characterized by bizarre structure.

The following dream scene typifies the appearance of bizarreness in form:

"I was on vacation by the sea, together with a woman and two men, all known to me. And, later on, several of them arrived there, at the hotel. I somehow got there earlier. Just then they came in. And somehow I sat with them at a table outside, and suddenly I saw the woman. And all of a sudden, I was sitting with both men at the table, and she somehow wasn't there anymore. First I thought I was staying down below, at the hotel, and then somehow those others arrived, and I suddenly lived further up."

(Female, 24 years-old, 3rd night, 4th REM phase)

What is striking about this dream is not content or actions, but its erratic transitions, the abrupt appearance and disappearance of people, and the inexplicable change in the dreamer's own accommodation. It remains an open question whether this lack of coherence was a feature of the original dream or whether its bizarre form developed later, during the process of recalling and reporting.

Figure 16 illustrates how frequently dream contents, within the framework of our definition of the bizarre, differed from everyday experience. We found that the bizarre was encountered in every content category, although distributed unevenly.

Most often, dream figures engaged in eccentric actions, with bizarre dream characters in second place. Odd locations, curious objects, unusual happenings, and strange speech appeared less frequently. This range is, however, also found in the frequency with which we observe specific dream contents. For example, we encounter more actions than people or settings in dreams. We may, therefore, conclude that the bizarre is not limited to specific content categories, but capable of remodeling all types of dream content.

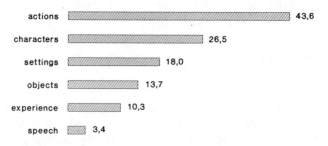

FIGURE 16. Bizarre Content in Dreams. Percentages of different bizarre content categories in 117 REM dreams.

What follows are dream segments that illustrate how the bizarre may appear in different content categories:

> "And my mother comes in and discovers that the upper part of the door is made of glass. And then she breaks the glass, in order to walk through the door. And I get panicky, or I simply know that she shouldn't get through, and I take a hammer and kill her."

> (Female, 24 years-old, 2nd night, 4th REM phase)

This dream scene is dominated by two unusual actions. The mother breaks the glass of a door, and the daughter kills the mother. In the first instance, the action must be considered bizarre, because it is not ordinary behavior and, in addition, does not evolve from the dream situation. In the second instance, the aggressive physical action violates social and cultural standards.

> "We had to move and tried to arrange something with somebody with a car to help us out. But then he couldn't do it, and then we were unable, and then Brigitte and I drove to the country, to recover a bit from all that stress. We parked the car, and a couple with simply thousands of kids turned up, with all of them having to get into the car, in order to move on. And they only had a VW Bug, and as they left they threw all the kids inside."

> (Female, 22 years-old, 4th night, 3rd REM phase)

In this dream, individual content items are not bizarre themselves, but the essentially ordinary event is shattered by the rude action of stuffing an enormous number of children into a small car of seemingly unusual capacity.

> "Three of us are inside an empty apartment, an older man and a woman and I. The woman and the man are a married couple who have separated. And now she has returned home, to see how he is doing. And now the whole apartment is empty. They seem, half-way, like animals. And I stand there as if I were a ghost: I don't touch the

ground, I float around. But they can see me. It seems as if they are putting on masks, each separately, in order to scare each other."

(Female, 24 years-old, 4th night, 2nd REM phase)

Everyone in this dream is a bizarre figure. The dreamer feels like a ghost, but can nevertheless be seen, while the couple has odd, animalistic features and hides behind masks.

"I was sitting in a WC, a public WC, where there were books. Next to the WC, actually inside it, there was a rack for pocketbooks. It was a mixture of all different kinds of pocketbooks."

(Female, 24 years-old, 3rd night, 4th REM phase)

Only the setting of the dream is unusual because public toilets are not, as a rule, equipped with pocketbook displays.

"I was sitting in the garden at night, with my family and my godfather, and I was the father of a little girl whom I had to keep looking after. And then my godfather discovered a giant hashish tree, some 20, 30 meters high. And my brother and I wanted to plant the tree. I placed it upright, but by then the tree started to tilt slowly toward the river, down a bit, to the slope."

(Male, 25 years-old, 2nd night, 5th REM phase)

Aside from the fact that the dreamer is not yet the father of a little girl, the dream scene centers on the oversized hashish tree, an object that is clearly strange, as hashish trees do not grow to gigantic size.

"I was sitting at a table somewhere, a train schedule in front of me, printed on a small white card, but I don't know what I was looking for. And as I put it down on the table, the schedule becomes enormous, turns into a huge black plate, with peculiar things on it, to stick in the departure time and destination, and that's what I very slowly did."

(Female, 23 years-old, 4th night, 5th REM phase)

What is odd in this dream scene is the sudden change of a quite ordinary train schedule into a large plate, reminiscent of train announcements at railroad stations, but actually inappropriate to the setting in which the dreamer finds herself.

"We were standing at a store's checkout counter, but just couldn't get to the front. There was just one person ahead of us, it seemed forever, and we simply had to keep waiting. And then it was closing time, and we slipped under the door, some kind of folding door, and got outside. And somehow, where we found ourselves there was going to be an assassination, or there had definitely been one, and we had to get to some other place."

(Female, 23 years-old, 4th night, 3rd REM phase)

This dream is notable for its particularly bizarre experiential quality, whereby the dreamer becomes aware of an assassination that has no rational origin within the dream plot, and remains unexplained.

"I was at a sort of holiday camp. And somebody grabbed my hair brush and crushed it in his fist. I ran after him, and asked him why he had ruined my brush. And now there was a woman, who said, well, about that brush, that wasn't so terrible, as I had frequently written to Brezhnev, and now I could write to Nixon and ask for a new brush."

(Female, 24 years-old, 2nd night, 3rd REM phase)

Events in this dream camp are not exactly ordinary, but not entirely unimaginable. Yet the spoken content is bizarre, a request to use this small incident in order to appeal to former leading politicians.

Unusual elements, while extraordinarily varied in design, appeared only sporadically in our dreams. Bizarreness was not a common feature of dream patterns, although our subjects did occasionally report such dreams; the following dream of a traffic accident illustrates this point:

> "We had a car accident, and a man got stuck under the car and was completely flat. And we just happened to have some chocolate with us, and scattered chocolate on top of him. And Ernest wondered whether one shouldn't spread some sand and gravel over him, so it would not show where he is and wouldn't be so conspicuous. And now we were inside a bus and decided that this was not okay, to simply hide him so nothing could be seen."

> (Female, 30 years-old, 4th night, 3rd REM phase)

This dream is not only marked by individual bizarre elements, but is notable from many points of view. It starts with a car accident, which, by itself, is not uncommon, but to which the dream figures react in a very unusual manner. Instead of summoning police and an ambulance, they act oddly and inappropriately, scattering bits of chocolate over their peculiarly flattened accident victim, and finally they make their getaway by bus. The accompanying notions of the dream characters, which center on an abstruse cover-up, further violate social expectations and contribute to the overall bizarre character of the dream.

A dream concerning an excursion illustrates the category of dreams which, according to our definition, lack strange elements and mirror episodes that could have taken place in everyday life:

> "A colleague and I visited Germany to go swimming. We lived near the German border and crossed the border by hitchhiking and by bus. It was terribly hot. Just now I was inside a bus and ran into a lot of people that I have known before. We watched them, and it was very lively, like a school outing. Everyone was chatting with every-

body else, quite noisy, and I just listened. I wasn't able to say anything myself, because my voice couldn't penetrate the noise."

(Female, 22 years-old, 2nd night, 5th REM phase)

Compared with the preceding example, this dream seems quite ordinary: it describes an event that could actually have happened. People are attuned to the setting, and their actions are logical and understandable.

Our results suggest that every aspect of dream events may be subject to bizarre admixtures. But they also clarify that the bizarre should not be regarded as either a general or a dominant dream feature. Dreams often seem a good deal weirder than they essentially are, because bizarre phenomena contrast strikingly with other dream events, so that ordinary elements tend to be overshadowed. Even where we encounter the bizarre, dreams retain generally intimate contact with the real world. We have collected only very few dreams in which coherent thought and experience were entirely lacking, which remained totally unintelligible or were even seemingly disturbed.

As a rule, the bizarre in dreams does not upset us, as our waking fantasy enables us to comprehend such unusual situations quite well. Instead, the bizarre elicits astonishment and even admiration of the caleidoscopic turnabouts in sleep thought, which succeed in reorganizing and transforming our waking experiences as part of a creative process.

Sensory perceptions function as the ever present creative medium of dreams, while thoughts co-determine dream events decisively. Emotions and the bizarre, on the other hand, no matter how striking they may be, should rather be considered as concomitant features in the total dream experience.

6

The Content of Dreams

Dreams are interesting and stimulating, because they offer a broad panorama of contents, because their themes are varied, and because they convey fresh, enriching impressions and experiences. This diversity is so prominent that one does not realize at first just how much dreams have in common. If, therefore, we want to characterize dream content and theme structure in a comprehensive manner, we need to organize and summarize the variety of dream experiences.

While psychotherapists concentrate their interpretations on individual dreams and on their origin in life histories, dream researchers collect as many dreams as possible, in order to establish how dream events may be commonly described and whether dreams differ in content and themes from everyday experiences.

Variety of Dream Contents

In the 1960s, Calvin Hall and Robert Van de Castle compiled a particularly comprehensive content inventory of 1,000 spontaneously recollected dreams. They selected five dreams each from the dream diaries of 100 male and 100 female students, to be coded in accordance with their content analysis method (Hall & Van de Castle 1966).

The dreams of these students preponderantly resembled realistic life situations, staged against a background of a setting and with different props. Next to the dreamer, additional dream figures entered the stage, and dream events were usually dominated by a variety of activities and interactions.

Over half of the dream settings were situated in alien environments, and only every third was familiar to the dreamer. Although people who appeared in these dreams were frequently known to the dreamer, just as many were strangers. Among the abundance of dream objects, no single category emerged as dominant. The variety of contents was documented by a listing of 1,170 different objects and animals, ranging from 'Accordion' to 'Zipper'. In the 1,000 dreams, for example, food and drink appeared 99 times, of which half were sweets or stimulating beverages. Animals participated in dreams 143 times, usually cats or dogs, while such exotic animals as lions or elephants enlivened the dream stage only rarely. Snakes, known for their celebrated role in dream symbolism, were encountered in this sample only 13 times.

These dreams were remarkably rich in activities. In every case, one-quarter of all actions fell into the categories of physical activities, speech and movements in space. Half the dream actions originated with the dreamer. Aggressive interactions could be observed in nearly half the dreams, whereby the dreamers were more frequently victim rather than the aggressor. Nearly every second dream featured friendly actions, with the dreamer as much active as passive. By comparison, sexual interactions appeared in less than ten percent of the dreams.

Thirty years later, Hall and his collaborators collected and evaluated a new sample of 600 dreams under comparable conditions (Hall, Domhoff, Blick & Weesner 1982). Surprisingly, the dream world's contents had not changed materially. Social changes that had taken place in the interim were not reflected in these categories of dream contents.

The inventory compiled by Hall and Van de Castle refers to dreams that were spontaneously recalled at home. But is the dream world described by them equally representative of dreams elicited in the laboratory? It has often been alleged that lab dreams are not capable of reflecting a 'natural' dream world, because even an awareness of the experimental setting may change dream creation, and because dreamers might only report on selected dreams.

In 1970 one of the first comprehensive studies was done by Frederick Snyder. The study evaluated 635 REM dreams, reported largely by young adults during 250 laboratory nights. One significant result of his study was that the contents of these lab dreams generally coincided with the statistics covering spontaneous dreams.

A study in our lab compared home dreams and laboratory dreams experienced by the same subjects. We evaluated these dreams according to the categories established by Hall and Van de Castle, and concluded that the contents of dreams elicited under these conditions did not show any basic differences.

In order to examine the appearance and distribution of contents and themes on a wider basis we coded the dream setting, the dream characters, the activities and social interactions in 500 REM dreams from our databank.

Our dreamers, too, usually created a scene of actions that formed the background for the dream happenings. Only 43 dreams did not show any indication of a setting, as when a dreamer simply thought about something or where an object was somehow viewed in a void. In most instances, the backdrop remained the same; still, every fourth dream changed scenery, when, for example, the dreamers were suddenly transported into a totally different environment or when they moved in the course of events to several different locations.

The circular chart of Figure 17 outlines the familiarity of different settings. The dream usually creates new decors as the dreamers found themselves mainly in alien locations or unknown landscapes. Only in second place do we find settings that are familiar and well-known to the dreamer. Sceneries might also remain vague when they are merely indicated or kept so unspecified that they could have stood

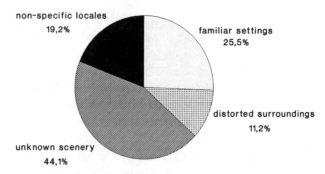

FIGURE 17. Dream Settings. 500 REM dreams were situated in 642 settings, subdivided according to their familiarity.

for a variety of environments, as when a dreamer says: "I was on a train." A particularly notable feature were oddly distorted environments. In such cases, the dream takes place in a setting which, on the one hand, is familiar to the dreamer, yet otherwise somehow transformed.

The first example is a dream that takes place in such a changed setting:

> "I found myself in this test situation. I got up and turned off the microphone. But the room was upstairs, on the third floor, and I stepped into the physician's office next door. And across the hall was another office, where something was running. Anyhow, I met a lot of people on the way to the basement, where you were kind of crouched next to your machine and I couldn't get in there. It was locked and I turned the microphone on again, in front of the door, and said, I am awake and I would really like to stop the experiment."

> (Male, 30 years-old, 1st night, 5th REM phase)

The dream environment is familiar to the dreamer in that it concerns the house in which the experiment is taking place. But when one knows the location, the environment is transformed in two ways: the bedroom is actually located on the ground floor, not the third floor, and there is no physician's office in the building. In this case, the estrangement of a familiar environment manifests itself in a change of rooms and in a transformation of the functions that are assigned to the various locales.

As the dream is a creation of the dreamer it is not surprising that the dreamer is present in nearly all dreams. But the dreamer does not usually appear alone, but surrounded by various dream figures. Only twelve dreams were completely inanimate. In an additional eighteen dreams, characterized by absence of the dreamer, events were solely in the hands of other dream figures. In the great majority of dreams, the dreamer dealt with several people; only in one out of ten dreams was the dreamer in a dual situation.

All kinds of creatures turned up in dreams; dreams displayed no particular preference, but offered a wide range of roles. The circular chart of Figure 18 presents the participation of all dream characters. First of all, dreamers surrounded themselves with people they know. They mainly sought contact with colleagues and with friends from their circle of acquaintances. To a lesser degree, they dealt with members of their immediate families, particularly parents and siblings. Prominent personalities only rarely entered dream scenes. Although dreamers encountered familiar people, they also often met new ones; or, in other cases, people

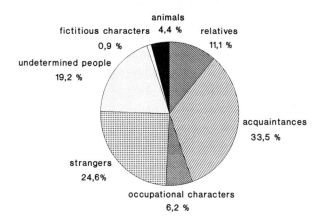

FIGURE 18. Dream Figures. 1410 dream figures, belonging to a variety of categories, appeared in 500 REM dreams.

appeared during the course of a dream who remained shadowy and undefined. Occasionally, people took part in dreams who represent a specific category, such as policemen or mail carriers, characterized only by their functions, but remaining anonymous as individuals. The smallest segment was taken up by dream figures whose origin was in fiction.

Compared to the numerous human beings, animals were not very prominent, but nevertheless appeared in every tenth dream. Dream animals fitted mainly into the domestic scene, while exotic animals were hardly present at all. Dreamers were mainly accompanied by dogs and cats, but they also dealt with other native animals, such as horses, rabbits and fowl.

When we examine dream characters within separate dreams, and not from an overall point of view, the most frequent combinations were familiar persons with strangers or anonymous characters. It is interesting, however, that in just about every third dream the dreamer encountered only strangers. By comparison, only one in five dreams was totally private, in that only people known to the dreamer appeared in it.

Concerning the range of persons who appeared in their dreams, we did not observe any striking differences between the 44 subjects. There were no single dreamers who only dreamed of strangers, or others who only dreamed of friends and relatives. Rather, throughout every dreamer's set, there were at times encounters with known as well as unknown people. Individual difference, therefore, did not concern the repertoire of role players, but only the proportionate part of the different character groups.

The circular chart of Figure 19 divides the dream persons with regard to their sex and age. The dream stage is largely occupied by adults who, in the majority, have established their identity. Men are present more frequently than women, but mixed groups of both sexes were also encountered often. The greater participation of men was, among other elements, due to the fact that prominent personalities or members of different occupations appeared more

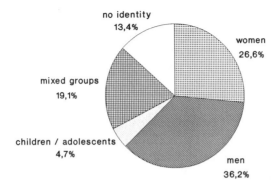

FIGURE 19. Identities of Dream Figures. Human figures in five hundred REM dreams, categorized according to sex and age.

often as men. Children and adolescents occupied the same status that they had for the dreamer in daily life. Dreams thus generally took place within the present existence of dreamers and did not take them back to their childhood.

The allocation of dream figures within individual dreams showed clearly that dreams do not unilaterally create 'male or female worlds'. Women as well as men played a leading role in two out of three dreams. All our individual dream series contained dreams in which males and females jointly influenced events. There were, however, certain subjects who, despite their enjoyment of social contacts, avoided dream encounters only with women; other dreamers never met only men in their dreams.

A dream featuring several people illustrates the distinctly social nature of dreams:

> "There was my father, my mother, three elderly women, of whom I know one, it is my grandmother, and my aunt from Germany, and a small miniature pincher, which apparently belonged to my parents and they had bought it that very day. And everyone sat around a table, one of those low tables with a group of leather armchairs, and talked about the advantages and disadvantages of cigarettes. The last thing my father said was something like, it didn't bother him if somebody in Israel . . . and the rest of the sentence was cut off. And before that it

was all about a new kid who seemed to live in my aunt's house, and she didn't want the baby to get sick, because my father sweats so terribly. And we also rode in an elevator at some point, together with some other gentleman."

(Male, 26 years-old, 3rd night, 6th REM phase)

The dreamer chats with his family members in a domestic setting, where they are joined by two strange women. The miniature pincher has also newly entered the family's dream world. The baby—his godchild, according to the dreamer—is not present in a sensory mode, but mentioned during the conversation. And finally, a strange man appears as companion on the elevator.

The dream sketches a conceivable, ordinary slice of life—with the exception that one would expect that the strange women might have introduced themselves, whereas it is quite realistic to ride in the elevator with a stranger who remains unidentified.

Dreams do not present themselves as a chain of stills, but create eventful and changing situations, wherein dream figures become active. Just as in everyday life, these activities encompassed a broad spectrum, ranging from extended movements in space, and communication with the environment, up to active internal processes. Mainly, dream figures were engaged in bodily movements, moving within the dream scene, largely under their own power, but also with the aid of vehicles, or engaged in activities right on the spot. Conversations took place in two out of three dreams. By comparison, activities that internalized the environment or coped with it internally, such as listening to music or mulling things over, remained in the background.

Only very few dreams might be described purely as dreams of speech, action or contemplation. As a rule, dreams are not one-track in nature, concentrating on a single activity, but devoted to several different ones.

Only every second dream featured social interactions marked by particular cordiality or aggression. Dream figures frequently dealt with each other in a rather neutral fashion, as when sitting in a restaurant and talking among themselves. Where dreams showed friendly activity, it was most frequently expressed in words and gestures, more rarely as concrete assistance or generous gifts. With aggressive actions, too, there were mainly verbal expressions of a disagreeable nature, rather than actual physical clashes. The ratio between giving and receiving was evenly balanced, both for friendliness and aggression; dreamers were just about as likely to be initiators as the recipients of social interactions.

Interestingly, sexual interactions were reported in our dreams only four times. The experimental setting may have caused censorship, either during the dream itself or later, when the report was made.

What kind of statement do such inventories make about the world of dreams? Dreams are not limited to one segment of the world, but contain all the elements that determine our waking experiences. It is, however, significant that dreams are created from a highly personal point of view. Few dreams take place without participation of the Dream Self, while we absorb many impressions in our waking world that do not immediately include ourselves. In a dream, the Dream Self is much more closely linked to a situation and less likely to focus on impersonal matters. Dreams are, therefore, highly personal, but not necessarily egocentric. The dreamer alone does not determine events and is not exclusively involved with closely associated individuals. Furthermore, the dream world is not particularly fantastic, as the dreamer is more likely to create a reality oriented world, which is only rarely equipped with totally odd backdrops, fantastic dream figures and unusual props.

It is, however, notable how many strange and only vaguely defined people appear in dreams and how often dreamers find themselves in an unknown or elusive environment. Of course, we encounter strangers in our waking lives as well, but we are able to fit them in, as soon as we begin to deal with them. While awake, we know where we are, even if we pay no particular attention to the scenery.

The dream functions apparently more sparingly, introduces dream figures only to the degree and develops backdrops only as far as they are essential to the progress of the dream script.

The Role of the Dreamer

The dreamer is the author of the dream, is featured in most dreams, but does not always play a starring role. Dreamers might function as mute extras, they might appear only marginally in a supporting part and remain otherwise mere passive participants in an event. Conversely, they may be central figures on the dream stage, acting decisively and able to determine the dream's progress.

We studied the different types of the Dream Self's participation more closely in 198 REM dreams. Over three nights, each of our 22 subjects contributed three dreams. For each dream we determined whether the Dream Self remained uninvolved, inactive or active. When we view these three categories as increasing levels of self-involvement, we are able to determine which form of self-involvement was achieved.

The upper circular chart of Figure 20 initially shows that the Dream Self appears in nearly every dream, as the person of the dreamer was absent in only 21 dreams. Greatest emphasis had dreams which, at some point, featured the dreamer as active. Dreams, experienced by the dreamer as taking place in his or her presence, although not as participant, and dreams where the dreamer played, at most, a passive role, were a good deal rarer than those featuring an active Dream Self.

Because the dreamer's activity, as such, does not reveal any direction, we further subdivided the large group of dreams that featured the Dream Self in some kind of active role. We classified these 140 dreams into four groups, designed to describe the dreamer's activity in relation to the prevailing social situation. The Dream Self may act

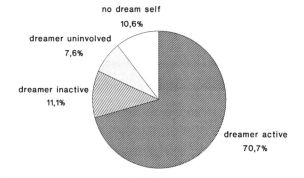

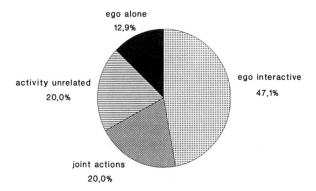

FIGURE 20. Participation of the Dreamer. Upper illustration records the appearances of the Dream Self in 198 REM dreams. Lower illustration notes the social relation of ego activity in dreams involving an active Dream Self.

'alone,' 'not related to others,' 'together with others' or 'through interaction with others.'

The lower circular diagram of Figure 20 discloses the social aspects of the dreamer's involvement. By far most frequently, actually in every second dream, did the dreamer and other dream figures find themselves in an interactive relationship. In every fifth dream, the dreamer was jointly engaged with others, but without any communication. Equally frequent were dreams in which the activities of the dreamer and of other dream figures were unrelated. Rarest of dreams were those in which the Dream Self acted entirely alone.

Action on the part of the dreamer, while lacking a social situation, may present itself as follows:

> "I went into the room. I was determined to dream about my relation to Alexander. And I did have a dream later on, but I didn't quite know what I had dreamed. And then it was somehow taped. And next I turned the radio on, which somehow was too loud, and I just wanted to turn it down. And then I wanted to look into this cookie jar, colored red and with a white heart, to see how many cookies there were, and I wanted to count them. And a toolbox was there, too."

> (Female, 23 years-old, 4th night, 3rd REM phase)

The dreamer appears here as the only thinking and acting person. Another dream character is involved, but only indirectly, through the dreamer's wish to dream about her friend Alexander. However, the radio transmission, which symbolizes possible contact with the outside world, is rejected by the dreamer as rather disturbing.

The same subject reported a dream that illustrates an unrelated type of Dream Self activity:

> "I was lying down at the Institute and was dreaming. And then a cleaning woman came in and didn't close the door. The cleaning woman wanted to take my temperature. Right then, I hear something on the radio about the visit of the Pope, that he had arrived and there was some kind of riot. Then, I got up quickly and went into the next room. And when I came back, my bed had disappeared and there was only a bathtub. And as I can't lie comfortably in a bathtub, I lay down on the rug in front of the bed."

> (Female, 23 years-old, 2nd night, 4th REM phase)

Although two dream figures appear during the first part of the dream, their activities are unrelated; no exchange takes place between dreamer and cleaning woman. At the outset, the dreamer confronts a situation to which she does not react directly. The cleaning woman is a nuisance and she even means to take the dreamer's temperature, but the dreamer ignores this intrusion and concentrates on the radio report. Later in the dream, the dreamer is on her own and adjusts uncomplainingly to the changed sleep setting, which remains unexplained.

Joint, parallel activities of dream figures are mirrored in the dream of a car with a stranger:

> "I was riding in a car, with a man. And I didn't talk to this man. And his face remained expressionless; I know, because I looked at him from time to time, glanced over to him, and otherwise simply at the speeded along countryside. And he and I, without a word between us, simply raced through the countryside. And then there was a sudden shift. Without having stopped the car or having stepped outside it, we were sitting on a small bank before a green ivy wall and, as if we were the audience, we watched a movie."
>
> (Female, 24 years-old, 4th night, 3rd REM phase)

Together with a strange man, the dreamer undertakes a long car ride, whereby, quite remarkably, there is no conversation. Even though the dreamer studies her companion now and then, neither the man's identity nor the reason for the trip are established. The anonymity of the social situation is retained during the second part of the dream. Even when the two dream persons jointly watch a movie, which is not further described, does the dream episode fail to advance any contact.

We most frequently received dream reports that showed the dreamer in contact with other dream persons:

> "I sat on a bed, together with other people; it was a big bed. And these were people I know, Ursula and Anya, plus two men, whom I didn't know. And we were eating ice cream, and Ursula bought a cake, but we weren't sup-

posed to touch it, as it was her private, personal cake.
Not much happened, we just talked to each other, Ursula,
Anya and I. And the two men were somehow always
there, on the bed. And just now one of them was lying
next to me, talking nonsense all the time, and I had the
feeling he had been drinking. And he asked me something, and I said, yes, we did pick red currants. He said:
'Weeell, then you'll all get pie-eyed afterwards.' And he
put his arms around me and tried to kiss me. Anyway, I
bit him, because he revolted me. Then he got scared and
took off."

(Female, 19 years-old, 3rd night, 3rd REM phase)

This dream differs from previous examples in that the
dreamer finds herself in the company of known and
unknown individuals and because, aside from joint activities, these people react to each other. Interaction in this
dream is particularly substantial and includes verbal as
well as motor activities. As the dream goes on, the relationship between the dreamer and the stranger becomes more
concrete and direct. Proceeding from an erotic skirmish of
talk and backtalk, interaction advances to sexual attack, to
which the dreamer reacts with a counter-attack that severs
their relationship.

Looking through the dreams in which the Dream Self
interacts with other people, we noted that communications
predominantly took the form of conversations that were far
from vague but dealt with utterly concrete themes. Relations expressed through actions or non-verbal signals were
far less prominent. What do dreamers and their dream partners talk about? Most conversations concerned everyday
things, such as food, clothing, appointments, plans. Other
people and relations were also frequent topics, particularly
when the dreamer's companions were friends, colleagues,
acquaintances and family members.

Professional matters were discussed much less frequently, and impersonal events of public life, or even political topics were practically ignored. In addition, it was

notable that talk about the weather, which so often initiates and maintains contacts while awake, was missing from our dreams. Clearly, the dream has no need to bridge gaps in conversation, as its own control determines the course of interaction.

Even when the Dream Self participates in a majority of dreams, becomes active and involved with other people in principally verbal exchanges on everyday topics, it does not necessarily mean that the dream is simply the unmodified portrayal of segments from a waking experience. We are better able to judge the realistic nature of a dream when we evaluate a dreamer's participation in the context of specific dream elements.

Dream Scenarios

While the inventory of dream contents provides insight into the location of events, the presence of the Dream Self and the participation of individuals who make their appearance, any experiential nature of a dream is actually revealed only through its choice of topics. In what kind of situation do the dreamers find themselves, and what are their concerns? Does the dream involve everyday situations, does it allow dreamers to experience holidays and leisure times, or does it transport them into an entirely remote existence? Are the dreams realistically constructed, or do they conjure up unfamiliar or even fantastic situations? What underlying themes dominate the dream?

We determined, in the case of each dream, whether it dealt with an everyday topic, with leisure, or entered a fantasy world.

A dream at a kitchen table illustrates how a routine situation can be managed in strikingly realistic fashion:

"I was sitting at a kitchen table and looked at a children's book. And Martin sat next to me and he was looking, too, and kept joking. And then I said: 'There are people who

understand such a book only when they are a bit older.'
And I was laughing as I said that, because I meant it
somehow ironically."

(Female, 19 years-old, 1st night, 3rd REM phase)

This dream scene creates playful interaction between
the dreamer and her friend. It does not show any elements
that differ from ordinary experience, and could easily have
taken place during the dreamer's domestic life.

In the next dream an everyday topic is more freely
approached:

"One of my friends called, and she had a terribly complicated telephone number, something like three times 6,
twin numbers, a telephone number that was incredibly
long. And my parents were still at home. And I decided,
I'm not going to make a call just then, with them standing
next to the phone. I'll just pack what my girl friend needs.
And down in the basement I collected all kinds of old toys
and put them in boxes, because I somehow wanted my
friend to have them. And then I packed the lot into shopping carts. When I had finished, I tried to telephone my
friend, but I dialed wrong."

(Female, 22 years-old, 1st night, 3rd REM phase)

At the outset, the routine situation is characterized by
the familiar environment of the parental home, where the
dreamer concerns herself with people from her daily life.
Making a phone call, thinking things over, packing up—all
these are activities that fit a domestic routine. The dream
thus represents a slice of daily life, but does not otherwise
truly simulate a realistic life situation. All individual dream
elements have their origin in the dreamer's daily experience, but at several points they are combined in a manner
that no longer reflects reality accurately. This applies to the
complicated and long telephone number, which could really
exist but is not the number at which the friend could, in
fact, be reached. Packing toys is not, of itself, an unusual

activity; yet, it does not fit the situation, as there is no convincing reason why, of all things, the friend should require toys.

The realistic design of a leisure time theme is realized in a dream about a bicycle tour:

> "I was riding my bicycle on a pebble road, out in the country. Was bicycling peacefully along, and then I was overtaken by a mother with her child. And suddenly I saw the bicycle race and two men who were changing a wheel. And I simply watched them for a while."

>   (Male, 26 years-old, 1st night, 2nd REM phase)

The dream represents leisure time activity as it might have happened during the dreamer's waking life. The theme of bicycling is acceptably varied and dream elements match appropriately: The dreamer cycles leisurely through the countryside, lets himself be overtaken and remains a mere observer as the bicycling turns into a sporting contest.

By comparison, a dream dealing with an exhilarating party presents the leisure theme in a more playful manner:

> "A group of people are at a party, dancing. And it is some kind of funny folk dance. And they keep slapping their thighs and dance some kind of polonaise. I am right in the middle of these people and take part in their celebration. Although I don't know just what they are celebrating. It is tremendously noisy and thrilling. Plenty of garlands and balloons are up in the air. Yes, a real celebration. Donald Duck was there, too, and he had pretty orange-colored feet."

>   (Male, 26 years-old, 2nd night, 2nd REM phase)

This lively dream joyfully captures the leisure situation. The dreamer is clearly familiar with festivities and gregarious dancing, but this dream, too, does not simply reactivate a remembered experience. Elements representing the festivities are playfully combined and colorfully embellished with Donald Duck. The dreamlike impression is not only created by the appearance of a cartoon figure, which might easily have been a disguised person, but because the dreamer does not know who the host is, where the party is taking place and what people had been invited.

In our sample of 500 REM reports, illustrated in the circular chart of Figure 21, three quarters of the dreams had everyday life situations as their theme, while nearly all other dreams fitted a leisure time pattern. Only six dreams dealt with fictional themes, stimulated by films or literature. Dreams are, therefore, largely based on experiences that engage us in our waking lives. Dreams are less likely to originate with events of which we are mere consumers, rather than actual participants, such as television shows. The dream uses our own world of experience as a starting point, neglecting alien worlds that remain fictional to us.

Above all, everyday situations included the rather intimate domestic realm, routine daily living, but also the laboratory setting. Professional environment stood in fourth place. Within these settings, dreamers were active in many ways, they kept busy, moved around, engaged in conversations and were thoughtful.

Dreams centering on leisure time themes dealt prominently with all kinds of social activities and relaxation. Next

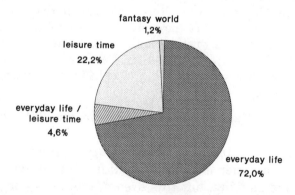

FIGURE 21. Topics in Dreams. Percentages of everyday situations, leisure time themes and fictional worlds in five hundred REM dreams.

came different sport categories and trips to near and far countries.

Conversation taking place in different situations played an important role in more than half the dreams. Dream persons usually discussed specific topics, quite often in actual speech.

Dreams dealt predominantly with themes of daily life or leisure activities, but were certainly not uniformly structured. The transposition of these themes moved within a dimension that ranged from decidedly realistic arrangements to quite fantastic creations.

In order to evaluate degrees of reality, we categorized all dreams overall, differentiating several levels that ranged from the realistic to the fantastic: we regarded dream situations as 'realistic' when they equalled experiences that might have taken place while awake; we judged them as 'fictional' when they combined familiar waking experiences in an unusual manner; and we evaluated them as 'fantastic' when they lacked all relation to the waking experience.

Degrees of reality in dreams are reproduced in the circular chart of Figure 22. We categorized only about every fourth dream as close to reality. Most frequent were dreams that combined realistic with fictional elements. Far less frequent were dreams that were entirely fictional; fantastic

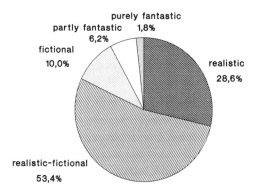

FIGURE 22. **Reality versus Fantasy.** Categorization of five hundred REM dreams, ranging from the totally realistic to the purely fantastic.

dreams, totally lacking in any relation to reality, were recorded only very rarely.

Realistic staging of an everyday theme may create quite a lively dream situation:

> "My father and grandfather were watching television together. Mother was frightfully nervous, because she had so much to do in the garden, where everything had ripened at once. And I seem to have upset her, too, and I had to help carry wood from the balcony, so she could hang up the laundry properly. As we were quite finished stacking, I said to her: 'Look, look, who's coming!' And there was grandmother, stepping firmly, a small parcel under her arm and a laundry basket. And she said, yes, if she had known mother had so much work to do, she would certainly not have come. As grandmother arrived, I had just started to rinse and polish a box of apples. They turned out absolutely gorgeous and good."
>
> (Male, 28 years-old, 4th night, 3rd REM phase)

These colorfully narrated everyday scenes of a dream family are all entirely naturalistic. Still, we are not dealing with a repetition of an actual experience, but with a milieu sketch in which familiar elements have been reshaped into a new experience.

A leisure time dream concerning Spanish dance instructions shows how smooth the transition from a purely realistic to a more imaginative staging can be:

> "In the evening, I was strolling with my Walkman through the outlying section of some town. There were two of us, and we were listening to Stephan Eicher. A Spaniard and his daughter came along. He was either a colleague of mine or of my friend, and he said we were moving our bodies so oddly, we should try and listen to some other kind of music. And we took off the Walkman and put on some other music, some kind of Spanish music. And, with his daughter, he danced to the music. All of us started to dance. And the Spaniard taught us how to dance, first

two firm steps with both feet together, and then one has to keep up one leg for quite a while, and use it to embrace the man's hip from behind. And next, step down hard, once more."

(Female, 27 years-old, 1st night, 5th REM phase)

The dream at first has the dreamer and her companion strolling along, with their Walkman, in a familiar manner. But their encounter with the Spanish family leads to a playful dance, complete with imagined acrobatic motions. This dream is actually a good deal less than realistic, because this kind of encounter and its subsequent events are, in this context, quite unexpected.

A step still further in modification of reality is taken in the following dream:

"I had traveled from Lugano, where I stayed with my parents, to Zürich, because of festivities. And, together with my girlfriend, I drove through the city for a spell, and there was quite a traffic jam, because of the festivity. And I ran into a lot of people, and my mother was there, too. Everybody was disguised in some wacky fashion, which was apparently the thing to do for this event. Among them was Anna, a female friend, and Jean-Luc Godard. They wore completely silly masks. And Anna had totally gray hair, and I couldn't tell whether that was part of her disguise. And my mother sits outside and talks with some friends. And I say, if my parents ever get rid of the apartment I live in right now, I wouldn't care, and I could find some other solution. And I discover that, just at this point, my mother was listening."

(Male, 27 years-old, 3rd night, 3rd REM phase)

This dream, too, contains some entirely realistic elements. The dreamer moves in familiar places and meets close acquaintances. It does not contradict reality that there are festivities, although, as a rule, the whole city of Zürich is not in gridlock, and not everyone wears a disguise. And the French motion picture director Jean-Luc Godard has probably visited Zürich, at one time or another, although not disguised and in company with the dreamer's friend. We placed this dream at a level ranging from realistic to fictional, taking into account that it mixes realistic and improbable events.

Far more fantastic episodes are embedded in a dream in which a moon rocket is baptized:

> "I am in a major American city, where there is a baptism of the rocket for a manned moon capsule. People have come from all over the world and expect something sensational to happen. My sister, and Suzanne and I have been invited. Everything took place at a harbor, and there was some kind of breakdown at the start, and the rocket took off ten or maybe a hundred meters beyond the ramp, and then simply fell back down. And we wondered what might have happened if it had toppled over, just plunged into the water, or if it had lifted 200 meters into the air, and maybe flipped over and had then fallen into the water. If it had gone as high as one kilometer, it might have fallen into the city and on top of a skyscraper. And then we fantasized whether the rocket might be propelled by the muscle strength of statesmen—Giscard d'Estaing was there, too—and thrown upwards like that, which would certainly have caused a debacle. And that's what happened. Several people representing all kinds of nations grabbed the rocket at its bottom, lifted it up and tried to propel it skyward. And the rocket did fly for about one-hundred meters, twisted, and returned toward the water, and everything was tried to save it. And they succeeded once more in putting the rocket into its orbit. Finally, it did fall into the water. All this time, we took photographs from all kinds of perspectives."

> (Male, 25 years-old, 4th night, 2nd REM phase)

This dream is fictional from the start: the dreamer had never been in the United States, and it is highly unlikely that a psychology student would be personally invited to such a state occasion. The dreamer participates in an event which, in reality, is known to him only by public information and through the images of film and television. The unfortunate and grotesque rocket launch develops into a distinctly fantastic event; interestingly, it begins as a fantasy within the dream and is subsequently transformed into a dream reality. Only toward the end does the dreamer reach again the solid ground of reality, by taking the traditional visitor's photographs.

The final dream, dealing with traveling swans, gives the impression of being quite fantastic, showing the particular creativity characteristic of dreams:

"It was all about different swans, which had to travel from a distribution center everyday to a designated town, to Chur, Solothurn and Geneva. The swans took different routes, and not everyone went the whole distance from the beginning, but at one point the routes are somehow divided up. I told Rudi that I would go dreaming. And he, too, was very interested in the swan routes, wondering where they would pass. Then I just told him about it. One swan had to go to Lausanne, destined for Peter. Anyway, I knew that, after a while, the route would be divided up, and that, altogether the swan needs about two-and-a-half hours to reach its destination. These routes were pretty-well marked. That's when I called Rudi, the only one who knew the owner, to tell him that his swan should get started slowly, and that it would be fed a steak on the way. He should see to it that the road is clear, so that the swan really passed by where the steak would be. When I called Rudi, his sister was on the phone, and as usual she was quite cool. And, ahead of this swan, the other swans had reached the goal. With them, things were less complicated, the route had been firmly fixed, it didn't have to be outlined by telephone. I had to make sure that they don't get off the road, and I found this difficult, because I'm not good at geography. And all this took place on rails, like on a narrow-gauge railroad, on which the swans had to travel."

(Female, 31 years-old, 3rd night, 3rd REM phase)

The swans, moving on rails, convey this dream's fantastic impact. Contrary to their nature, swans are mechanically directed by a distribution system and receive steak to nourish them on the way. This exceedingly bizarre theme is, however, placed within a pattern of events that could fit the tasks of a public transportation system. The dreamer's activities, designed to inform the owner and to keep within the travel schedule, are quite realistic and reasonable, if one ignores their aims and the fact that they do not match the dreamer's actual occupation. Scattered among this fantastic dream story are two distinctly realistic elements: the episode where the dreamer tells her friend about the dream experiment, and the time when the sister reacts to the phone call in her usual cool manner.

Everyone of our 44 subjects experienced several 'fictional' dreams, but there were differences in the ratio of the two other categories. With five dreamers, reality-oriented dreams were most prominent; twenty-three dreamers incorporated fantastic elements into their dreams; but only three dreamers did not experience any realistic dreams at all. Individual dream styles pointed mainly toward either a more realistic or a more fantastic dream creation.

Our REM dreams were imaginative, as far as their concrete content was concerned, but did not, as a rule, contain any 'tabloid news' flashes. In only nineteen dreams did we encounter crimes and misdemeanors. In one instance, the dreamer himself engaged in blackmail; in another, she committed matricide. In the rest of the dreams, other dream figures were involved in different crimes, ranging from theft to kidnapping. In only a few cases did the dreamer actually witness a criminal act. For the most part, he was faced with a fait accompli.

Dreams were not particularly fateful as they dealt with assorted everyday mishaps, rather than with existential threats. Only five per cent of dreams featured either illness or accident; interestingly, it was usually not the dreamer but someone else who became the victim. Dreamers occasionally suffered slight injuries but they did not undergo life-threatening illnesses and they never experienced a lethal accident. Dreams also did not contain natural catastrophies; neither were dreamers involved in war actions, nor did they suffer severe losses or deprivations. But dreams were also lacking in outstandingly good fortune, surprising successes or distinctions.

The rare occurrence of fateful events among our dream material might be due to the fact that our dreamers were young adults. As dreams reflect actual life experiences, these dreamers' relative youth might account for the limited presence of an illness theme. We were nevertheless surprised that existential concerns, which occupy much of the waking awareness of this generation, were so little in evidence in their dreams.

Books dealing with dreams often report a preponderance of specific themes and contents, such as metamorphoses, falling, being unable to move, flying, and loss of teeth. Many people claim to have had such dream experiences at least once in their lives. Still, in collections of spontaneously recalled dreams, as well as in REM dreams, such so-called typical dream phenomena are not particularly frequent. At any rate, in our REM dreams such themes were extremely rare. Only five times did a dream figure undergo a metamorphosis, and only three times did dreamers encounter themselves or did not know who they were. Of the remaining contents, the theme of flying or floating appeared in four dreams, and once did a subject dream of losing two teeth. These particular dream contents are not, therefore, part of everyday dreaming; rather, it is their extraordinary nature that makes a lasting impression on a dreamer's memory.

The panorama of actual dream events, which permits the dreamer a wide latitude of activities, encompasses the entire extent of human experience. Dreams are, on the whole, neither entirely close to reality, nor completely fantastic—above all, they represent a creative elaboration of the waking experience.

7

Dreams in Different Sleep Stages

We know today that dreams accompany all of sleep and are experienced during all stages of sleep. As the sleep stages differ markedly as to physiological features, one wonders whether there exist correspondingly varied types of dreams. If bodily changes and specific psychological phenomena are complementary, dreams ought to differ in structure, quality and perhaps in content, depending on the sleep stages during which they appear. Can we, therefore, recognize whether a dream originated with the onset of sleep, belongs to NREM sleep, or was experienced during REM sleep? Are there stage-specific dreams or does the sleep experience tend to be uniform, little influenced by changing physiological conditions?

Dreams During Sleep Onset

The transition from waking to sleep is particularly well suited to the study of changes in consciousness; the onset period permits us to note the appearance of phenomena, up to a point, and to follow the progression of events with expectant observation.

For this reason, the period of sleep onset has received attention from the very beginning of dream research. Ladd and Maury observed their thoughts as they fell asleep, programming themselves to awake shortly afterwards. They were thus able to recall images which, with the onset of sleep, slowly faded from conscious control. Maury referred to such onset experiences as 'hypnagogic hallucinations', as he was impressed by the vivid sensory qualities of these phenomena.

These early studies left undecided whether the recalled experiences had, in fact, originated with the relaxed waking stage or the sleep onset phase. Only accompanying EEG measures made it possible to differentiate between waking fantasies and sleep onset dreams. With that, it became possible, more specifically, to assign the onset experience to different physiological phases.

Wolfgang Kuhlo and Dietrich Lehmann published a study in 1964 which showed that consciousness changes during sleep onset are accompanied by a slowing-down of brain wave activity. They studied the onset experience by means of controlled awakenings, but they also asked their subjects to press a button whenever hypnagogic phenomena appeared.

An outstanding feature of these onset experiences was their sudden appearance: they surfaced without any logical links to preceding thoughts. They were primarily experienced as visual or auditory impressions, with a preponderance of visual perceptions. Despite their vivid qualities, these impressions remained elusive, were experienced with a certain feeling of remoteness, were emotionally neutral and generally rather fragmented and disorganized.

Gerald Vogel, David Foulkes and Harry Trosman (1966) used systematic awakenings in their study to examine the full spectrum of sleep onset, from the relaxed waking stage to the onset of Sleep Stage 2. In addition to the typical qualitative features of sleep onset, they described a progression which, within different phases of sleep onset, indicated changes in ego functions.

During the initial phase, the Ego is still capable of exercising a certain amount of control over the hypnagogic hallucinations. Gradually, control over the emerging images recedes, although awareness of the experimental situation continues and contact with the outside world remains uninterrupted. During the second phase, awareness of the experimental situation fades. At this point, the Ego views itself largely as a passive observer, but does not yet regard the onset images as a dream. The sleeper loses this reality-consciousness only during the third phase, as dreams replace the outer existence and the Ego finds itself more closely involved with the progress of dream events.

This psychological process often ran parallel to increasing depth of sleep, but might also be displaced; changes in consciousness could, therefore, not be unequivocally attributed to physiological conditions.

During these earliest experimental studies, researchers concentrated mainly on the graphic phenomena of the onset experience; they did not analyze in detail links between hypnagogic hallucinations, thoughts and abstract images.

The following sleep onset experiences, recorded by us after awakenings from Sleep Stage 1, at the beginning of the night, provide insight into the range of experience that encompasses thought as well as perception.

> "Put a test together, with items. Had to arrange the items and interview people. Something like a psychotest."
>
> (Female, 25 years-old)

This example, from a psychology student, is limited to considerations concerning a realistic, professionally-oriented task. Questioned later on, the student stated that she had experienced no visual impressions and had been able to guide her thoughts.

> "Saw kind of yellow fringes, and then brooms, America, next the Italian flag appeared. And then I thought, I hope you don't wake me up just now."
>
> (Female, 27 years-old)

Compared to the first example, this sleep onset experience contains both visual impressions and thoughts. Control over thoughts during sleep onset recedes at first, as images appear that seem to have no apparent connection. These images are succeeded by a reality-close consideration that is related to the experimental setting.

> "Something about food. And it had to do with a big cake, which looked like a big Gugelhupf cake, but with some orange and pink coloring. And several people were sitting around and got a piece of cake."

> (Male, 24 years-old)

This sleep onset experience covers a complete, coherent visual situation, including unknown people, and with the Self participating as observer. Although the distribution of cake slices suggests action, the scene as such appears quite static.

These examples come from a study designed to examine different dimensions of the sleep onset experience. We awakened twenty subjects during the course of three evenings, twice during the onset phase, once 30 seconds after the onset of Sleep Stage 1, and again 20 seconds after the beginning of Sleep Stage 2. At the end of the report the subjects categorized their experiences on different scales.

Although awakenings took place during two different stages of sleep, the formal and content features of the onset experience showed rather uniform character. We were unable to fit them into the two physiological conditions beyond mere coincidence.

This sample of sleep onset dreams contained all the means of expression that are also encountered in dream experiences during REM sleep. Visual impressions dominated, followed by thought processes, with other sensory perceptions far behind. Three out of four reports contained thoughts as well as images, while onset dreams that featured exclusively either thoughts or sensory images were quite rare. As far as their structure was concerned, these dreams were categorized as monothematic and, content-wise, as largely reality-oriented. One notable feature of sleep onset dreams was, however, a reduced control of consciousness, as these phenomena appeared out of nowhere and the subjects usually felt that they were unable to guide them.

Consciousness processes during the sleep onset phase encompass a wide range of form and content features. Because of their brevity, they might be labeled as 'little dreams' or as precursors of dreams; compared to REM sleep dreams, they lack narrative structure, differentiated composition and, frequently, a dreamer's active self-involvement. In its quality of expressions, the sleep onset dream does, however, qualify as a dream experience. Because of its nearness to the preceding waking condition, this sleep experience occupies a special position, as waking thoughts are more likely to blend into these dreams.

Herbert Silberer (1919) has made the interesting attempt of interpreting the sleep onset experience psychologically. He described several forms of symbol creation, which express the transition from a thoughtlike to a visual experience. According to his concept, so-called threshold symbols transform the momentarily prevailing consciousness of sleep onset, the transition from one mental condition to another, through the utilization of images. Moving across this threshold may be expressed by visualizing a bridge that links one shore with another, as viewing a departing train or the unlocking of a door.

Non-REM Dreaming

Dreams during Non-REM sleep (NREM) were overshadowed, from the start, by REM sleep dreams. Even now, they are not often regarded as 'genuine' dreams. During the first few years following the discovery of REM sleep, many dream researchers actually maintained that dreams were linked to REM sleep only, and they designated it as 'dream sleep' exclusively.

The existence of NREM dreams was originally doubted because, during initial experiments, control awakening from NREM sleep resulted only in intermittent and fragmentary

reports. These reports were disregarded as memory rem-
nants from preceding REM phases or as thoughts that did
not develop until awakening.

These assumptions had to be revised, once David
Foulkes published his study in 1962, proving that dreams
during NREM sleep were reported prior to the onset of the
first REM phase and that the frequency of recall increased
when he did not specifically ask about dreams but more
generally what had gone through the sleepers' mind before
awakening. From then on, NREM awakenings were scheduled in order to ascertain more precisely whether experience during NREM sleep is characterized by particular features and how it stands in contrast to those during other
sleep phases.

In several studies, dreams from all stages of NREM
sleep, including deep sleep, were described as rather brief
experiences, with fragmentary and disconnected impressions. They tend to be thoughtlike, usually refer realistically to the waking world, with the dreamer often emotionally uninvolved. In their formal features they therefore
resemble the sleep onset experience, but are less vivid and
sensory in their expressive qualities.

We collected NREM dreams in our laboratory as part of
a psychophysiological study, measuring mimic activity during sleep and relating it to emotions while dreaming. We
awakened five subjects during REM sleep and NREM sleep,
but asked them to limit their report to what "only just, as
the very last thing" had come to mind. We thereby sought to
establish an identical point in time to which each recall
referred. We undertook 64 REM awakenings and 80 NREM
awakenings and received 59 REM and 48 NREM dreams.
The recall rate of 92 percent and 60 percent, respectively,
reestablished that recall of REM sleep experience occurs
most of the time, while it is more frequently lacking after
awakening from NREM sleep.

NREM dreams were characterized by reduced abundance of dream elements, by a rather fragmented structure
and by predominantly static impressions. While REM

reports, on the average, contained six dream elements, NREM reports showed an average of only three elements. Four out of five NREM dreams were classified as fragmentary, as their dream elements were isolated or disconnected from each other. REM reports, on the other hand, presented two-thirds of dream experiences as coherent scenes. It fits the fragmentary nature of NREM reports that their dream elements appeared quite static and lacking in dynamic connections. By comparison, slightly more than half of the REM reports showed dynamic progress.

Figure 23 illustrates the expressive quality of dreams in both sleep stages. The majority of NREM dreams, too, was exclusively made up of sensory impressions, they were followed, in second place, by reports that contained only thoughtlike images. The smallest number were dreams that combined sensory with thoughtlike elements. By comparison, REM reports contained an overwhelming number that reflected sensory expressions, much more frequently linked with thought. However, purely thought-oriented REM reports were encountered only rarely.

NREM dreams featured reality-oriented themes most prominently; only every fourth dream offered deviations from reality or bizarre elements. Themes akin to reality dominated REM dreams as well, but dreamlike elements appeared in greater number. Both types of dreams revealed

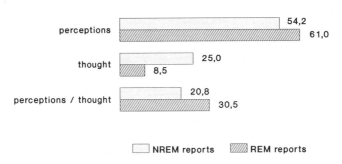

FIGURE 23. Perceptions and Thought in REM and Non-REM Dreams. Percentages of sensory impressions and thoughts in 48 NREM reports and 59 REM reports.

a marked difference in self-participation and emotional involvement. Barely every second NREM dream featured the Dream Self, emotionally related to the dream situation, whereas four out of five REM dreams involved the dreamer emotionally in its events.

Our results regarding the quality of NREM dreams correspond to earlier studies. However, earlier interpretation of results tended to emphasize differences. Yet, even when such differences between NREM and REM dreams are repeatedly encountered, similarities should not be ignored. Not every NREM dream is brief, thoughtlike, disconnected or directly related to waking thought; NREM dreams may well be convincingly 'dreamlike.'

To begin with, two dreams, recalled by a 31-year-old woman during her fourth experimental night, illustrate typical differences between NREM and REM reports. She narrated the first dream when she was awakened from Sleep Stage 2, after one-and-a-half hours of sleep; the second was recalled about one hour later, after awakening from the first REM phase.

NREM Dream:

"It was all about books, actually about books from a lending library. I don't know why, but they were real library books, they all had this number pasted on the back. I arranged them at home, I don't know how I happened to be arranging library books. Pile-high."

REM Dream:

"There was a real street. And on it were all kinds of small wooden cars, and to the left and right were all sorts of cardboard houses, as thin as a sheet. Then I walked in the street, and one of those things came at me, all by itself, half baby carriage and half car. And I wanted to make it stop and stood right in its path, in the middle of the street. The baby carriage was coming straight at me, although the street was totally level, but I didn't manage to catch it. Slowly, the baby carriage was transformed into a small car and proceeded to scoot, hither and yon, behind me. Later, it turned around and traveled toward me. And I thought: 'Heck, you're going to catch the damn thing after all.' Next, it grew a handle, like a pram, and came at me again. And I thought: 'Go ahead, throw yourself on top of it, regardless of how.' And it came at me again, and, like a goalee, I hurled myself on it, but it eluded me again, and, bang, I fell to the ground."

The NREM dream is brief and resembles a snapshot from daily life. The dream scene is fragmentary and limited to the dreamer's own activity: arranging books. The dream is neither enlarged with regard to environment, nor does the action fit into a wider framework.

The REM dream, however, is more detailed and eventful, and has a sequential structure. Although the dreamer finds herself alone on the dream stage, the setting proves to be quite differentiated. In addition, the dream possesses a dramatic quality, centering on the duel between the dreamer and the animated vehicle, which transforms itself and avoids her grasp ingeniously.

The next two dreams, recalled by a 44-year-old female architect during her fourth laboratory night, illustrate what a communality may exist between REM and NREM dreams. She reported the first dream about 4 a.m., after awakening from Sleep Stage 2; the second dream was reported three hours later, following awakening from REM sleep.

NREM Dream:

"I was at an exhibition, downstairs at an institute. There were frames of great depth, and if one did not like a picture, one could press down, the picture disappeared and the one below came up. Outside was a black piece, like iron, a button. What happened was that these pictures were totally different: if there was a romantic picture, and one pushed, then an extreme modern, cold one came up, with few colored spaces. And when the picture was one of those, then something like a Rubens came up. And then it was again at the institute, no longer an exhibition, but there were people who were relatives whom I had never seen before. And they kept running around, terribly busy, saying: 'Sure, that will have to be organized quite differently. The whole thing is terribly unprofitable. Crazy, all this waste of time.' And I kept thinking: 'What are they talking about? I don't understand what's bothering them.' And I was actually quite angry that they should suddenly turn up as managers, trying to organize something I did not understand."

REM Dream:

"We had a house with a large, altered basement. And my friend Rita had prepared a children's party, with innumerable trays of cute sugar easter bunnies, everything quite lavish. And they all really threw themselves on these delicious things. Then my son brought his stuff home with him, and had a tartan skirt of mine, a very soigné one, where he had torn the folds right out. And, anyhow, my daughter had dirtied my things in the most incredible manner and wrecked them, too. So I started to shout at them something fierce. Over and over again, I found new items of clothing that could hardly be used any more. Afterwards, they all stood around inside an office. And my co-worker, Helmut, he stood there and brushed his teeth with a new kind of cleansing solution. Whole cartons full of this stuff had arrived, together with dental glasses. And then my daughter, or somebody else, wanted to try the toothbrush with the new solution. But I said: 'You can't take that away from Helmut. Go and use one of your own.'"

The two dreams are about equally long and offer scenic staging that is linked to a situation change. The dreams also share the feature that the Dream Self is part of the event and emotionally involved. In addition to the dreamer, both dreams present other people, engaged in different activities. Both examples also show certain incongruities: for example, the bizarre picture selection apparatus in the one dream and the many dental glasses in the architect's office in the other dream.

Aside from the properties they have in common, the dreams differ as to the concrete nature of their arrangements and of the animation of the dream stage. The REM dream contains more action, more known people appear in it, they are more clearly identifiable and the dreamer is in direct contact with her environment. The NREM dream, on the other hand, offers greater uncertainty in its dream course, and the dreamer plays more the role of observer and commentator.

Mental activity during NREM sleep is, in one way, characterized specifically by a marked presence of thought elements, which, as in the sleep onset experience, are reality-oriented and demonstrate a rather fragmented structure. Otherwise, longer NREM dreams resemble the scenic experience of REM sleep, even when their dramatic arrangement is less differentiated.

REM Dreams

REM sleep dreams, which permit the easiest access to the sleep experience, have always been the reference point from which other types of dreams were judged. Dream researchers have also made numerous attempts to differentiate dream life within REM sleep by linking it to the physiology of REM sleep. They have sought to determine whether the means of expression and qualities of REM dreams are related to activation patterns or whether specific experience contents actually correspond to salient physiological features.

Such relationships appear quite obvious, as REM sleep, while clearly different from other sleep stages, is in itself far from uniform: a general EEG activation level is superceded by short-term phasic changes in other body functions. Thus, phases of eye movement alternate with phases of eye rest, intermittent muscle twitches occur, and breathing, pulse rate, and other body signs may show fluctuations.

Consequently, the variability of physiological phenomena during REM sleep has prompted numerous questions. Are visual dream experiences accompanied by eye movement and are thoughts likely to correspond to eye rest? Are dramatic, emotionally charged dreams accompanied by increased phasic activation and do everyday dreams originate with less 'hectic' REM phases?

Apparent though these considerations seem, results have shown little agreement. There were constant hints of relationships between physiological activation and intensity of dream experiences, but more strongly activated REM sleep was not necessarily accompanied by particularly vivid and intensive dreams.

Actually, the concept that observable body phenomena might provide clues to the dream itself has engaged dream researchers from the very beginning. Back at the end of the last century, George Trumbull Ladd wrote the following:

> "As we look down the street of a strange city, for example, in a dream, we probably focus our eyes somewhat as we should do in making the same observation when awake, though with a complete lack of that determined teleological fixedness which waking life carries with it." (1892, p. 304)

Experimental dream research seized on this concept quickly. It is an enticing hypothesis that eye movement during sleep is directly related to a dreamer's viewing pattern within a hallucinated dream world, as this might permit tracing the dream's content. William Dement and Nathaniel Kleitman noticed during their initial experiments that there were occasional striking correlations between dream content and directional changes in eye movement. They reported the impressive example of a sleeper who had moved his eyes accurately from left to right and who reported on awakening that he had just watched a tennis match.

Sleep researcher Howard Roffwarg was the first to systematically pursue the question whether, on the basis of eye movements during sleep, it was possible to predict any looking around of the sleeper within his dream world (Roff-

warg, Dement, Muzio & Fischer 1962). Following characteristic sequences of eye movements, sleepers were awakened by one experimenter and then questioned about their
dreams by another one. The second experimenter predicted,
on his own and on the basis of the dream report, the numbers and the directions of eye movements, as they should
have been recorded in the sleep protocol if eye movements
actually signal a space orientation within the dream. In this
initial study, matchings were obtained in four out of five
cases, particularly in the case of dream scenes that subjects
had recalled vividly.

Some subsequent studies could confirm these encouraging results, while others failed to do so. The relationship
between eye movements and viewing direction within a
dream is apparently not close enough to accurately predict
the specific viewing direction of a dreamer, merely on the
basis of individual series of eye movements.

In addition to eye movements, other physiological signals were related to the dream experience. For example, a
research group checked whether phasic muscle activations
in arms and legs, which occur during sleep, indicate how a
dreamer moves about within his or her dream world. On
the one hand, there were specific correlations, here too; for
example, they noted activation of arm muscles and the
dreamer stated that he had just been rowing on a lake. On
the other hand, dreams with manifold movements were
reported that did not coincide with muscle twitches. Conversely, not all recorded motor activity was accompanied by
dreams in which the dreamer was physically active (Gardner, Grossman, Roffwarg & Weiner 1975).

Two Japanese sleep researchers at Osaka University
inquired whether speech during a dream might signal activation of muscles involved during speech while awake
(Shimizu & Inoue 1986). They awakened their subjects,
either when only 'speech muscles' showed deflections or
when, for a period of time, they did not observe any speech
muscle activation. Their results showed correlation, beyond
coincidence, between covert mimic expressions and speech

while dreaming. However, here too, correlation was imperfect. There were dreams during which the Dream Self spoke, while the respective muscles did not react; conversely, motor activation of speech muscles were recorded when there was no speech within the dream.

We pursued the question whether phasic activations of face muscles, which occur during sleep at irregular intervals, might reflect emotions experienced during sleep. While awake, emotions are accompanied by facial expressions. Such expressions can be directly observed, but may also be measured by specific muscle activations. Such activations occur even when the emotional expression is not apparent, as, for example, in the case of imagined emotions. Might we, then, assume that negative emotions in dreams are accompanied by a hidden wrinkling of the forehead and are positive dream emotions echoed by invisible smile activity?

During these experiments, we awakened our subjects immediately following activations of the forehead muscles, or of cheek muscles and, as a control, during phases of mimic rest; we asked them to describe the final dream scene and its accompanying emotions.

One dreamer, whom we awakened from REM sleep after activation of her 'laugh muscles,' reported the following scene:

> "I was sitting in class, at school. The woman teacher, up front, was saying that she was waiting for a patient who had been admitted because of an accident. And all of us were laughing and finding it quite amusing. The teacher was terribly embarrassed, as it hadn't worked out, but she laughed right along with us."
>
> (Female, 26 years-old)

If we assume that recorded muscle activation is most likely to indicate emotions experienced by the Dream Self, then this dream provides correlations. The dreamer experiences a positive emotion, expressed by immediate laughter within the dream. The negative feeling of embarrassment, attributed to the dream figure of the teacher, was not reflected by an appropriate physiological recording.

Another dreamer, whose activation of forehead muscles we observed just before she was awakened from a REM phase, reported the following:

"I was inside a flower shop and was just buying some cut flowers. I had actually told them I wanted a particular kind and, as the cashier went to check me out, I saw that there were other flowers which I would really have preferred. And that really upset me a bit. And there was a colleague, who holds up the other flowers, which I had not noticed. And she is surprised that I had not selected those."

(Female, 24 years-old)

The upset felt by the dreamer, concerning her hasty selection of flowers, could be related to the observed wrinkling of the forehead, whereas the surprise of the dream colleague was again not reflected in any covert mimic expression of the sleeper.

Even if such examples suggest that emotions experienced by the Dream Self are linked to respective muscle activations, such correlations are not very firm; independent judges, who evaluated all reports, were unable to assign reported dream feelings to the observed muscle twitches beyond chance.

The problem presented by such psychophysiological studies is compounded, because the matching of concrete expressions of bodily phenomena during dreams is more difficult than while awake: dreams are reported retrospectively, and are not always recalled with the same clarity. In addition, we cannot be sure just how space and time are experienced during the dream, whether they more closely resemble perception of the real world or of fantasies while awake, or whether they adhere to their own rules.

Psychophysiological approaches to the dream refer not only to the dream experience, but also reflect simultaneous bodily processes. This comprehensive approach seeks to validate the dream experience on somatic grounds. The dream experience would gain in credibility if it could be proven that features of its experience are mirrored by bodily phenomena. Studies have thus far confirmed that dreams develop during sleep and not at the time of awakening. But it is also evident just how little correspondence exists between dream experience and physiological phenomena. The difficulty in arriving at clear cut results is rooted in the fact that here are two systems, being related to each other, which have their own rules and forms of expression.

Efforts to define different types of REM dreams on the basis of activation patterns during REM sleep have not been particularly successful until now. Do REM dreams perhaps vary with increasing sleep time, from sleep cycle to sleep cycle, by growing more dreamlike and escalating from close-to-wakeful themes to fresh creations, enriched by fantasy?

Sleep researcher Milton Kramer and his associates have investigated whether dreams of a single night indicate their succession (Kramer, Hlasny, Jacobs & Roth 1976). Three judges received fifty dream series, each consisting of three randomly mixed dreams; they were asked to arrange them into accurate succession. This organizing effort did not succeed, as the dreams of one night apparently failed to yield any progression pattern.

The following REM dreams series was reported by a 23-year-old female student in her fourth laboratory night, whom we had awakened from REM phases 2 to 5, which had lasted five, ten, fifteen and twenty minutes respectively:

> "I was living with my parents at Thalwil. And we kept driving with our car across this interchange at Thalwil. Usually, I accompanied one of my parents, who was at the wheel. Just then it happened that I was driving. And my father, now and then, was involved in local politics. He had once had an election victory and one could still see posters at the interchange, publicity for himself. We passed this interchange often, and once I drove by myself, without a parent."

"I was together with two boys, about 17 years old. They were fixing an enormous steak, a T-bone steak. I noticed how they had prepared it. It was a gigantic piece, one might have thought from an elephant, incredibly huge. And they kept talking about it. One could see how, on one side, they had used a saw to cut away several bones. We were all quite fascinated by this piece of meat, which was still raw. And they planned to have some kind of competition with the Americans, and had convinced themselves that it would turn out well for them."

"I thought I was awake again, and that you weren't the experimenter, but a student of Asian appearance. Then I was awakened and got up. I was able to take off the electrodes by myself. That's when he called out: 'Hey, you shouldn't do that; I'll do that all right.' But I did it myself, because I thought that it is quite simple to take off those electrodes. Everybody can do that by themselves. It is a lot easier."

"I was at my sister's, got up quite early, had awakened too early. That's how I managed to confuse her experiment. And, to please her, I went back to bed, with the electrodes on, and went back to sleep. And we discussed dreaming and the household. She said that the things one can buy these days are of inferior quality. I quite agreed with her. Next we talked about her husband who is conducting this dream research. And she was disappointed that he does not treat the subjects properly, so that she has to settle with the subjects that he has ruined. I decided that this went beyond her duties as a spouse. She should really not get mixed up in his research matters. She agreed; she would stop doing it from now on. But she would have to admit that she had been lucky with her husband, who was quite lovable and did a great deal for her. Next we were in her bathroom and she showed me a new mouth-rinsing device. I found it very interesting and was surprised that she owned something like that, as she doesn't think much of dental care. My dentist was there, too, and said that it was a good mouth-rinsing device. I was wearing some kind of pullover, and she said: 'Well, well, you have been shopping again. You don't look after your money.' So I said: 'As long as I've got it, I can spend it. But the pullover had only cost 25 Francs, I hope it holds out.' She decided that I was a bit unrealistic. She had bought the same kind of pullover, which costs 140 Francs. Those that cost only 25 Francs would not really last frightfully long."

The first dream represents a situation that could come straight out of waking life. The dreamer makes car trips into a familiar neighborhood, while, for the most part, close relatives are at the wheel and she, herself, drives only once. The frequent passages across the same interchange are notable; they appear condensed in time and do not fit into a wider framework of action. Furthermore, it is not as such unusual that political posters are placed at roadside. But at this point, the dream incorporates an unreal element, as the dreamer's father, who campaigns for himself on the poster, in reality has nothing to do with politics.

The second dream deals with a totally different topic. It pictures, in extra vivid terms, the invented situation of preparations for a bizarre competition. The dreamer, in a vague setting, observes with fascination how two unknown youths triumphantly prepare an extra-dimensional piece of meat, a symbol of the animalistic.

The third dream starts from the situation in which the dreamer finds herself at the time. However, it varies from reality in that an exchange of persons takes place: the position of the experimenter is taken by a foreign-looking man. In addition, the dreamer is not cooperative, as a subject is supposed to be, but frees herself from the electrodes, thus keeping the experimenter away from her.

The fourth dream transports the dreamer into the familiar home of her sister. A lively exchange ensues, with the dreamer being agreeable as well as critical. On the one hand, the dream is not unusual, as the sisters talk about household items and clothing, and the sister's marriage is also discussed. On the other hand, several dreamlike elements are interwoven. The sister's home is the setting of a dream experiment, and her husband, in variation from reality, is a dream researcher, and the dentist suddenly appears in the bathroom, intruding into the conversation.

The night's dreams are impressive in their scenic cohesion, in the changes of the dream stage and of its actors. In viewing the whole dream series, however, no linear escalation of dreamlike quality emerges from the first to the last dream. Dream topics also do not change in any progression from everyday themes to the fantastic. Rather, we encounter unusual elements in every dream, which, with the exception of the second dream, are always mixed with realistic situations. The different durations of the REM phases, which preceded awakenings, do not stand in clear-cut relation to the manifold levels of the dream experience. The final dream, which emerged from the longest REM phase, does actually differ in extent from the rest of the dreams; yet, it is not the most fantastic dream, but ranges behind the animalistic competition of the second dream, which was reported after the ten minute REM phase.

There are, of course, examples in which the dreams of one night provide obvious transitions from waking-near and waking-removed themes, as well as a gradual increase in dreamlike quality. Nevertheless, a single night's dreams do not, as a rule, offer such predictable changes; they tend, rather, to represent coherent and integrated units of experience.

Similarities and Differences

In one way, dreams of the sleep onset phase, NREM sleep stages and REM sleep vary so markedly from each other in quantitative and qualitative terms that it seems logical to speak of different types of dreams. Still, the overlapping of these dream categories indicates that a division of sleep experiences is not always clear-cut. Dream research nevertheless retains the classification of dreams from different sleep stages, because the particularly interesting question is: do different psychophysiological states control the dream production in different way?

One research team used a matching procedure to ascertain whether one might generally be able to use a dream report to determine from which sleep phase it originates (Monroe, Rechtschaffen, Foulkes & Jensen 1965). In this study, independent judges were successful in matching nine out of ten cases of REM and NREM reports correctly. The success rate was highest with pairs of REM and NREM dreams, reported by the same dreamer, during the same experimental night and in temporal proximity.

One of our series of REM and NREM dreams, as recalled by a 45-year-old educational secretary during her fourth experimental night, illustrates such matchings.

1st Awakening 1:15 a.m.: REM Phase

"This was about a married couple, where the husband was no longer around. And she was now down and out. What they did was like a game. And she was always quite oppressed, while he showed a mean character streak. And one day, when one dreamed it, it was all over. She may have talked about it, or I may have observed it retroactively. Anyhow, they lived in this house together. And she had to turn on some kind of lamps, which glared something fierce. Anyhow, she said quite triumphantly: 'If he had lived today, he would not have survived it.'"

2nd Awakening 2:36 a.m.: Sleep Stage 2

"Somebody, I don't know who, said: 'Next time, when you dream about sex life, we'll have to set it up differently.' And then it was set up as if all kinds of breakfast rolls were lying there, five or six in a row. And numbers were written underneath, like a big blackboard."

3rd Awakening 4:12 a.m.: REM Phase

"A woman was brushing my hair, and it was not as short as it is now, but longer. She brushed it quite hard, and I thought: 'It certainly won't stay in place.' And she looked it over, once more, and said: 'That is no kind of hairdo.' 'Yes, I know, it just does not stay in place, you'll have to brush much more inwards.' That is what she did, and then it stayed in place."

4th Awakening 5:16 a.m.: Sleep Stage 2

"Examination plans. Examination plans are just coming up. All this means school. Again, one gigantic scheme was subdivided, and I couldn't figure it out, with all those numbers. I wondered, and then I recalled: of course, examination plans. Suddenly I had grasped it fully, although it made no sense, being divided into segments, evenly back to front, and finally nothing except numbers could be recognized. I felt that this was perfectly in order and correct, and did not find it difficult in any way."

5th Awakening 5:53 a.m.: REM Phase

"We were standing on the street and many cars were parked there, so close together that one couldn't get out. One car, which we would liked to have out of the way, suddenly began to move, neatly forward, so that there was a space. We were chatting, just standing around. And I said: 'Well, if one drives real fast in France, the Flic-Flacs come.' Somebody next to me said: 'They aren't coming; they're already here.' And I said: 'Well, do they really stop every car?' 'Yes, whether somebody is French or anything else, it doesn't make any difference.' Then I walked with the policemen, quite arm-in-arm. Female colleagues of mine joined us and said: 'Now, they are going to be bribed, those two cops.'"

6th Awakening 6:52 a.m.: Sleep Stage 2

"A lot of young girls were walking ahead of me, one could only see them from the back, marching all jumbled, like geese. That's when I said: 'What's going on there, up front?' Somebody, a man or woman, gave me a whole bunch of index cards and said: 'Those are the progressives.' And I suggested: 'Oh, because they are progressing, walking forward.' The other one said: 'Certainly, everything is written on the cards.' I: 'Are they all on there?' 'Yes, they're all on there.' Then I looked into the cards and said: 'Those are all men. This is a mix-up.' And I quickly checked and said: 'Yeah, sure, it'll be alright with these girls.' At that point they turned around and I said: 'But these are really men, and I am in the wrong school.'"

Although the six dreams of this night vary in extent and imagery, none of the reports is sufficiently notable as being so exclusively fragmentary or thoughtlike to be considered a 'typical' NREM dream. Still, if we compare them in pairs, we are more easily able to separate NREM and REM dreams.

The first two dreams during this night share several features. Scenic imagery is only partially presented, there is spoken language, bizarre elements appear, and the Dream Self acts merely as observer. The REM dream is more extensive, but contains only one clearly visual element, the glaring lamps, while the pre-history of the married couple is presented as implicit knowledge. The NREM dream is more abstract in theme, but transforms the problem of sex life arrangement into a graphic image of breakfast rolls. Despite similarities, a correct distinction might perhaps be achieved, as the NREM dream is notable for its greater disconnectedness and as the identity of speaker and environment remain vague, whereas the REM dream embodies more activity and clearer scenic touches.

The second pair of dreams shows the most striking differences. The REM dream offers a short but concrete beauty parlor scene, with the dreamer directly involved. During the NREM dream, however, the dreamer only sees the examination scheme, while considering it realistically. Interestingly, although in a different form, the theme of division, noted in the first NREM dream, makes a reappearance in this dream.

The two last dreams, recalled toward morning, present greater similarities. They are comparable with regard to length, concentrated activities and the presence of other dream figures with whom the dreamer engages in lively conversations. Both dreams contain certain inconsistencies: the car starts to move suddenly, the policemen are called Flic-Flacs, and the supposed girls are actually males. Similarities are prominent, and only when we devote attention to differences do subtle variants emerge, pointing toward greater solidity in the REM dream. The REM dream is distinguished by a somewhat clearer environment, while the scenery in the NREM dream remains less clearly defined. The REM dream features more clearly identified characters, such as colleagues and policemen, while the individuals in the NREM are not only anonymous but are also undefined as to their sexual identities.

An overview of the total dream series further reveals that all NREM dreams contain elements that, in one way or another, refer to the dreamer's job situation: an arrangement, an examination scheme, or index cards of pupils. The REM dreams, on the other hand, present themselves as situations without a thematic connection and they select ever-new slices of life. This example may suggest a significant difference between the production of REM and NREM dream: dreams during NREM sleep seem to circle around the same theme, whereas REM dreams draw on more abundant resources.

The research team of David Foulkes presented a systematic comparison of form and content features of dreams from different sleep stages (Foulkes & Schmidt 1983). They collected sleep onset experiences, NREM dreams and REM dreams, employing 23 subjects, each during three separate nights. This was followed by segmentation of all dreams into action units; for each unit they decided whether the Dream Self or other persons were involved, and in what environment they found themselves. They then evaluated, beyond these units, the continuity of coded contents within each dream.

As expected, the three types of dreams differed in their extent. REM dreams were, on the whole, four times longer than either sleep onset experiences or NREM dreams. They also featured greater continuity: places and individuals, once introduced, remained engaged in dream events for a longer period. Regardless of how many action units a dream might contain, NREM dreams featured fewer dream characters and the Dream Self was more frequently not involved: in this respect, NREM dreams resembled sleep onset experience more closely than REM dreams.

So far, these results confirm only differences, established during earlier researches. In order to study more intensively what impact the extent of dreams might have on its copiousness, Foulkes and Schmidt selected pairs of dreams of equal length from different sleep stages. They were able to show that, given comparable lengths, variations between dreams of different sleep stages are less significant. During NREM and REM dreams, continuity as well as richness in content depend on the extent of dream events. No matter what sleep stage its origin, the longer a dream, the more coherent and filled with experience it is likely to be.

At the University of Bologna, Corrado Cavallero and his colleagues engaged in a series of experiments to ascertain whether, during each different sleep stage, dreams utilize different memory data (Cavallero, Cicogna & Bosinelli 1988). They elicited dreams from the onset phase, from NREM and REM sleep. They subsequently asked their subjects to freely associate to individual dream segments. The dreamers' spontaneous impressions were then placed into three classes: episodic memories concerning actual life experiences; statements regarding general knowledge; and associations concerning the dreamer's own personality. Dreams from different sleep stages offered varying emphases concerning dream sources: associations to REM dreams were more often related to general knowledge, whereas dream onset and NREM dreams were more closely related to memories of actual life experiences. But, even in this study, differences became elusive, as longer NREM dreams as well incorporated data from a general knowledge.

Dream researcher Alan Moffitt and his team devoted a study to self-reflection in dreams (Purcell, Mullington, Moffitt, Hoffman & Pigeau 1986). They encoded dreams from Sleep Stages 2 and 4, as well as from REM sleep, according to a scale that described various levels of thinking. During all sleep stages, dreams were experienced that were accompanied by thought processes. However, during REM dreams, dreamers more frequently thought about the dream and about themselves, whereas, during NREM dreams, they tended to go along with events without reflection.

Dream researcher John Antrobus maintains that NREM and REM dreams are generated and stored according to identical rules, but their retrieval is more or less difficult. Accordingly, NREM reports are only shorter and less elaborate because it is more difficult to transmit these dreams to the waking state (Antrobus 1983). David Foulkes also emphasizes the impact which the ability to recall exercises on different types of sleep experiences. But he feels that it is too early to tell whether different activation, characteristic of separate sleep stages, is not simultaneously reflected in specific shadings of the dream experience.

Even when the link between dream experience and sleep stage is not particularly close, an interesting correspondence could be found in the specific category of night terrors. Night terrors are intensive anxiety experiences, related to abrupt awakening. Such sudden awakening may be accompanied by shouting and writhing, intensive bodily excitement and difficulty in adjusting to the waking environment. People who experience night terrors usually cannot remember what triggered their fears. When there is some recall, it usually refers to such basic themes of fear as claustrophobia, fear of falling, dying, or being threatened. These fears are, for the most part, lacking in scenic detail and notable for their archaic character.

Charles Fisher, a New York psychiatrist and the first to undertake a detailed study of the night terror phenomenon in a sleep laboratory, has noted that night terrors are exclusively linked to deep sleep (Fisher, Byrne, Erwards & Kahn 1970). He observed with many sleepers who suffered from such anxiety attacks that, during quiet deep sleep, their pulse rate quite suddenly doubled, the sleepers awoke in fear and needed minutes to realize where they were. The night terror experience was particularly intense when the preceding deep sleep period had been of long duration.

Night terrors are rather rare experiences, they appear sporadically, particularly among children and adolescents, and continue only infrequently into adulthood. They differ markedly from the more frequent nightmares or anxiety dreams. In his book, *The Nightmare*, the psychiatrist and sleep researcher Ernest Hartmann dealt with physiological and psychological aspects of anxiety dreams and with their demarcations from night terrors (Hartmann 1984). Nightmares are mainly experienced during REM sleep and are rather part of everyday dreaming. They may be accompanied by considerable excitement, but in this case sleepers awake without motoric unrest, find it easier to orient themselves and remember vivid anxiety-oriented dream content in detail.

On the basis of current knowledge, the initial question, whether experience during sleep is quite uniform, or whether there are dreams that fit specific stages of sleep, cannot be answered conclusively. Dreams from the onset of sleep, from the NREM stages and from REM sleep do, in fact, show specific proportions of formal and qualitative properties, but there are also overlappings, which prevent any clear-cut classification of individual dreams. As we are only able to study dreams that are available to recall, we just cannot be certain whether differences between stage-specific dreams are not, after all, just the result of easier or more difficult access.

8

Sources of Dreams

Dreams continue to surprise us, because they create situations that do not relate to our daily lives in realistic terms. We gain this impression in particular when we view the dream in its totality. If, however, we look at its different components, we note that all of them originate in our waking experience and do not make their first appearance in the dream. We can recognize these dream elements, we are able to describe them, they are not totally alien, and it is only their encapsulation within the dream situation that makes them unusual. The variations from reality that puzzle us do not refer to the dream's building blocks, but to the manner in which these have been reassembled.

It is the dreamer who invents the dream, and the sources of all dream patterns do, therefore, originate in the dreamer's memory pool. Dream contents are entirely determined by the dreamer's own knowledge, by lifetime experiences and by thoughts about self and world. Yet, though a dream can only incorporate what the dreamer's memory has stored away, in one guise or another, it is fair to ask what temporal relations exist between dream repertoire and waking experiences. Just how often does the dream unearth events from early life experiences? To what degree are dreams determined by actual life situations? What impact do immediately preceding daytime impressions have on a dream; and, furthermore, up to what point may the dreamer absorb stimuli that exert an influence during dreaming?

Temporal References in Dreams

When we try to recall the sources of dream contents, we usually encounter multileveled connections that may reach from immediate past back to early childhood. We are, however, likely to observe that dreams prefer stimuli from preceding days. Sigmund Freud called these dream sources 'day residues.' His detailed dream analyses showed how each dream is linked to such a residue, although it is, in turn, linked by association to earlier life experiences and unconscious wishes.

In order to define the temporal references of a dream episode, we have to question the dreamer about origins of dream contents and find out how far back these experiences go. Tracing such dream sources is often quite difficult, as it not only makes severe demands on the dreamer's introspection and memory, but because dreams and life histories are tightly and intricately interwoven.

Even a short and clear dream may require complex dating, as shown by an example from the dream diary of a 28-year-old woman:

> "I am inside my apartment with Anita and Bruno, preparing a meal. Bruno is moving close to me, and I try to push him away. Next, I am with strangers at a big party, where red hats are handed out. I meet Doris and Helen there, and they tell me about their stay at a psychiatric clinic. I understand, later on, that this whole event occurs at a place in England."

Temporal comments of the dreamer defined just when, in reality, she had encountered the various dream elements most recently in real life. The individuals, Anita and Bruno, referred to immediate day residues: she had seen both friends the day before. She had prepared a meal at home, the last time, three days earlier, when she invited Anita and one other acquaintance. The action ('Bruno is approaching—I reject him') refers to an incident that had occurred four days earlier; it involved another visitor, who did not appear in the dream, but had made an undesirable advance. The content of "strangers at a big party" could not be fixed in time, as the dreamer was unable to relate this rather unspecific situation to any actual experience. The element of "red hats" had a dual temporal link. Six days earlier, the dreamer had lent Anita a red hat to wear at a carnival event; a day earlier, and just for fun, she had tried on a similarly-shaped but differently-colored hat at a store. The dreamer had met her acquaintances, Doris and Helen, three weeks earlier. Doris had been at a psychiatric clinic two years before, and she had mentioned this during their meeting. The English location went farthest back into the dreamer's past, as she had made a trip to England ten months earlier.

This dream contains day residues, events from the preceding week, as well as experiences going back over several months. Time elements are linked, so that events of a few days ago become revitalized by the previous day's happenings. Differing temporal references do not permit us to categorize this dream overall, as the location of the dream events lies further in the past than the positioning of people and objects. It is of additional interest that the affect-oriented dream situation of the unwanted advance is not a day residue but based on an event that occurred several days earlier, although, by employing a switch in personalities, the dream managed to incorporate this situation into a daytime remnant.

In this case, the dreamer sought to connect the dream's setting, individuals and actions with real life experiences. But dreams are not only stimulated by actual events but just as well by the thoughts and imagining that absorb a person. That is why, in determining time relations, we must also ask when dream elements were last present within a subject's thoughts. This is quite difficult, as a multitude of things pass through our minds during the course of a day. Thus, the dreamer post-dated the unwanted advance in her dream as an actual experience by four days; but she might well have remained concerned about it for several days thereafter, and it is also possible that she thought more recently of her acquaintances, Doris and Helen, whom she had met three weeks earlier.

We pursued the multi-level nature of temporal relations by questioning laboratory dreamers closely to which sources they traced the contents of their dreams. This study allowed for the fact that the building blocks of dreams are not only prompted by perceptions but by imaginings and thoughts as well. We therefore asked the subjects in the morning to indicate two time references: First, when they had last encountered, in real life, the very individuals, locations and objects that had made an appearance in their dreams; and, next, just when these elements had last entered their minds. Finally, they were supposed to state when such a dream element had appeared in their lives for the first time. These questions were designed to ascertain from what storage dreams obtain their patterns, regardless of any personal significance they might have in connection with a dream plot.

On the basis of two REM dreams by a student of Germanistics, we provide an example of how manifold such time specifications can be:

> "I was somehow in a room with somebody. And he kept saying: 'No, that's impossible, that is not the correct setting for my film, the finish has to have something else, we can't do it here.' And then we went off together, strolling down a street with beautiful houses. It was a residential type of street, in a quiet city neighborhood, with few gardens, not very lively. And he carried a big black briefcase. Then he walked ahead a bit, entered one of the row houses, came out again and waited for me up front. And I walked rather slowly up to him and looked around a bit, and suddenly discovered that everything was much more lively than I had thought. People stood at the windows of the house, others came out of it, and other people were walking around. I did not see who these people were, and that bothered me. I had the constant feeling

that I was too far from the house to recognize these people. And I felt that I could not get any closer to the house, although it was strenuous to run toward the house, and it also seemed to grow larger. And then I started to chat with the man, but don't remember what it was about."

(Female, 24 years-old, 3rd night, 2nd REM phase)

The dreamer was unable to connect any details of this dream to a specific episode in her life. The man was a stranger, and the other people were too vague to be identified. The dream environment resembled any number of possible settings she might have encountered in her life, but she did not recall having been in such a neighborhood, either recently or earlier. Finally, while the dreamer knows, of course, what a briefcase is, this particular black dream briefcase did not seem familiar.

This example illustrates that a dream may start from models that are rooted in general knowledge of the world. Houses, a man, shadowy people, walking along a street—all these are everyday experiences, which vary in ever novel arrangements, but need not reflect specific episodic moments.

When building blocks of dreams cannot be fixed in time, this applies only to their immediate manner of appearance, but not to their symbolic content and meaning. A dreamer's associations could trace the origins of such dream elements back into a life story, which our inquiries had categorized as non-specific. In this case, the briefcase did not provide a temporal connection, but it might have reminded the dreamer of a briefcase her father had owned, referring to their relationship, or it might have been the symbolic expression of a career ambition.

In a second dream, the dreamer was able to relate most elements to episodic waking experiences:

"I was sitting in a room, at a big oval table. Markus sat at the other end, and was drawing. He had a piece of paper in front of him, and two cardboard boxes. One box was closed, and the other was half-open on top, inside were all kinds of drawing utensils which he had taken out. And music was playing, some kind of tape. And I was sitting at the other end, while we had to wait for something. There were other people somewhere around who had to wait, too. We didn't know for what. And then I got up and walked over to the left, where there was a book rack with many white shelves. They were not only filled with books, but with a pile of other stuff, some kind of old toys. And I got some paper from there, sat back down at the table and asked Markus whether I might use some of his colors. There were water colors, crayons and chalk. And he sort of nodded. And I picked up a crayon and drew the first lines on the paper."

(Female, 24 years-old, 2nd night, 4th REM phase)

The dream environment corresponds to a room in Vienna, where the dreamer had lived for several months, although the dream room was partly furnished differently. While the oval table fitted to the Vienna setting, a book rack of this type stands in her parents' house, although not as big as in the dream. The dreamer had left her Vienna apartment nine months earlier, but keeps thinking of it, consciously the last time four days previously. She last saw her parents' book rack two weeks before, but shelves and books are part of her daily life. The shelves partly contained books that the dreamer owns, but also others she has only on her shopping list. She sees most of these books daily, but some of the books are stored in a loft and she saw them last a week earlier. Markus is a friend of the dreamer; they had met four days before, but she had thought of him a day earlier. The other people in the room, whom she had viewed only as shadowy figures, were unknown to her. The cardboard boxes and drawing utensils are the dreamer's own property. She had dealt consciously with the boxes, which contain all kinds of things, five days before, but handles drawing materials daily. The toys have dual temporal links: first, they were toys that are, in fact, stored in a book rack at her home; second, they were objects she had seen the previous week at a flea market and would have liked to have bought. The scene of sitting at a table with Markus, while drawing, reminds her of a situation a week earlier, when she and Markus were sitting at a different table, and he was also drawing something.

Time relations in this dream are closely interwoven. Setting, people and objects of the dream are, in their relations to most recent reality encounters, situated on a time axis that extends from the previous day to nine months before, and that includes the future as well. However, this time relationship becomes foreshortened when we take into account when the dreamer last thought about those contents. Probably all dream elements are somehow related to the preceding day, even when they do not emerge as identical images within the dream. All of the dream is, therefore, basically stimulated by day residues, although these occupy different temporal positions in the dreamer's life story and, furthermore, are assembled into a new dream construct.

Our study is based on fifty dreams, reported by five subjects. During subsequent inquiry, a total of 80 leading figures, 39 extras, 74 settings and 298 objects were dated. Figure 24 initially shows how often subjects related different

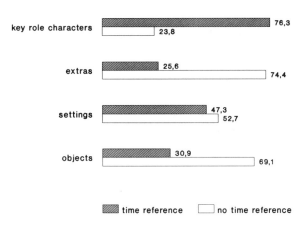

FIGURE 24. **Temporal References of Dream Elements.** Comparison of dream elements, with and without time references, in 50 REM dreams. Percentages refer to 80 leading figures, 39 extras, 74 settings and 298 objects.

dream building blocks to specific episodes in their life histories. Most frequent were time relations for characters who played a key role in the dream, while walk-ons on the dream stage could not, for the most part, be placed in a specific time slot. Among settings, barely half, and among objects, just about one-third could be given a temporal marker.

The numerous elements that are lacking a time relationship indicate two strategies in dream staging: on the one hand, the dream utilizes general knowledge, while, on the other hand, the dream outlines single elements only in a sketchy way, making multiple realizations possible. The theatrical stage offers a close analogy: extras, props and stage décor are less focused than leading parts, and may even be interchangeable.

Figure 25 shows how time-fixed dream experiences fit on the time axis; in this evaluation we have only considered the most recent memory of a building block, regardless of whether it was encountered in reality or thought.

The results emphasize the considerable significance that events of the preceding day have in dream construction.

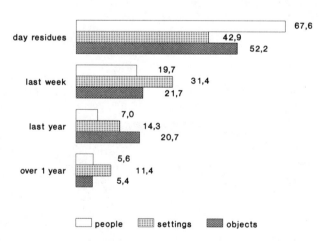

FIGURE 25. **Temporal Sources of Dream Elements.** Arrangements on the time axis of 198 dream building blocks from 50 REM dreams. The most recent memory was considered, regardless of whether it involved real or imagined encounters.

Day residues are clearly dominant. In particular, dream figures were mainly people with whom the dreamer was somehow concerned during the previous day. By comparison, people of whom the dreamer had lost track of for some time appeared only rarely in dreams. Dream environments and dream objects, while also related largely to the preceding day, were more frequently connected to earlier memories.

It becomes difficult to decide whether these different distributions are due more to dream organization or dream evaluation. The dreamer is inclined to incorporate familiar individuals into a dream, people who are significant to the dreamer's actual life situation. At the same time, settings and objects provide a mere framework for the progress of dream situations. It is, of course, possible that dreamers quite simply take particular note of dream persons; it is relatively easy to remember just when they have most recently encountered or thought about an individual, while they pay less attention to the details of everyday environment.

Furthermore, it is notable that dreamers rarely referred to time relations that reach back over more than one year. Neither did any reference by our young adult subjects delve into early childhood; at most, they reached back into their adolescence. Thus, the dream does not, as a rule, call upon life's total experiences. Instead, it makes a selection that is guided by personal interests and current impressions.

The distribution of temporal references within the fifty dreams revealed that only nine dreams lacked time references entirely. An additional nine dreams tended to be oriented toward the past, with all time specifications going back more than one day. Day residues had entered the vast majority of 32 dreams. These residues did not, however, permeate the whole dream in all cases; rather, they were associated with the dreamer's memories that could reach back over several days and weeks, or even over many years, without having been central within the preceding day's consciousness.

Even when day residues occupy a particularly prominent position in dreams, they do not, as a rule, concern new experiences that entered memory for the first time the preceding day. These residues were not new to the dreamer, but familiar elements that had only recently been refreshed.

It cannot be ruled out, conclusively, that all aspects of a dream are somehow activated during the preceding day. As a day's impressions and thoughts are of limitless variety, and for the most part not at the center of attention, it is just not possible to recall every one of these references the next day.

Impact of Pre-Sleep Experiences on the Dream

The influence which events of the preceding day have on a dream may be experimentally studied by specifically structuring the previous day, by varying the situation immediately prior to sleep, or by instructing the dreamer to realize particular dream topics.

Dream elicitation in the sleep laboratory is a standardized, fixed situation, where subjects who participate in such experiments encounter identical framework conditions and demands. The environment of the experiment is just as fixed as are the procedures of the experimenter in preparing sleep measurements and dream elicitation. The laboratory situation also represents a new and, for all subjects comparable, experience; it is particularly interesting to observe how dreamers absorb and deal with this situation. In addition, the experimenter is a good judge for identifying whether, and in what way, the features of this situation are incorporated in dreams.

A dream experiment may enter into the sleep experience in a variety of ways. Our first example deals with a dream that has the laboratory situation as its continuous topic:

"You had just come in, and I thought I was awake. And a second person stood at the door, but I don't know who it was. Next, you dragged a mechanical device into the room, and said it would help me sleep better. And then I said I did not want any special treatment. And the device was a box with switches and metal cables, to be fastened to the head, designed to sleep better, or sleep at last."

(Male, 22 years-old, 2nd night, 2nd REM phase)

On the one hand, the experimental situation is presented realistically in this dream, as the dreamer finds himself inside the familiar laboratory and talks to the experimenter. On the other hand, the dream has in many respects imaginatively altered the prevailing situation. In reality, the experimenter does not suddenly, at night, bring in an additional apparatus, and there is obviously no strange observer standing in the doorway. The box, which is supposed to induce sleep and help the dream researchers gain their data, also belongs to the dream world; the dreamer, as one can well understand, would want to resist such experimental manipulations.

Quite often, the experimental situation provided only the framework for events that expanded into other locations and contents:

"I woke up here, in the morning, and I was frightfully angry that I had not dreamed more. And there were inside this house quite many people. They were frying eggs, and all kinds of things. And that bothered me a lot, all these people around. I walked about, wearing my electrodes, and sometime I lost sight of you. You had very thick red hair. And then I left the house and, in my pyjamas, walked around town and wondered whether I would meet you. And then I saw you, on a bicycle. You wore a dressing gown and make-up, fire-red lips and red cheeks. And then I asked whether I might not, to start with, take off my electrodes. And you decided that sure was a good idea. And then we traveled back home. On the way home, we encountered a woman and her mother. The woman had two small children with her. They each sat in a kind of sled that one could pull with a string. And then, while we rode on the bike, she threw the sleds at us, with her children on it, so we could catch them and take them in the opposite direction. She asked us: 'Can't you take my children along?' It went uphill, and we had to stop, because it was so dangerous. And then we said that we could not go ahead, because it was too icy. And the woman decided we were just plain stupid. That's when I got furious and said to her: 'Don't you realize how dangerous this is? Why don't you take the kids with you?' And I very nearly threw the sled at her. And she was quite surprised. And then we went on and came back here, to the Institute."

(Female, 23 years-old, 1st night, 4th REM phase)

The first sentence refers realistically to awakening in the laboratory. However, the dreamer finds herself surrounded by strange people, and the experimenter is, at that point, nowhere to be found. Looking for her, the dreamer, while still equipped as a laboratory subject, goes for a walk and finally encounters the quite altered, equally inappropriately dressed experimenter. Together, they face a new situation which absorbs their attention totally. Only when they have refused the imposition of the demanding mother, to take her children on a dangerous journey, are they able to return to the laboratory.

This dream illustrates particularly vividly how aspects of the laboratory situation are freely seized and linked with other events. The awakening in the laboratory, the chagrin of not having dreamed enough, the wearing of electrodes and the desire to take them off, express themes which, on the one hand, are linked to the experimental situation. On the other hand, the experimenter is equipped with fresh attributes and, together with the dreamer and the items, electrodes, pajama and dressing gown, is transported in a different context that gives the dream a bizarre character.

Quite frequently, suggestions that originated in the laboratory situation—as in this dream about a bee—are represented in a figurative manner:

"I was lying in bed and, with people I know from sport, was watching some kind of film. And then, suddenly, a bee comes from somewhere and tries to build a nest in my hair. I try to shoo it away, but it just won't work."

(Male, 26 years-old, 4th night, 2nd REM phase)

Lying in bed and watching a film are everyday events. By themselves, they do not necessarily point toward the sleep laboratory situation. However, during our preparations for the night, we had, by attaching the electrodes, in a way been 'building a nest' on the subject's head. It makes sense, therefore, that the irritating bee acts as an allegory for the EEG connections.

Even odder was one aspect of the experimental situation transformed in the crochet pattern dream, in which the topic dreaming is presented as a metaphor:

"I was on the telephone with Sandra, and when she called we decided she would come at a certain time, and then we would first go swimming and, in the evening, to the theater. But when I thought about it I wondered whether this would work out, as I had already planned the whole day. And that's when I found an U-shaped old crochet pattern, worth a great deal. I wanted to transpose it to a canvas. However, I was unable to do that, because with my last dream I had not advanced that far. It had not yet been rolled up, and I needed nearly all the space for it. And right now I was eating a carrot and threw the garbage into a garbage pit."

(Female, 30 years-old, 4th night, 4th REM phase)

In this dream, domestic activities are loosely interwoven. In between is a reference to a dream elicitation, although in disguise: in this case, dreams are not narrated but obviously transferred to canvas.

Dreams do not only select various aspects of the experimental situation in direct or alienated ways, but they also indicate how participation in such experiments affect the subject and how the participant deals with it:

"You came in here and I was supposed to fall asleep again, but somehow more quickly. I asked you whether I should put on some lipstick, because I thought I might look better in front of the camera, or otherwise. And then you said, sure, if I wanted to put on lipstick, that would be fine. But I said: 'No, I don't want that, I only mean, so you can see everything better.' And finally, by mistake, I bit off half the lipstick and that was quite disgusting."

(Female, 24 years-old, 3rd night, 3rd REM phase)

In this dream, the subject strives to make things easier for the experimenter, by trying to fix herself up properly. But this willing cooperation is not particularly supported by the experimenter and ends with a clumsiness that expresses the dreamer's discomfort with the experiment.

Some dreams nevertheless succeed in recasting the subject's role, permitting entirely different reactions to the laboratory experiment to be expressed:

"I was just having a big argument with you, whether people who are all enthused about these experiments are awakened more often, and that additional electrodes could be attached. We disagreed and argued about whether it was proper to glue on one more electrode. Until now there were four of them, and I wanted five, one more. These electrodes would have to be attached in rows: one back row, one in the middle and one up front. Each would be responsible for one dream."

(Female, 25 years-old, 5th night, 2nd REM phase)

In this dream scenario, the dreamer rids herself of a dependent position, putting herself on the same level as the experimenter and entering into a discussion concerning the professional application of electrodes. The dreamer, who was spending her fifth night at the laboratory, emerged in the meantime as more competent than the researcher, in that she felt sure that a fifth electrode would yield an additional dream.

In another dream, problems arising from a dream experiment were solved ingeniously:

"I was here at the sleep laboratory. I could not go to sleep, so I went outside to go sledding. My boy friend went along. I decided to come back around 8 o'clock, so you could wake me up. And I suddenly had a small motorbike, on which we could ride together. But I could not find my way back, and it simply got too late. We got lost. We came to a spot, a narrow pass, where everyone was lost."

(Female, 24 years-old, 1st night, 5th REM phase)

The recipe of this dream is: 'If you are unable to sleep, simply get up and do something that's fun.' The dreamer, though, does not entirely escape, because she plans to return for a pro forma awakening. But at this point the dream plays a trick on her and she is unable to find her way back in time.

Laboratory dreams may also reflect anxieties caused by the experimental situation:

"I was inside the sleep laboratory, and I was awake. And we were disturbed by people, by police, there had been some kind of break-in. The room was searched, and there were many policemen who emptied the closets in this room. And you were plenty upset. It was not really a room, but a tent; it was light outside, daylight. That's when I got up. You unplugged me. I walked around outside, on a meadow, in my pyjamas, with the wires on my head. There were people who were fixing a picnic. I talked to them and told them that I had trouble with falling asleep and with dreaming. And then you said I should go to sleep again. You needed it once more. And now I was going back into the tent and trying to sleep and to dream."

(Female, 23 years-old, 1st night, 4th REM phase)

The experiment is presented here as a situation that is ripe with threats and insecurity. At the outset, the danger to privacy is dramatized as a break-in and a police search of the bedroom. The experimenter, having lost control, is forced to halt the project. The sleep laboratory itself is no longer a secure room, but a tent, out in the open. The dreamer finds herself in this disagreeable situation, and unable to escape it. She simply tries to tell others about her difficulties, but finally submits to returning to the tent, in order to continue the experiment.

As everyone deals differently with the laboratory situation, the qualitative manner in which dreams picture the experimental setting provides insight into different dream styles. The themes of these dreams also reveal emotions that are triggered by the experimental setting, and they show how each dreamer handles them. The manner in which the laboratory situation is managed may well be allegorically related to a dreamer's life situation.

A series of studies repeatedly confirmed that dreams show a preference to incorporate elements of the experimental situation, although the frequency of such references varied greatly. We can, however, expect that just about every third dream contains some kind of reference to the experiment.

In one of our studies we examined the impact of the experimental situation on the dream contents of 112 REM dreams, as reported by twenty subjects during each of two laboratory nights; among these, as the circular chart of Figure 26 shows, nearly every second dream contained a reference to the laboratory.

Most frequently was the inclusion of the experimental situation in individual dream scenes; next came dreams which used the dream experiment as a major theme; about every tenth dream contained only isolated elements of the experiment, scattered among dream events. Quite rare was a direct and realistic inclusion of accurate experiences from the preceding evening, as of other day residues; for the most part, the laboratory situation was transformed in an alienated fashion.

On the one hand, the preceding day acts as a particularly significant source for the selection of dream contents;

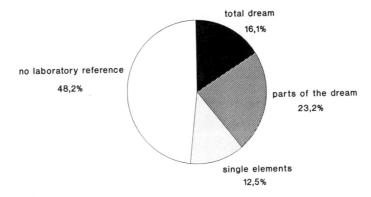

FIGURE 26. Laboratory References in Dreams. Frequency and degree of references to the experimental situation in 112 REM dreams.

on the other hand, not every dream is equally influenced by events of the previous day. But when day residues enter the dream, they are not incorporated without revision: the sleep's imaginative activity deals with such impressions creatively, either transforms them or transfers them to a different context.

In our dream study concerning the influence of the experiment, we did not guide our subjects specifically toward dreaming of this experience. In addition, the laboratory situation is quite complex, encompassing a broad spectrum of impressions and enabling the dreamer to choose among the most diverse stimuli. But if we structure events of the previous day more specifically, we are much better equipped to define whether and how they might influence the dream.

Howard Roffwarg undertook an ingenious experiment, designed to manipulate the color perceptions of his subjects during the waking state: for several days, they had to wear goggles that made them see the world around them in red coloration (Roffwarg, Herman, Bowe-Anders & Tauber 1978). This altered perspective found expression in the more than triple presence of red color elements in subsequent dreams; these increased from the first to the third night and were most evident in the first REM dream per night. It is an indication of the creativity of dream formation that these dreams not only colored scenes in red that had previously been viewed in this manner while awake, but earlier experiences were also seen in this new light. Interestingly, the wearing of these color filters had no lasting effect. Even during the first night, following normal perception, the dream world appeared once again in 'normal' colors. The manner of daytime perception was, therefore, crucial to dream perception. It remains open to question whether the red tinted dreams were simply the result of a rose-colored waking perception or whether the subject's consideration of this novel situation had been the decisive factor. In this instance, control experiments proved informative: the subjects were given the strong suggestion that their dream would most likely contain green as a complementary color. However, the dreams were not influenced by this maneuver, and the red component remained prominent.

While Roffwarg altered the view of the waking world and not its content, a whole other series of experiments has introduced specific experiences into the pre-sleep situation. In particular, different films were presented, which either projected tranquil-relaxed or exciting and threatening themes. The assumption that emotional reactions to these films would be reflected in dreams could not be consistently confirmed. There were always some dreamers who, following an anxiety-inducing film, experienced more anxiety in their dreams, but no such reaction could be immediately observed in others. Such manipulation of the pre-sleep experiences is, of course, burdened with the problem that a specific film does not necessarily create the desired reaction in every viewer; in addition, an emotional reaction might well take place during the waking state, prior to the subject's sleep.

More direct efforts to guide the dream experience are made in experiments where the subjects are supposed to dream about personally significant themes. Dream researcher Rosalind Cartwright guided experimental subjects to dream of a desired personal attribute (Cartwright

1974). At the outset, subjects were asked to use prepared lists to check off their real and desired attributes. Next, a personality dimension was selected that stood in stark contrast to the subject's self-appraisal. If, for example, the subject maintained, "I am petty and would like to be more generous," she was supposed to concentrate on the topic, prior to sleep, "I should like to be more generous." During this study, dream commands were effective, inasmuch as judges were able to recognize selected attribute dimensions beyond coincidence. In most instances, however, dreamers did not realize the desired attribute but its counterpoint.

While Rosalind Cartwright based her study on the discrepancy between a real and a desired personal attribute, we gave our subjects two types of dream commands. During one night, dreamers also decided before going to sleep that they would dream about a desired personal attribute; during another, the suggestion concerned a personal quality which the subject valued highly, such as, "I'd like to remain cheerful." We sought to use the second group of dream commands to determine whether auto-suggestion was more effective when it referred to a quality the subject already possessed.

Over a period of two nights, and using ten subjects, we initially obtained dreams without specific instructions. This was followed by one night each, devoted either to the suggestion of a desired or of an already existing attribute. Independent judges were unable to evaluate whether and what kind of dream commands had been given. On the one hand, desired attributes were developed in unstimulated dreams; on the other hand, dreams with dream commands did not predominantly reveal the specific incorporation of a desired attribute.

Another study indicated that personal matters, of immediate concern to an individual, and thus more directly related to the waking existence, found much easier access to dreams than did the induction of abstract attributes. We observed eight subjects for three nights, recording 105 REM dreams. We asked the subjects, prior to the second night, to describe their current concerns and problems. Next, they selected their most pressing worry and expressed it in question form, as in, "Will I pass my exam?" During one of the following nights, they were asked to focus on this question, by using it as a dream command, whenever they were about to fall asleep. During the other night we gave no particular instructions.

A specific or symbolic reference to the selected problem could be observed, in four out of ten dreams, during nights that had been subject to prior stimulation. During the two other nights, at least every fifth dream contained some kind of reflection of the special theme. Therefore, similar to laboratory situations, personal concerns seem to influence dreams more strongly than other conditions of the pre-sleep situation. Themes that were significant for daytime experiences did not, however, determine the dream experience consistently, as dreamers were able to turn them off or to select other contents freely.

Results of these studies confirm the everyday experience that we cannot simply choose our dream themes. A dream may be stimulated by matters that concern us during the day, but it will not be dictated to in its selections, in how it responds to stimuli or into what dream situations they are transformed.

Stimulus Incorporation into Dreams

Stimulation during sleep is the oldest method of dream research. While, during the past century, it was assumed that direct stimuli could provoke dreams, we now use this method to find out whether such signals are seized by the dream and incorporated into events in progress.

Even today, acoustical signals are employed primarily, but scents and tactile stimuli are also used occasionally. Stimuli may vary in degree of complexity, as when we use single tones or brief melodies; they can also differ in meaning, as when we run names forwards or backwards. And, finally, stimuli may convey a general emotion, as in the case of a deep sigh, or they may be personally important, as with the name of a close friend.

One of our studies was designed to ascertain whether a neutral or emotionally negative sound, presented during REM sleep, would find entry into dreams. Five minutes after the onset of REM sleep, we played either the increasing and decreasing sound of a jet fighter or the weepy sobbing of a person. We introduced these sounds, softly, three times. We awakened the sleepers thirty seconds later and asked about their dreams. For comparison, we practiced awakenings during one night, without prior stimulations.

Independent judges had the initial task of establishing whether a dream had been stimulated at all. In half the stimulated dreams they found indications of reception and incorporation of the sounds, but they also surmised the impact of sounds in one-third of the control dreams. Next, the evaluators were to define which of the two sounds had been involved. In only every third dream were they able to recognize whether the 'jet fighter' or the 'weeping' sound had been absorbed. They also established erroneous correlations, assigning the incorrect sound to stimulated dreams.

As this limited number of hits suggests, a direct stimulation of dreams is apparently no easy matter. Several reasons suggest themselves: a dream may ignore a stimulus or incorporate it in so disguised a manner as to make it unrecognizable. There is the additional problem that auditory impressions, together with their related images, also appear in non-stimulated dreams, and that these may erroneously be evaluated as incorporated stimuli.

Whenever dreams showed the influence of a signal, incorporation either resulted in a scenic rearrangement of the environment from which the stimulus originated, or in a manner and quality of the sound itself, which was placed within a different context.

When we had introduced the 'weeping' sound into a REM phase, one subject reported a dream that dealt with a funeral:

"There was some kind of funeral in the town where my parents live. There was an open grave, and one had to step on a bridge, and then look down into the grave. And somebody had been buried there. I slouched past it, and wasn't being very dignified. And next to the grave stood a horse. So that the horse couldn't take off, they had placed a tree trunk across the street. And then I somehow ran and the horse ran along with me. And suddenly I knew that the horse would have to jump and didn't see the tree. That's when I gave it a push, so it turned sideways. It somehow hit its leg halfway, but everything turned out alright."

(Female, 24 years-old, 4th night, 5th REM phase)

In this dream, the weeping was neither directly incorporated, nor transformed into another sound. But the sound is absorbed to the degree that the funeral theme reflects the weeping by association and setting. It is, however, notable that the dreamer takes no part in the funeral, behaves inappropriately and turns to other things—which is understandable, inasmuch as we had smuggled the stimulus into her dream.

Following presentation of the 'jet fighter' sound, we received the following dream report:

"We were inside a hospital room, and there was Hans, who was asked by his colleagues whether I would not like to try out the bed. There were many children, supposed to witness how a medical examination is done. And they took off my overcoat and jewelry, but stopped halfway. And now Hans is my father. And he and a friend talk about their travels, because this friend also wants to get away. He tells me what he still has to finish, that he has to drive seventeen kilometers before he can board the plane. And my father makes a slip of the tongue and says that it would be below 3,000 or that we had started with 3,000. And I understand that it means he actually wanted to say that, a week ago, we had reached a height of 3,300 meters. And then everybody laughed."

(Female, 24 years-old, 4th night, 5th REM phase)

In this dream, too, we encounter only the general environment of the stimulus: the subject did not hear either a jet plane, or another sound. The theme of flying occurs in a humorous conversation, which appears in a disconnected manner, following the scene in a hospital room. One gains the impression that the stimulus interrupted the dream at a specific point, and we may speculate further whether the triple stimulation was transformed into height levels of 3,000 and 3,300.

An original and alienated transformation of the stimulus 'weeping' appears in a dream of squeaking footsteps:

> "Another woman and I were inside a small self-service store, and we were just about to get to the cashier. It was about whether I buy another liquid to gargle with. And we kept walking around the store, and everytime I took a step with my right foot, it squeaked like an old door. It was like a regular whistle sound, so that, with every step I took, it was as if I squeaked like an old piece of furniture. And somehow I tried to fix that with the gargle water."

> (Female, 24 years-old, 4th night, 6th REM phase)

While a sound plays a major role in this dream, the squeak which the dreamer produces while walking, conveys strikingly the physical quality of the stimulus. In the dream, emotional aspects of weeping were not reflected, nor any impressions connected with mourning. The origin of the sound was not linked to a human voice, but transposed to the feet, although the reference to gargle liquid suggests the sound's actual source in a disguised manner.

In a number of cases, the stimulus 'jet fighter' was transformed in inventive manner, as in the following gas stove dream:

> "There was a gas stove someplace, and it didn't function any longer. There were people around, and you were one of them, and everyone sat by themselves, in front of their stove tops and were cooking something up. Independently

of each other, we discovered that the gas stove doesn't work any more. And we had just told Rita to look into it. What was funny was that it sometimes worked again, and then stopped. I had the feeling, at times, it simply spits, the flame was sometimes lower and sometimes higher. And then somebody came in and said the same thing happened with him yesterday. And then came the owner of the stove. And she said the same thing had happened to her. And then it was fine, suddenly the flame was high again."

(Female, 24 years-old, 4th night, 3rd REM phase)

In this case, the sound's acoustical features were incorporated into the dream. The spitting gas stove is a transformation of the jet fighter into a similar sound. The lower and higher flame provide a picturesque image of the increasing and decreasing sound of flight, but perhaps also of the repeated stimulation.

Our results stand in accord with other studies, which also encountered stimulus incorporation in only about every third dream. The dream does not only appear autonomous in relation to the pre-sleep situation, but also direct signals do not influence dream structuring decisively. If external stimuli are considered at all, they are, for the most part, not absorbed directly, but transformed and adjusted to dream events—often to such a high degree that we can no longer identify the original stimulus.

9

Dreamers and their Worlds

Dreams always have an individual touch: they absorb waking experiences that reflect a dreamer's personality and life situation; but dreams also bear a collective imprint, because people are comparable in thinking, feeling and behavior and, under certain conditions, have similar experiences. This enables us to select common personal features, or different phases of life, in order to discover whether such criteria determine typical patterns and specific groupings of dreams.

Children's Dreams

Researchers had always found the dreams of childhood particularly fascinating, as they may illuminate the beginning and development of dreaming. This has posed several questions: Do the phases of cognitive and emotional development, through which we pass during childhood, correspond to different stages of dream structuring? Is the dream stage enriched by increasing life experience? Does the dreamer play different roles parallel to the development of self and identity?

The study of children's dreams is confronted by the initial problem of ascertaining at what age children are capable of recognizing the dream as a dream and do not confuse it with a waking experience. Then, too, the verbal capacities of children have to be sufficiently developed to translate the

181

dream experience into an appropriate report. This second condition does not, of course, apply only to children's dreams, as the dream reports of adults also depend on a capacity of being aware of internal experience and to transform it into language.

Eliciting dreams from children does have one advantage: children display a less inhibited attitude toward dreams and convey their dream experiences more directly and openly than adults, who view their dreams more critically and may relate them to others in an edited or even censored version. Freud noted early that children's dreams are simpler and, with regard to interpretation, more transparent, as they express wishes in an undisguised manner.

David Foulkes performed a remarkable series of experiments for the systematic study of content and structure of dreams during childhood development (Foulkes 1982). A group of fourteen children visited his sleep laboratory initially between the ages of three and five years. Their dreams were studied twice more at intervals of two years.

During each period of this longitudinal study the children were awakened from different sleep phases three times during eight to nine nights and asked about their dreams. Foulkes also used comprehensive test procedures to cover each child's state of development and life situation. Sixteen other children participated in a parallel study, starting at ages ranging from nine to eleven, and these dream experiments also continued twice at two-year intervals.

Foulkes' longitudinal studies therefore cover the development of dreaming from ages three to fifteen. His results are based on the impressive total of 1,500 REM awakenings, 908 awakenings from NREM sleep and 303 awakenings from the sleep onset phase.

Even the 3 to 5 year-old children reported dream recollections from all sleep stages, although at this age, dreams appeared only very rarely: only about every fourth awakening from REM sleep resulted in a dream report. Recollections from the two other sleep stages were even less frequent. Frequency of dream recall from all sleep stages increased during the first life decade. At ages 7 to 9, every second REM awakening, every third awakening from sleep onset and every fifth awakening from NREM sleep were successful. Between ages 9 and 15, dream recall was not yet as frequent as among adults, but it began to approach it, as two of three awakenings from REM sleep and from the sleep onset phase were accompanied by dreams, while recollection of dreams from NREM sleep increased to 40 percent.

Consequently, dream recall in early childhood is rather sparse and increases only with advancing age; but, as with adults, children are from the start likely to recall dreams more easily that originate from sleep phases that are close to the waking stage. Foulkes concluded from these results that the capacity to dream runs parallel to psychological maturation and that dream recall does not simply improve because verbal skills are enhanced.

In his book, *Children's Dreams*, Foulkes summarized the characteristic dream features of every age level. Dreams of the 3 to 5 year-olds were very short, predominantly static and emotionally neutral. In 40 percent of their dreams, animals were present, while people appeared only in about every fifth dream. Dominant were familiar figures and objects, occasionally already creatively transformed. If any action occurred, it was carried out by other dream figures: the Dream Self was either not mentioned or presented as passive, such as sleeping on a fire engine.

The dream reports of children between the ages of 5 and 7 were substantially more encompassing, more vivid and presented first signs of scenic realization in form of simple activities, although these were still mainly undertaken by other figures, with the dreamer largely in the role of observer. Every third dream included animals, often in humanized form; but known individuals were also increasingly present, and strangers made their first appearances. Interestingly, even at this early age, sex-specific differences could be observed: girls reported more agreeable dreams of positive social events, while boys' dreams contained more negative feelings, strange dream characters and wild animals.

The most significant advance in the dreams of the 7 to 9 year-olds were a differentiated scenic structure and an increased activity of the Dream Self. The dreamer participated in numerous activities, engaged in occasional speculation and experienced emotions. By then, animals appeared only in every fifth dream, while, in addition to family members, other known and unknown individuals increasingly played roles.

During ages 9 to 11, dreamers were fully and equally integrated within ample dream events. As with adults, animals appeared only in every tenth dream. Primarily, dreamers' relations to other dream figures were cordial, and aggressive activities were left to other dream figures, who also had to suffer the consequences.

The impact of socialization was particularly evident during the ages of 11 to 13, as girls dreamed more frequently of girl friends and boys of male peers; with boys, aggressive themes increased, while girls continued to emphasize positive relations. Only from this age level on did dreamers begin to participate more actively in conversations and generated thoughts while dreaming.

During ages 13 to 15, dreams showed little changes from the preceding study. While with boys there was an increased number of conflict themes and of bizarre dream designs, their dreams still contained preponderance of cordial social interactions and of positive dream conclusions.

From childhood to youth, dream experience undergoes several stages, and dream development may be traced on different levels. Formally, brief and static dream fragments appear at the start, followed by scenically more vivid impressions, the dream world slowly expands to include dynamic and more eventful stories. The creative forces of earliest dreams are sensory impressions, and only with the passing of time are dreams accompanied by emotions and imbued with thinking and reflection. The Dream Self changes from passive observation to fellow-traveling and active intervention. On the one hand, the repertoire of dream contents is enlarged by increasing life experience; on the other hand, dream themes are determined by changing interests at different age levels.

These stages of dreaming reflect an expansion and differentiation of cognitive and emotional capacities in the course of development. The great number of dream animals which dominate children's dreams during the first decade and taper off later on, seem to serve a particular function. During the dawn of dreaming, when children are not yet able to place themselves inside their dreams, animal images that display childlike attributes and particularly absorb the interest of children, provide a projection screen for self-representation. The role of animals seems to expand during the course of individual development, in that animals symbolically represent humans to whom the dreamer is closely attached. Finally and naturally, animals appear in dreams simply as animals, just as they have their own place in the world, as do other dream building blocks.

In a recently started project in our sleep laboratory we study the dream and fantasy world of children in their second life decade. Until now, five girls and five boys, aged 10 to 12 years, have dreamed in our laboratory. They also recorded spontaneously recalled dreams on tape at home. During the evenings at the laboratory, they told a story to match a theme given to them. We awakened the children a total of 68 times from REM sleep and obtained 55 dream reports, representing a recall rate of 80 percent, which comes close to an adult level.

We evaluated these children's dreams just as we did adult dreams, to ascertain whether the dream world of children realizes childlike themes and stagings appropriate to their ages, and to observe how realistic or fantastic these dreams might be.

Initial insight into the manner in which children devise dreams is given by three reports that illustrate variants in the degree of realism in dreams:

"We were at a boys' camp, me and other kids from my class, but there were also a few I did not know, and Claus, too, and several adults. And during the first night we couldn't fall asleep. And, during the second night we fell asleep right away. There was some kind of wooden ladder, and on top there are the upper beds and underneath the below ones. And those who want to sleep on top put their sleeping bags up there and went up the ladder, and there were such tiny mattresses. And those who want to sleep below have their sleeping bags down there and can simply step inside them. And afterwards everything was quite normal. And then there was always such totally strange food, something Chinese. That was really great fun. And we kept looking at books with Tintin and Snowy."

(Boy, 10 years-old, 1st night, 4th REM phase)

The dream about a boys' camp is realistic and refers to specific leisure time activity, which this boy has experienced several times in a similar manner. The boys get ready in their sleeping quarters, with their two-level bunk beds, and pass their time with comic books, while adults remain in the background. The dream event is promoted by several individuals, but they merely engage in collective action and no one has a speaking part. The only exceptional and invented element in this Swiss dream camp is the exotic provender, Chinese food. Quite obviously, sleeping at the laboratory and concern about falling asleep had intruded into this dream, but were turned into a familiar, age-appropriate situation and transformed into a community experience. This dream represents the category of children's dreams where a realistic starting point is embellished by invented episodes.

One episode from everyday life is transformed, quite undramatically, into the dream of a street encounter:

"I was at Bühlstreet, with my mother, and we met a woman there. She kept talking to herself, not to anyone, just to herself. And there were other people on this street, but they probably did not hear it. And my mother said:

'Good morning.' And she answered: 'Good morning!', and kept mumbling to herself. And we looked after her, puzzled."

(Girl, 11 years-old, 2nd night, 5th REM phase)

This dream could just as well have happened in real life. The dreamer finds herself on a street in her neighborhood, where one might easily run into someone who mumbles, and it is certainly common to say "good morning", and quite normal that her mother should greet the woman, with the dreamer just standing by.

The dream of a picnic is, however, a good deal more fantastic, when a routine family outing takes place in the company of a fairy tale guide:

"Some Emperor or other took us on a trip, that's the four of us, my mother, my father, my sister and I. And, just like always, we quite simply fixed a picnic in an unknown forest. But there was no meat, only fried and another type sausage."

(Girl, 11 years-old, 1st night, 5th REM phase)

The girl is on a picnic with her family where, with natural culinary instincts, she is concerned about the food, but does not express any wonderment that their host is an Emperor. The fairy tale elements, the Emperor and the unknown forest, remain in the background, as compared to the not-so-unusual leisure time situation. This dream, too, is based exclusively on group activities and there is no communication between the dream individuals.

The general evaluation of realism in our children's dreams is illustrated in Figure 27; for comparison realism in the dreams of adults has been placed next to it. It is notable that the circular chart for the children shows little difference from that for adults. The results not only indicate an identical range of categories, but frequencies are comparable in that about half the dreams scripts were realistic-fictional and every third dream realistic. Dreams with fantastic references were

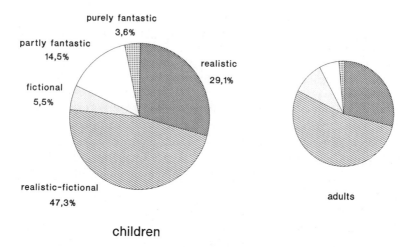

purely fantastic
3,6%

partly fantastic
14,5%

fictional
5,5%

realistic
29,1%

realistic-fictional
47,3%

adults

children

FIGURE 27. Realism in Children's Dreams. Categorization of fifty-five REM dreams by children, ranging from the totally realistic to the purely fantastic. Results of adult dreams are presented for comparison.

actually somewhat more frequent among children than among adults, but the children as well had only occasional dreams that were located in a totally unrealistic environment.

From an adult point of view, the children selected predominantly leisure time themes, as illustrated in Figure 28. In approximately every second dream, the children played games or engaged in sports and excursions. Everyday topics, such as lessons at school or home activities, were prominent only in every third dream. This ratio of leisure time to everyday activities in the children's dream world should not be interpreted as a preference for entertainment, because leisure time activities in these age groups occupy a larger segment during waking hours, too. Compared to dreams of everyday and leisure time activities, those in which the children created a fairyland had a rather minor position, although such fiction-type dreams were somewhat more frequent than among adults.

The dream of a missing fried sausage is set in leisure time and conveys an absurd atmosphere, as it contains bizarre elements within several realistic episodes:

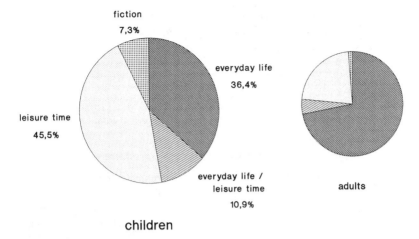

fiction
7,3%

everyday life
36,4%

leisure time
45,5%

everyday life /
leisure time
10,9%

adults

children

FIGURE 28. Topics of Children's Dreams. Appearance of everyday situations, leisure time themes and fictional worlds in children's dreams. Results of adult dreams are presented for comparison.

"A friend of my brother wanted to organize a party, and then he invited a lot of people. And he wanted to set it up in the basement of our house. And suddenly we were inside the school building, where I used to go to school. I think I was the tallest. There were some small children and my needlework teacher. And then we fried a lot of sausages. Everyone had a little suitcase, with a gift inside, and in the middle of it an indentation, so one could put a sausage in there. Next, I was suddenly in the house where we used to live, and there were Theresa and my brother. And I asked: 'How shall I do that with the grilling, shall I put it on a spit or on the grill?' And then my brother gave a long explanation, how he first has to grease my sausage, then puts it on the grill, and finally cooks it inside some kind of box. And then he simply took the sausage and took a bite out of it. And the friend wanted all the time that we should write 'Welcome' on the wallboard, and the name right with it. We sat in a circle, and it had turned into the needlework room. And then I suddenly could no longer find my sausage and started to weep. And then all the kids started to look all over for it. And after the meal, I did find it, under a windowsill, together with a little toothbrush. And it was whole again. After this birthday I was back at home, ill and with a high fever, lying in bed and listening to loud, totally wild music, which I did not like at all."

(Girl, 11 years-old, 2nd night, 5th REM phase)

Quite normal preparations for a children's party present the opening for this dream. It is, of course, puzzling from the start that it was supposed to take place in the basement of a house, then starts to get going in the needlework room of a school, and in between continues at a previous residence. Familiar people are involved in this dream, and they act quite normally. Totally absurd, however, is the key role the fried sausage occupies in this dream. It is being grilled rather awkwardly, further placed in the plush-lined partition of a gift suitcase, a piece of the sausage is being bitten off, it disappears under obscure circumstances and is finally located, undamaged, under a windowsill, in the company of a toothbrush.

The sausage dream contains three bizarre categories: abrupt changes in setting, unusual actions, and strange objects. As Figure 29 indicates, most of the children's dreams were structured in a bizarre manner in two to three cate-

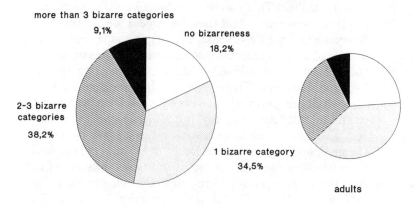

FIGURE 29. **The Bizarre in Children's Dreams.** Frequency of bizarre feature categories, as coded in fifty-five REM dreams. Results of adult dreams are presented for comparison.

gories. Nearly as many dreams were unusual in only one category, and every fifth dream contained no bizarre elements. Compared to adults, the bizarre occurred in children's dreams more frequently, with fewer dreams containing none and more dreams featuring an abundance of the bizarre.

Whatever roles the dream figures occupied in children's dreams is shown in Figure 30. The children filled their dream stages, much like adults, with all types of dream figures. The larger segments of family members was to be expected, because the children live with them and deal with them daily. As with adults, other known persons also appeared most frequently, although they were, quite naturally, mainly children—just as, with adults, dream acquaintances belong predominantly to the dreamer's own age group. It is interesting to note that children's dreams not only included many strange persons, but that many people in their dream world remained undefined and shadowy. Animals and fictional figures were still represented in these children's dreams, but no longer to any remarkably high degree.

One particularly significant feature of children's dreams was their high degree of active self-involvement.

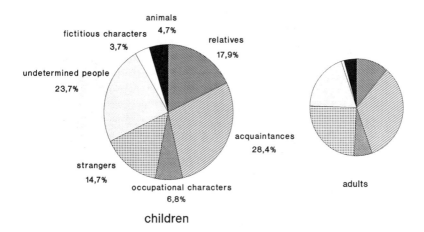

FIGURE 30. **Figures in Children's Dreams.** Division of 190 dream figures in 55 REM dreams. Results of adult dreams are presented for comparison.

Children would seem to want to participate in their dreams at all times: in nine out of ten dreams, the Dream Self was directly linked to events, the Dream Self remained passive only four times, and was a remote observer in just two dreams. During dreams of our young adults, the dreamer was also primarily actively engaged in dream events, but in nearly every third adult dream the Dream Self was either passive, uninvolved or actually absent. Adults are apparently more easily able to create dreams that are independent of their own participation.

Active ego participation in children's dreams did not, however, and in contrast to adults, occur predominantly on an interactive level. As Figure 31 indicates, children's dreams most prominently featured actions that were undertaken jointly with others, although lacking in mutual relations.

A dream dealing with a birthday party illustrates how joint activity may be expressed in a child's dream:

"We were at a birthday party for my former friend, who lives in Thurgau. They served baked bananas, with honey. And that was pretty good. Next we divided some sweets and other

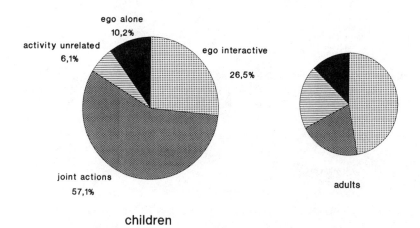

FIGURE 31. **Ego Activity in Children's Dreams.** The social relation of ego activity in forty-nine REM dreams (in six dreams, the Dream Self was not involved). Results of adult dreams are presented for comparison.

stuff. We did a lot; we blew up balloons. One of us had to blow them up until they busted, and inside was an arithmetic puzzle he had to solve, and he had to give the solution to the mother, so he could go further in the game. Finally, my Mum came by train and picked me up, and we drove back."

(Boy, 10 years-old, 2nd night, 4th REM phase)

The dreamer spends a pleasant afternoon at a birthday party, away from home, that fulfills all childlike wishes: there is something to satisfy his sweet tooth, and they play exciting games together. The dreamer is involved in everything, but does not stand out in any activities. The children also do not interact with each other, but are totally absorbed by their joint activities. It is typical for someone in this age group that, at the end of the dream, his mother comes to pick him up and takes him home.

While, in the dream about the birthday party, the Dream Self does not emerge from his group, a dream about a boyish prank assigns a specific role to the dreamer:

"I was together with several pals. And then we ran through a street, and one of the guys said to another boy: 'Run ahead and ring the doorbells and yell our names.' He laughed when he said that; it really was just a joke. And then this woman and that man looked out, and the other kid hid behind the pillar, and she sees me. And she looks at me, and I really wasn't the one who had done it."

(Boy, 11 years-old, 1st night, 5th REM phase)

This dream starts with a communal activity of peers, but a prank is initiated by their leader and carried out by a follower. The dreamer, initially just a hanger-on, is the innocent target of suspicion, becomes the center of the dream event; yet, surprisingly, he displays no reaction to it.

In contrast to the preceding, a dream that transported the dream laboratory into a school, features the Dream Self as engaged in an active interchange with his dream environment:

"A boy came along and asked: 'Do you remember the key fob? I have the same in green, as the one you found.' And then I said: 'Yes.' And we somehow were on the school corridor, with sleeping bags, Tina, Anya and I, and we tried to go to sleep. But it just wouldn't work, because it was much too narrow, although it was a wide corridor. And then Tina said: 'You take up too much space. I now want to get some sleep myself'. Then I went into another corner, and the other two came over, too. That's when the teacher called."

(Girl, 11 years-old, 1st night, 2nd REM phase)

In this dream, the dreamer is addressed twice. She does react to the boy's question, although in a decidedly taciturn manner, and she silently responds to her friend's complaint. While the dreamer is active as a person, dream events still proceed largely as a communal experience.

Compared to the dreams of adults, the children's dreams contained distinctly fewer conversations. Although speech took place in nearly every second dream, conversations were largely carried on by other dream figures; the dreamers themselves took the floor only in one out of five dreams.

As with adults, the children's dreams we elicited in the laboratory reflect a dream world that dips into actual life situations and employs fantasy in dealing with them. The structure and content of children's dreams evolve, parallel to the development of fantasy activity and differentiations in thought and emotion. In their dreams, children do not prominently display their ability to come to cope actively with the waking world, but do express any conceptions they may have of themselves and of the world around them.

'Female' and 'Male' Dreams

Dream researchers have long wondered whether a dreamer's sex exerts an influence on the content and selection of dreams. Do the dream worlds of men and women differ, or are dreams tailored so individually that biological and socio-cultural conditions, which determine the waking existence of both sexes, fail to have an impact on their dreams?

As our 500 REM dreams originated with 18 men and 26 women, we examined whether the dreams show any sex-specific differences among the features evaluated by us. Let us, right at the start, present a significant result of these analyses: we noted clear-cut sex-specific differences in only a few content categories, although women's dreams generally showed a greater multiplicity of events and were more abundant in their contents than men's dreams.

The dreams of women and men featured an equally wide range of stage settings and dream figures. While sceneries were similar with regard to localization and familiarity, dream persons varied with regard to identity and familiarity.

The bar chart of Figure 32 indicates that there was no general discrimination of sexes in dreams; both samples predominantly showed female and male figures in joint

FIGURE 32. Identities of Dream Figures in Dreams of Women and Men. Percentage of frequency of females and males in 331 REM dreams of women and 169 REM dreams of men.

appearances, with a shift in accentuation emerging only in the other categories.

With men, an interchange with exclusively male dream figures stood in second place, followed by dreams in which they were by themselves, while encounters with women followed only in fourth place. With women, 'dream men' had a slight advantage over any get-together with members of their own sex. These contrasts are not, however, particularly striking. We may simply record them as a male tendency to be surrounded more frequently in their dreams by men only, while the dream world of women is more varied and contains a less 'selective' companionship.

The chart of Figure 33 illustrates the degree of familiarity among dream individuals, showing the same rankings for dreams by men as by women. In most dreams, known people were present, while exclusively strangers appeared comparatively rarely. Only in the smallest number of these dreams was the Dream Self all alone. The chart suggests, however, that women preferred a more familiar social environment in their dreams than did the men, who were more frequently alone or associated only with strangers.

The quality of social interaction in the dreams of women and men is illustrated in Figure 34. The dream world of men showed relations that were more restrained, with altogether

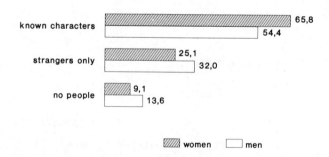

FIGURE 33. **Familiarity of Dream Figures in Dreams of Women and Men.** Degrees of familiarity, in percentages, in 331 REM dreams of women and 169 REM dreams of men.

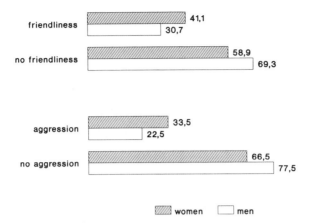

FIGURE 34. Friendliness and Aggression in Dreams of Women
and Men. Friendliness and aggression, in percentages, in 331 REM
dreams of women and 169 REM dreams of men.

fewer friendly or unfriendly activities than in women's
dreams. The stereotypical viewpoint that women are more
cordial in their contacts with others and that men are more
forceful, found no confirmation in these dreams, as both
groups engaged in more friendly than antagonistic contacts.

The expression and reception of friendliness was balanced among both sexes. However, female dreamers were
more frequently recipients than executors of unfriendly acts,
while male dreamers were more likely to play the role of
perpetrators. There were no differences in the type of
unfriendly actions, as men and women showed an equal
balance of physical and verbal aggression in their dreams.

There was no difference in male and female dreams,
concerning any participation of the Dream Self in events
and in the social relation of ego activity.

Specific emotions and mood states, as well as the intensities of experienced feelings, also closely resembled each
other. We only encountered sex-specific shifts in the quality
of emotions experienced within the dream. As Figure 35
illustrates, women had more dreams containing negative
affects, while men's dreams were more frequently accompanied by positive emotions.

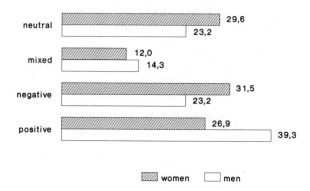

FIGURE 35. Qualities of Dream Emotion in Dreams of Women and Men. Percentage of frequency of emotional tone in 331 REM dreams of women and 169 REM dreams of men.

Whether women actually experience disagreeable dreams more frequently than men cannot necessarily be deduced from this result, as women may be more readily inclined to observe and report such negative emotions.

The dreams of men and women also showed a comparable distribution among everyday and leisure time themes, as well as an identical range from realistic to fantastic dreams. As the bar chart of Figure 36 reveals, men within this range experienced a higher percentage of realistic

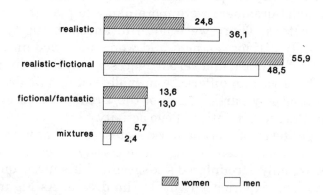

FIGURE 36. Realism in Dreams of Women and Men. Characteristics of reality, in percentages, in 331 REM dreams of women and 169 REM dreams of men.

dreams. Taken by itself, this result might reflect the continuity of an everyday stereotypical assumption that ascribes a more realistic attitude to men; still, this difference should be qualified, as men's dreams also featured, clearly in first place, a combination of realistic and fictional elements.

The few differences that emerged from our comparisons did not reveal any sharp contrasts between the dream worlds of men and women, but only a few different degrees of emphasis. That is why we are often unable to decide whether the author of a dream is female or male. To document this point, we appropriately selected the following two dreams:

"I was standing out in the garden, listening to birds and to cars, which passed at a great distance. And suddenly I was at a parking lot, driving a big, heavy motorbike, and I wore a white helmet, with a visor that could be smartly tilted up. And cars, placed on wooden blocks, were parked to the right and left of a wall, and one could drive around the wall. Viewed from the center, there was another circle of parked cars. And I drove around and parked my motorbike in one of the parking spaces. But it didn't suit me, and I pulled my motorbike out of there, and, just as I left, my father took the parking space. The parking lot was all filled-up, but at one spot there was a tiny Fiat, on these wooden blocks, with half a space open next to it. And there, in a triangle, stood three little wicker baskets, and another three on top. And then I parked my bike, put the three baskets on the side, and simply lifted my motorbike up. And then I left, together with my father."

(Female, 24 years-old, 3rd night, 3rd REM phase)

"I was watching a junior hockey match. And they were playing with extraordinary dedication and enthusiasm. There were a few spectators, and next to me two rather young folks who were also excited and enthusiastic, and I kept watching them. And whenever somebody missed, I heard all those 'Ahs.' Actually, I did not understand much about the whole game. On and off, I asked the others, and they looked at me with surprise. I stood next to the boards, but it was not made of tin but of snow. And the whole game of ice hockey took place on the roof of some kind of house. I only got on the roof by accident, as I wanted to take a rest, walked a few steps, and that's why I went on the roof."

(Male, 23 years-old, 4th night, 4th REM phase)

Both dreams deal with leisure time themes that center on sporting activities. The themes of driving a motorbike and of an ice hockey match are realistically structured, but embellished by some bizarre elements. The parking spaces in the motorcycle dream are impractical and impassable, and in addition, inappropriately blocked by wicker baskets. Surprisingly, the hockey match takes place on a roof, and the playing field is bordered by a snow wall. In both dreams, the Dream Self is involved in the events: in the first dream, as an active biker; in the second, as an interested spectator.

By conventional standards, both dreams might have originated with men, because they deal with rather 'masculine' leisure time activities. Above all, the first dream gives a quite 'masculine' impression, as the Dream Self proves to be a rather accomplished biker, capable of lifting a heavy machine up the ramp. The second dream is less obviously masculine, as the Dream Self apparently does not know the rules of the hockey game and creates bewilderment among the other spectators by his kind of questioning.

The young woman who reported the motorcycle dream actually is not able to drive a motorbike; the man, who had dreamed about the hockey match, knows little about the game in reality. Both dreams have captured, on the manifest level, themes that do not reflect the dreamers' waking interests. Only an interpretation of the dream might yield links with the dreamers' wishes and needs, although these don't have to correspond to any sexual stereotypes.

In their book, *The Content Analysis of Dreams*, Hall and Van de Castle presented dream statistics, in each case, separately for female and male dreamers. Basically, the home dreams of men and women did not differ in either breadth of experience or scenic designs. There were, however, distinct differences among dream personalities: the dream worlds of men contained more male than female figures, while the dreams of women showed a greater balance between the sexes. This result appeared among our own laboratory dreams only as a tendency, as male dream figures were also more prominent among women's dreams, although not to the same significant degree.

In the home dreams, too, women created a social environment that was inhabited by more familiar than strange characters, whereas contact with strangers received greater emphasis among men. Here, a sex-specific emphasis and direction of aggressive interactions became notable. In men's dreams, aggressive conflicts turned more frequently into action, while women's dreams featured non-physical aggressions more prominently—a result we did not encounter in our REM dreams. When aggressive interactions were involved, the home as well as the laboratory dreams of both sexes tended to feature male dream figures.

The sex-specific difference, whereby men dream more frequently of male dream figures than do women, has been widely confirmed. Calvin Hall, when scanning the dream literature, encountered this difference in 29 empirical studies. The prominence of male dream figures was characteristic for home and laboratory dreams among students of several generations, but also for male youths and older men, as well as for dreamers in several other countries and cultures (Hall 1984).

How is this difference to be explained? A psychological interpretation might suggest that dreams express whatever concerns individuals personally. Given this assumption, men would dream more frequently of other men, because they are largely oriented towards a masculine world and the male self-image is either strengthened or challenged by other men. By contrast, women would dream of both sexes in a more balanced way, because their self-image is not only governed by female principles, but they must also face the dominant standards of a male society.

A more sociological explanation could take into account that dreams reflect people's actual waking experiences. With this as background, men would dream more often of other men, when they encounter them more frequently in their professions and in public life. This sociological hypothesis might be checked empirically, but until now it has not been studied whether men who, for example, work professionally mostly with women also tend to encounter more female dream figures in their dreams.

While the dream worlds of children in different stages of development show clear differences, the variety of dreams is less easily organized when we contrast the dreams of women and men. The closer relationship between the dream worlds of men and women shows that sex, as such, does not find expression in specific dreams.

Could particular life situations or decisive life events possibly have a significant impact on dream creation? Although this question has been dealt with in a number of studies, which evaluated dreams recalled at home, or in case reports, only few systematic laboratory studies are available.

Rosalind Cartwright has inquired whether the dreams of women in the midst of divorce reveal characteristic features in dream structuring (Cartwright, Lloyd, Knight & Trenholme 1984). Three groups of women spent several nights in a sleep laboratory: women undergoing divorce, who either rated themselves as depressive or as not particularly affected; and a group of happily married women. The emotional coloring of REM dreams among women undergoing divorce was more negative than that of the married women, but only those who actually suffered from their divorce presented a restricted, past-oriented time perspective in their dreams. This study suggests that it is not a decisive life event, as such, but the individual response to the situation, that is likely to have an impact on dreams.

The question of whether illness as a common fate tends to shape dreams has been examined in many studies, obviously for the most part in cases of psychological disorders.

Up to now, these studies focused on sleep structures and aspects of dream recall, and there exist no comprehensive analyses of the nature of such dreams.

Most intensive has been the study of depressive patients. Characteristic for these cases is a strongly reduced dream recall. A research unit at the Central Institute for Mental Health in Mannheim, Germany, has reported that only every fifth REM awakening resulted in a dream report. In more than half of the awakenings, patients maintained that they had not dreamed, and after every fourth awakening did they remember having dreamed, although without recalling the dream's content. The dreams were brief, consisted of fragmentary everyday episodes and reflected a basically negative mood; however, depressive symptoms of self-criticism and self-damage were not transformed into concrete dream events (Riemann, Löw, Schredl, Wiegand, Dippel & Berger 1990).

Ultimately, it cannot be determined whether dream activity is generally reduced during depression, or whether a predominant depressive symptomatology tends to block dream recall and to shape dream content from a depressive perspective.

Individuals with psychological impairment are apparently only able to create dreams that reflect these changes. It is therefore obvious that the dreams of individuals suffering from schizophrenic illness should reveal disturbances in thought and experience.

Dreams are interwoven with life situations in a multi-leveled fashion, as it is the dreamer who creates a dream against the background of waking experiences. Dreams are easiest to group when dreamers differ markedly in thought and experience. Therefore, children, during different stages of development, in many respects have other dreams than adults, as their imagination, and their ability to think about themselves and the world, have different dimensions. The dream world of the psychologically impaired has its own distinguishing marks, as they already experience the world differently while awake. As women and men are apparently not altogether different in their experiences, their dreams present more similarities than contrasts. Even decisive life events do not appear to change dream structures drastically, but at most influence the thematics of dreams, which nevertheless retain the individual imprint of the dreamer.

10

Dreams and Waking:
A Continuity

As sleep and wakefulness succeed each other constantly, dreams are at all times embedded within the waking experience, and so one might assume that this temporal propinquity encourages a relatedness of psychological activity, a continuity in structure and content of dream and waking experience. But such an assumption fails to consider the different states of consciousness that affect the dream and waking experiences. Dream consciousness might well create a unique experience, a self-contained world of its own, quite apart from the daily flow of thoughts and images.

The question of how unrelated or how interwoven dreams are, and whether their appearance is marked by specific features, has been studied in the dreams of a single night, as well as, more globally, by comparing dream and waking experiences.

Interrelatedness of Dreams of the Same Night

Elicitation of dreams in the sleep laboratory has provided new opportunities for an analysis of continuity within dream series. While earlier researchers, seeking to explore the interrelatedness of dreams, had to depend on spontaneously recalled dreams, the laboratory enables us to collect several dreams during the course of one night, dreams that are more closely adjacent to each other than those that are sporadically recalled. This permits insight into successive dream activities, and we may ascertain whether dream series reveal connections in form and content or whether their designs and themes are unrelated.

Shared features may appear on the manifest level of the dream, in that single elements recur, a particular theme is repeated in different contexts or when an event unfolds in installments; however, similarities may not be recognized until a later interpretation of a dream, when an underlying psychodynamic content is distilled.

The study of experimental dream series needs to consider that multiple awakenings during a given night tend to interrupt the 'natural' progress of dreams. This can lead to a variety of results: recall of a dream, which requires a waking stage, might stimulate the resumption of a theme during the following dream, as if it had been a 'day residue'; conversely, awakening might hamper continuation of a theme, as if, in a way, it had been checked off by being reported.

In 1958, William Dement and Edward Wolpert inquired, for the first time, whether REM dream series showed an interrelated content on a manifest level. They surveyed the dreams of 38 nights and discovered variations of a theme in about every fifth series. They noted crossover links of individual dream elements much more frequently, although these did not seem to follow any particular rules.

We studied 36 dream series of 24 subjects, to see whether their REM dreams of a single night were linked directly. We analyzed each dream series to see whether they were connected by any common themes and whether individual contents recurred. We found thematic links in fourteen dream series, although only six series represented a theme that was featured consistently. An additional eighteen dream series contained individual elements that appeared repeatedly at different points of the series; in this case, the dreams had selected properties from a limited assortment. During four dream series, we were unable to locate links in content on this manifest level.

The following three REM dreams, which a 28-year-old male reported during his first experimental night, do not present any clearly apparent linkages:

"I was traveling on a train. They were old-fashioned cars, with a passage and compartments. And I don't know what my destination was. Anyway, I had been on this train for quite a long time. I had a pile of luggage and settled down pretty solidly. It was rather noisy on this train, and it rocked a great deal. There were many people aboard, but I did not talk to anyone, but simply kept looking out of the window the whole time."

"I was sitting with a few acquaintances from the university in the garden outside a villa, and we exchanged experiences. We talked about our vacations, and what had happened to us. These acquaintances came mostly from the early semesters and did not know each other particularly well. And that's why it was somehow very funny that they all sat together."

"This was a house that looked like an educational institute, but it wasn't one. And several youths were rooming in one part of the house. For some reason, they started to quarrel. And this developed into an actual fight, which affected the whole house. They busted up a lot of things in this house, and they actually tore doors from their hinges and slabs from the walls, with which they hit each other. It looked to me like a real gang war."

Each one of these three dreams represents an individual stage production, with different players, new settings and changing plots. During the first dream, the dreamer is on a routine train trip, surrounded only by undefined individuals, and he silently enjoys the countryside. During the second dream there is a cordial exchange of experiences among acquaintances, in the garden of a villa, with the dreamer as active participant. The final dream, inside some kind of educational institution, climaxes in something of a gang war, with aggressive escalation, which leaves the dreamer uninvolved.

These three dreams appear to be totally different, and there is neither any overt thematic linkage, nor are individual dream elements repeated. Even the escalation, from the initial neutral mood of the first dream to the pleasant contact of the second and the violent destruction of the last one, does not cause any increasing apprehension on the part of the dreamer. Although this dream series does not offer any obvious linkage in its staging, it would certainly be possible to locate, in the dreamer's associations, latent dynamics that might connect these dreams.

A series of three dreams, reported by a 45-year-old American woman during her third experimental night, illustrates close linkages between the dreams of one night:

"I was in the park and two strange people gave me $271. First they were trying to give me $261, and one of the two said: 'No, we'll give you $271.' They gave it all to me in dollar bills, and I couldn't get it into my purse."

"You got married and you changed your name from S. to K. and you were wearing a little red woolen suit with a diamond pin on it and two platinum diamond rings. We were working with another girl and instead of lying in bed, I was sitting up in a little booth with you, with a table between us, and you had a little brown hat on. Prior to this, I was in a country somewhere, walking, walking, walking, trying to find where you were. And I went by a place where I said: 'Oh this is such a nice scenery, mountains and such.' And while I was looking at it, it all fell apart, because it was made out of cardboard and they were making motion pictures out of it."

"I was awfully busy trying to get you married. Any time I got you all dressed up, getting hats and gloves together, we could never find the man. Then I was together with two little babies. They were twins and they were part negroid and one had bright red hair and blue eyes. I kissed the baby and my lipstick got all over his hair, and instead of having hair, he had silk floss on his little head. The parents of the children were popular singers and I was living at Carnegie Hall; and there was all kinds of confusion, because the building was so old. The little babies were so nicely dressed, so clean and I was taking them out in their buggy to the park."

This series of dreams is composed of five scenes. The first dream contains only one situation, where unknown individuals are making the dreamer a money present in a park. The second dream takes place, initially, in a stage landscape, with the dreamer unsuccessfully in search of the experimenter. During its second episode, the experimenter gets married and the dreamer has advanced to the status of a collaborator in the experiment. In the third dream, the dreamer starts by trying to get the experimenter married off, but the dream changes to Carnegie Hall, where the dreamer gets involved with two strange babies and takes them to the park.

The two scenes that deal with the experimenter's marriage provide the most obvious link, although with different endings. During the second dream, marriage is an accomplished fact, but reversed in the third dream, when a wedding is abandoned for lack of a bridegroom. The experimenter also appears during the second scene, with the dreamer searching for her. The first and last scene of the series differ markedly in theme from all others, although linked by the 'park' element. Additional specific elements recur in different dream scenes: dress, color and appearance are emphasized in the two marriage scenes, and they also appear in the discussion of experimental tasks and in the description of the babies.

Although the dreams during this night are partly linked by themes and various elements, the dream series does not convey the impression of a consistent story line. Despite their shared elements, the scenes are rather disconnected, as locations, people and situations change and the dreamer fails to be involved in dream events in any consistent manner. During the first dream she has the luck, without any action on her part, of receiving a money gift, although she cannot quite accommodate it. In the second dream she is unsuccessful in her search for the experimenter, and the landscape she admires turns out to be a movie set. Next, she finds herself facing the now married experimenter and successfully engages in an active role in the dream experiment. Initially, the third dream represents a backward step, the dreamer tries unsuccessfully to marry off the experimenter, but she does not realize that, without her intervention, the marriage has taken place during the previous dream. The final dream scene, with the babies, assigns a role to the dreamer that does not involve her directly and is not characterized by either success or any particular failure.

Even though this dream series is not consistently marked by common themes and recurring elements, it nevertheless suggests a psychodynamic leitmotif. The alternating successes and failures suggest unfulfilled wishes, linked with a problem of self-fulfillment, against the backdrop of a world where not everything is genuine.

The following series of four REM dreams were reported by a 51-year-old woman during her fourth experimental night. On the basis of this example, we shall comment in some detail on how dreams of a single night may be multileveled as well as closely interwoven.

"There were children who belonged to an impoverished old castle. And there was some kind of mother, who was a bit wretched. They were airing their chamber, which contained old things, hanging them all outside. There were oddly embroidered gowns and eyelet decorations. And then the children took some of the things away and put on disguises. One had two halves of a celery on the ears, looking like a bird mask. I kept praising them, saying how smart they managed to look. There were incredibly many children, not all of them from this woman, all boys, fourteen years old and younger. They looked like tawny owls, kept rummaging around, but were quite peaceful."

"It was a house in the country. There was a family with children who no longer stayed at the house. Still, two daughters and a foster daughter remained. The foster daughter was quite lively and adored dancing. She always wanted to give parties, but the mother was extremely clever in blaming everything she wanted to avoid on her leg ailment. There was a party just then, with dancing, where they had invented very funny things, like poems. I was permitted to take part in the dancing, but I was somehow old and not much liked. The young ones were nice to me, but the old lady didn't like me. There was another one who wanted to put on a play. That didn't work out, because one could never find anyone to play a specific part, as the characters did not match somehow.When I tried to help the old lady to set the table, she wanted none of it. And so she said: 'We'll meet some other time when it's more relaxed.' And then I joined those who were having fun. And a man ordered pretzels, piled way up, beautifully, high in a bag."

"Everything was terribly complicated. My son was my brother and my daughter was our daughter. All of us were simple peasants and did not own any real technical equipment. And then my son said he had examined everything the father had made, and had seen that he had created wonderful inventions for the household, and all that would one day go to his sister. Earlier, something else happened, at the beauty parlor. The owner said: 'Today we have to ask the ladies who came last to leave. We cannot accommodate them.' So one had to leave; it was 5:30. One lady could not walk very well, and I wheeled her on a pushcart. And then I pushed our neighbor's baby in a pram, a bit sadistically, across stones that had just been unloaded for roadwork, so that it was terribly bumpy."

"It was somehow in the mountains, with many people whom I didn't know and rather disliked. There were women who were difficult to figure out. The house was disorganized; there simply were several rooms. An acquaintance with whom I usually get along very well, did not side with me but with those women. And there was one who did incredible things, but one could never see them. Just once, when she came out of her room in the morning, I noted that she simply pushed herself off the ground and flew through the air. And then a man gave me a piece of paper, which said that, since January, my daughter had been in a seriously life-threatening situation. At first I didn't believe it, and then I remembered that she had been up here with me, and that she left on her bicycle in the midst of a horrible storm. And next I thought that maybe some horrible person had grabbed her and is now holding her for ransom. And if I don't pay, he will kill her. I told the people about that, and none of them gave a damn. And one of my girl friends turned up, and I pleaded with her: 'Please help me. What am I to do? No one will help me, and I have to do everything possible to get to this child.' She simply shrugged her shoulders and said: 'I don't know what to do, either.' That's when I said: 'You used to really care when someone was in trouble.' But she just replied: 'I don't do that any more. I am a happy person, and want to have fun.' And the weather was just as awful as before. I had to face the weather, and I didn't have a bike, either, and I could not find anything to put on. So I rummaged in a clothes hamper of those women. Down at the bottom was a roll with a zipper, and inside a snazzy rain cover, and I swiped that."

This dream series is not like a novel in installments; every dream tells a separate story. Although the four dreams originate with the same author, they represent different slices of life. Each one contains integrated events, with the exception of the third dream, which encompasses several scenes.

Aside from these self-contained dream stories, the series offers numerous common elements that cover and interlock the dreams like a large-meshed net. At the outset, it is notable that all dreams take place in enclosed places. At all times, the dreamer finds herself inside a house, although at different locations. The first dream takes place in a castle, the second inside a country house, and during a scene of the third dream the dreamer lives with her family in a simple peasant cottage. The final dream finds her at a mountain villa. None of these houses is familiar to the dreamer and she clearly does not feel 'at home' within this alien environment: the castle is old and rundown, the peasant cottage is primitive and insufficiently equipped, she is only a guest in the rest of the houses, and, moreover, not really welcome.

The dream series is thus distinguished by limited spatial expansion. Events take place within a restricted inner space; there are few indications of any loosening or expansion of spatial dimensions.

Central and emotion-laden roles are played, throughout the dream series, by own children, other's children, and mothers. In the first dream, boys play an odd game of disguises. The second dream features two grown daughters and one foster daughter. During the third dream, the dreamer is incestually involved with her own children, creating a complicated relationship, and a baby turns up in the end. During the final dream, concern about a kidnapped daughter provides a crucial element. The children-theme is linked to the repeated appearance of mother figures. During the two early dreams, strange mothers are woven into the dream action, while the two final ones feature the dreamer herself in the role of mother.

Repeatedly, the dream series features female figures who are somehow physically or emotionally damaged or who are frustrated in their undertakings. The mother in the first dream is described as "wretched," the hostess in the second dream is moody and tyrannizes her environment with her illnesses, and another woman in this dream is unable to put on a play. The third dream features a peripheral woman who also suffers from a leg handicap and who, together with the dreamer, is rejected by the beautician. In the final dream, all women are disagreeable and lack consideration, and even one of the dreamer's close friends shows no compassion.

The 'mother-child' theme, as well as the related 'old-young' theme, run through this dream series like a red thread. It is quite evident that the older female figures tend to be presented as ill, disagreeable or disliked, while the young ones are viewed as lively and well-liked.

Finally, the individual dreams also repeat specific means of interaction. The first two dreams feature forms of 'play-acting,' with children putting on disguises in the one, and performances in the other. All sorts of 'role-playing' is connected with these events: in the third dream, this element appears in that the roles of individual family members are not clearly defined. The last three dreams contain the contrast of 'help and rejection.' During the second dream, the dreamer wants to help in setting the table, but is rejected by the hostess. In the third dream, the dreamer is sent away by the beautician, but aids a woman who is having trouble with her leg. During the final dream, the dreamer is desperately looking for help for her daughter, but her pleas are ignored by the whole group.

Similarities within this dream series, covering the three areas of space, dream figures and interactions, do not result in thematic stagnation; rather, they lead to a dramatic progress of events, which provides the overarching connection between the dreams of this particular night. The four dreams present the gradual development of a conflict situation, which reaches a dramatic point, but lacks solution.

The first dream of the series provides a harmless prelude. The dreamer observes a disguising scene from the sidelines and dispenses, apparently rather uninvolved, kindly praise to the children. The dream offers a rather playful and friendly ambience, although set against the background of an impoverished and somewhat wretched milieu. But by the second dream the dreamer is already confronted by a tense situation. The company in which she finds herself accepts her only tentatively. While she retains good contact with the young, she is not much liked by the older contingent: she is even brushed off when she offers help. Despite her readiness to be accommodating, the dreamer experiences a rejection to which she reacts evasively by turning to those "who were having fun." The third dream shows, for the first time, a change in the dreamer's pattern of action. During the first scene she remains in balanced contact with her environment, even though it is complicated and far from clear: she is linked to the son, while the father looks after the daughter. During the second scene she is once again rejected by her environment when she is not seated at the beauty parlor. She is acquiescent, once again, and this time offers help to a handicapped woman. Only in the final scene do we observe a sudden reversal. For the first time, the dreamer shows herself as aggressive, but her aggressive action toward a baby is spontaneous, rather than a reaction to a specific attitude of the environment.

The final dream leads to a climax of tension. By now the dreamer finds herself in an environment where she is totally rejected. Everyone is antagonistic toward her. As the situation reaches a critical point the dreamer is forced to ask desperately for help, but her plea falls on deaf ears. Even her friend would rather have fun than provide assistance. While, during the second dream, the dreamer herself avoided unpleasantries and preferred to have fun, she now encounters the same attitude from her environment. At the end of the series, the dreamer is entirely dependent on her own resources and it remains uncertain whether these dramatic developments will culminate in a solution.

From the first to the last dream, the progress of this dream series reveals multiple changes in the dynamic of events. Although each dream reflects the same underlying problem, it initially emerges only carefully and surreptitiously, but ultimately ever more undisguised. The originally peaceful situation becomes increasingly serious. What at first was an impersonal ambience passes from mounting tension to a specifically personal danger. An environment, originally cordial toward the dreamer, divides into two separate camps, up to the point when no one sides with her. In the beginning, the Dream Self is kindly, relaxed and rather detached, while at the end she displays a fierce desperation. In between there are moments of passive defiance and of misplaced aggression.

Even without any data concerning the personality of the dreamer or any additional associations, problems concerning aging, as well as of the dreamer's contradictory attitude toward motherhood and social environment, become apparent. Her emotional volatility, seesawing between attraction and rejection, between acquiescence and aggression, leads to tensions that find expression not only within the Dream Self but may also be found in the behavior of other dream figures. The repetitive themes and elements contained in this dream series define and identify this conflict, just as its progress mirrors the intensity and emotional dynamics of the conflict.

Milton Kramer and his colleagues have examined the relationship of dream series on an interpretative level (Kramer, Whitman, Baldridge & Lansky 1964). They described two dream patterns: progression and stagnation. Their material indicated that every second dream series provided a progressive dynamic unfolding of unconscious problems. The conflict solution that was achieved within a single dream appeared to form the foundation for a dynamic structuring of the subsequent dream. In every third dream series, however, individual dreams of one night consistently seemed to invoke a basic conflict, whereby the central problem varied in different aspects, although no evolution or solution could be observed.

Successive dreams of a single night may, on the one hand, center on one leitmotif, which either stagnates from dream to dream, showing slight adjustments, or which advances toward either a negative or positive climax. On the other hand, there are dream series wherein each dream appears to stand entirely alone. Between these two types, numerous mixtures may be observed: dreams of a single night are separated by caesura, develop within a specific framework, are linked adjacently or, disjointedly, by common elements, which may be either central or peripheral.

The stagnating or progressive developments of a single night's dreams appear to be related to each person's contemporary condition. Depending on whether the psychological position is at a standstill, overshadowed by conflict or characterized by a lively advance, one may expect dreams to display rigid or flexible, constant or changing patterns.

Waking Fantasies and Dreams

In order to define specific features governing the world of dreams, researchers have always compared dreams with the waking experience. Dreams were either related to the perceived waking world or to induced and spontaneous fantasies.

If we measure dreams against our real experiences during the waking state, the special nature of dreams seems particularly striking. The dream represents a momentary experience, detached from life's everyday continuity, with retrospective contacts to the past and future perspectives being less essential. Locations, persons and objects, as incorporated into dreams, may not be unknown, but are often combined and fashioned in a manner that differs substantially from any immediately available waking experience.

If we do not compare dreams to a perceived waking world, but to thoughts and images that appear in fantasy, dreams no longer seem quite as unique. Within our free-flowing fantasy we find it rather easy to emerge from a realistic situation, ignore limitations of space and time and to turn our experiences into something entirely novel.

Answering the question of how dreams differ from the waking stage depends largely on selecting a point of reference. Fantasy, therefore, provides an obvious comparison, as dreams and fantasies create an internal existence, not imminently linked to perception of the outer world.

How do dreams differ from waking fantasies? This is a question that will probably never find a fully satisfactory reply, because the manifold nature of dreams faces an unlimited expanse of fantasy potential. While dreams always appear to make a choice, as they do not incorporate everything we contrive or imagine while awake, our fantasy actually knows no boundaries.

We sought to approach a comparison between dreams and fantasies by eliciting waking fantasies in the sleep laboratory, using the same criteria of evaluation that we apply to our REM dreams.

Under varied conditions, five females and five males
provided us with 120 waking fantasies. Each subject spent
four afternoons in the sleep laboratory, lying in bed and trying to relax. In each case, and during a five-minute period,
we obtained three fantasies. During two afternoons, the
subjects verbalized continually whatever happened to cross
their minds; during the other two afternoons they reported
their experiences retroactively. In addition, we stimulated
their fantasies during half of the trials, using an introductory phrase, such as: "Imagine you are standing at a window. What do you experience?" During the other half of the
tests we provided no such stimulus.

Two waking fantasies should indicate how manifold
the experiences are that may appear during a relaxed waking state. Both fantasies were reported retroactively by a
25-year-old male; the first one occurred without stimulus.

"I was inside my old school, on the floor where the art
room is located, and looked across the staircase. On the
steps sat two odd figures whom I had once painted, seated
at the same angle that I was looking now. On the floor
below were people who laughed at me. Near me was someone else, or figures that nudged me a little. And in the
nearby area, as if in the background, my art teacher was
looking for my drawing of an apple. And then some young
people came sliding down the bannister, very fast, a whole
lot of them. I then entered a workroom, shaped like a
hose, like a cave, narrow at the back, large and wide up
front. This turned into an express street in Tokyo, with me
standing below. A miserable grey structure of pillars. It
begins to shake and keeps crashing down. I keep trying to
get away, but my feet are underneath. And as I have my
feet down there, they become like a spirit that emerges
from a bottle. And then I get to be like smoke, on top. And
the spirit changes shape, first into a pointed rash, which
turns into a bird's beak and then becomes a beautiful bird.
It melts, later on, and turns into a sticky mess that drib-
bles downward. On the other hand, it is as if it pulls itself
apart, whereby its upper part remains intact. There are
three levels, with down below a sort of nothing, at the

center the base. And on top the bird, which flies around
quite happily. The level spreads out, somehow, into a wide
formation, permeated by an intensive light that reaches
far back, like some sort of road. The more I try to get close
to the light, the more it suddenly moves toward me. And
the return later turns into a fountain, and now I am back
in reality, in the midst of Tokyo. But the fountain is also
like a throne that seats a big, bearded man who might be
Saint Nicholas."

This fantasy is introduced by a situation from the past:
the Fantasy Self feels that it has returned to a familiar
school setting. These revived memories are fantastically
developed, with scattered early experiences combined and
transformed in an unusual manner. Thus, the painter's previously experienced view of the model is transported from its
art room context onto the staircase. The familiar workroom
changes dimensions. It is puzzling that the Fantasy Self
finds itself inside the old school, is laughed at, and is
annoyed by elusive figures. Following this initial scene,
images evolve to an utterly fantastic degree, whereby all
contact to reality is eliminated: once the Fantasy Self has
been threatened and trapped by a cement mass in earth-
quake-like events, it dissolves and all aspects of familiar
reality relation are totally lost. A light leads the Fantasy
Self back from this chaos into a new reality, where a throne
for Saint Nicholas appears quite odd, but is no longer life-
threatening.

The second fantasy followed the introductory sentence,
"Imagine you are standing at a brook."

"I saw the brook outside my house, and I was walking
along the brook with Barry, a St. Bernard dog. And along
another brook, as well, which is actually the brook where
the dog usually walks. I kept changing back and forth a
bit, between this brook and the other one. At the brook I
recalled the situation where my friend had said he wanted
to return to Spain, which made me sad. But once, I also
saw the brook when I was going home, when it had grown

cold for the first time and there was white hoar frost on the trees, which I liked a great deal. Then I was at the other brook and saw this woman who was frightened of the big dog, and who picked up her little pinscher. The two dogs were barking at each other. Later I was thinking that Barry smells a bit, and that the apartment also smells of Barry a little. And that I had once forgotten to take my towel to the volleyball training, and that Barry's owner gave me his, and I asked him whether he had dried Barry with it, because it smelled of dog. I remembered the last game, when I was, once again, upset with the umpire and got terribly excited that he had denied me a beautiful point. Had imagined that I'd pull him off his seat. Next I practiced a hit and recorded a match, and then I thought that I once had to write up a match, although I would rather have watched another game and met somebody there. Then I walked from the gym to the school building, and noted how I slouched across the square, although it was actually time for a lesson. I thought that the French teacher might denounce me to the principal. But then I saw myself sitting at the brook, once more, together with our work team. And finally I thought how you had pasted the electrodes on me, and how much white glue is actually being used."

The suggested image is absorbed into this fantasy, with the Fantasy Self walking along the brook in front of his house, as well as another familiar brook. This walk awakens emotional memories of different situations that are linked to the setting by association. The St. Bernard who accompanies the Fantasy Self prompts memories that cause a switch of scenery to the gym. The new topic, sports, prompts further memories, enriched by the wish of punishing the umpire for his unfair decision and the notion of playing hooky. The fantasy fades back to its beginning at the brook, and finally the subject's thoughts return to the actual experimental setting.

Although both fantasies originated with the same subject, they show remarkable differences. During the first fantasy, images of memory not only merge but expand into a threatening vision, leading to a collapsing world and a dissolution of the subject's identity; this enhanced drama only fades at the end of the fantasy. This waking fantasy is comparable to a dream experience in that memory contents are freshly combined, although their visionary structure is actually a great deal more fantastic than is usually the case in dreams.

By comparison, the second fantasy proceeds much more evenly, and its content simulates everyday experience. It lacks any dramatic climax, but links remembered incidents and images which are quite affective but remain firmly rooted in personal experience. This fantasy is more clearly akin to consciousness, as its associated links are coherent and remain firmly based on reality.

Evaluations of all waking fantasies showed, at the outset, that fantasies, as well as dreams, draw on a full range of our means of expression, with all their sensory modalities, thought processes and emotions. Dreams did not, in fact, differ greatly from waking fantasies in their sensory aspects, as fantasies also consist mainly of visual images, followed by thought processes, auditory impressions and bodily feelings.

Dreams also shared with waking fantasies range, differentiations, and quality of emotional experiences, reflected in varied specific feelings and mood states. Interestingly, fantasies also showed little individual variety and offered a balanced relationship between positive, negative and neutral moods. In waking fantasies, too, specific feelings were more frequently of a negative coloration, whereas mood states favored more positive tendencies. These similarities stood in contrast to two significant differences: while three out of ten dreams were experienced without emotional involvement, this was only the case in one out of ten waking fantasies. Not only were waking fantasies accompanied more frequently by emotions, these emotions were experienced with particular intensity.

Waking fantasies were also characterized by a greater variety in content than dreams. As a rule, fantasies took place at several locations; rarely did the environment remain constant. Figure 37 shows that fantasies most frequently took place in familiar settings. In fantasies, every second environment was familiar, but in dreams only every fourth setting was well-known.

Only occasionally did familiar locations become alienated in fantasies. Just about as frequently as dreams did fantasies occur in a new environment. It was additionally noticeable that in waking fantasies, although less frequently than in dreams, the environment was not always clearly defined and might remain elusive.

Fantasies were also more densely populated than dreams, featuring a greater number of people, animals and other creatures. Only rarely was a fantasy world restricted to self-reflections or descriptions of nature. The first circular chart of Figure 38 shows that fantasies are primarily populated by human beings. Animals did appear more frequently in fantasies than in dreams. The quota of fictional figures was also higher, supplemented by the category of 'fabulous creatures.' This latter category, which included dwarfs and water sprites, was unique to waking fantasies and never

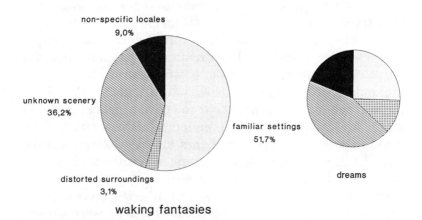

FIGURE 37. Fantasy Settings. Division of 323 locations in 120 waking fantasies, according to their familiarity. Results of REM dreams are presented for comparison.

appeared in our REM dreams. People who enlivened fantasies included not only acquaintances and relatives but nearly just as many people remained undefined, were identified as strangers or simply as members of their professions.

The positions of fantasy figures in individual waking fantasies showed that familiar persons appeared most frequently with other figures; but here, too, as compared to dreams, every fourth fantasy centered only on unfamiliar figures.

As seen in Figure 39, the identity of individuals in waking fantasies showed a remarkable similarity to dreams. Fantasies as well as dreams featured more women, men or children, while mixed groups or people of undefined identity were mentioned less frequently. As in the case of REM dreams, men were more numerous than women, due to a male preponderance in occupational categories. Generally, fantasies created a lively world that did not only center on the subject itself but assigned roles to others as well.

Waking fantasies were more likely to use leisure time rather than routine everyday situations. Quite often, they

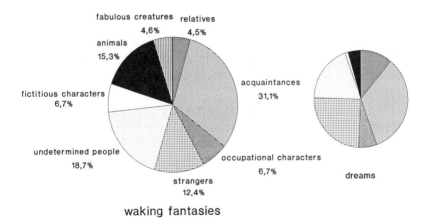

FIGURE 38. **Fantasy Figures.** Division of 582 fantasy figures in 120 waking fantasies. Results of REM dreams are presented for comparison.

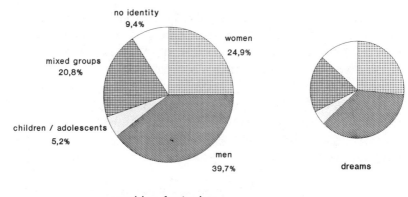

waking fantasies

FIGURE 39. Identities of Fantasy Figures. Division of 466 human figures in 120 waking fantasies. Results of REM dreams are presented for comparison.

extended into fictional worlds, which might feature either colorful fairytale elements or come to a threatening climax. In this respect, dreams differed markedly from waking fantasies in that they tended to emphasize specific everyday events. Fantasies more often contained such threatening situations as illness, accidents, crime or death; here, as in dreams, other people were more likely to be affected.

Waking fantasies tended to progress erratically and often combined everyday themes with leisure time and fictional elements. Dreams were more straightforward, developing a single situation and were less likely to change their thematic framework.

The Self participated in nearly all fantasy images. Being closer to consciousness, fantasies excluded the narrating individual less frequently than was the case in dreams. However, compared to dreams, social interactions were less prominent in fantasies. Although the Fantasy Self was not isolated inside a fantasy world, it made less active contact with fantasy figures, perhaps because events were not experienced as real as in dreams.

Bizarre features are certainly not limited to dreams; they infiltrate the waking fantasy activity in manifold ways.

Two out of three fantasy reports contained such unusual contents as unrealistic settings, extraordinary abilities and peculiar figures. On the whole, the bizarre was encountered less frequently in fantasy than in dreams. We should not, however, conclude that dreams are more bizarre than waking fantasies, as unusual phenomena were more heterogeneously represented in fantasy reports. Moderately bizarre elements could be more generally found in dreams, whereas entirely sober fantasies were contrasted by numerous fantasies which appeared in an entirely unrealistic world. While we are able to insert bizarre elements deliberately into the waking state, dreams cannot be consciously devised, and so we must let the bizarre come as a surprise.

Awake and Dreaming: Individual Continuity

Dreams and waking fantasies are experiences that are not directly related to external existence, but which use images and thoughts to create an internal reality. This common origin leads to similarities in the structure and appearance of dream and fantasy. They do not, therefore, differ basically, even though they vary in degrees of self-involvement, reality characteristics and structure. On the one hand, this variation is related to different states of consciousness and, on the other hand, it reflects individual forms of experience. As, despite all their similarities, dreams and waking fantasies offer substantial individual differences, only comparisons within a single person will facilitate more precise conclusions as to how the psychological activities of both states of consciousness differ in detail.

One of the few studies designed to examine the individuality of REM dreams and of the waking experience originated with Milton Kramer and his collaborators (Kramer, Roth & Palmer 1976). They pursued the question of what kind of motives appear in dreams and waking narratives. The researchers elicited 214 REM dreams from 12 female and 12 male experimental subjects. While awake, the same subjects were presented with pictures of the Thematic Apperception Test and asked to invent a story. The basis of the research team's evaluation was a list of ten different motives. The most frequent dream motives were 'Dominance,' 'Affiliation,' 'Aggression' and 'Achievement.' The prominence of these four motives was not limited to dreams, as they also led the list in the waking stories. The observation that dreams express the same motives as waking narratives should, however, be regarded only as general guidance; different emphases in motives need to be considered. For example, among women the dominance motive stood in first place, both while awake and in dreams. With men, dominance was only primary during waking narratives; in dreams, the affiliation motive took first place.

In evaluating our dream collection, we actually observed inter-individual as well as intra-individual differences in all features. Up to now, we only performed individual comparisons of waking fantasies and dreams with a few subjects. Here we encountered the interesting indication that dreams are more creative: although young adults, as well as children, employed individual bizarreness to different degrees, bizarre elements in dreams were always more marked than during their waking fantasies.

The following example illustrates how a waking fantasy and a dream are individually structured. One evening, a female student, 24 years-old, reported a fantasy during a relaxed waking state, stimulated by the image that she found herself on a meadow. She narrated her dream after awakening from the 4th REM phase.

Waking Fantasy:

"There is a meadow in front of the house, almost a garden, which is pretty wild, where many plants grow. I sit in front of the house, at a wooden table, with people who live near Bern. One can hear the river, it is sunny and we look around and decide that we'll go for a walk. And we go ahead and look at all the plants. And there is a bamboo forest, very cool and high. I have the feeling one could get lost in it. There are nettles, too, and cats are playing, and there are stones that make walking difficult. We go ahead and see some quite unusual flowers and plants. One of them is shaped like a chalice from which one could drink. Inside is a bulge, black and hot, with which the plant attracts insects, devours them, and after pollination, lets them go. It is really very quiet, we walk and chat, because we haven't seen each other in a long time."

Dream:

"Three of us are aboard a ship: a woman who is the captain, Henry, and I, and we are entering the port. It is as covered as if we were moving into a house. I sit up front and hold the clutch in my hand. We are entering a narrows, and we go much too fast, the shore and the building wall are getting close. There were two clutches, and we did not really know how to find the reverse, and the captain shouted that one has to pull it backwards. And she helped us get into reverse, and guided our hand. The ship stops suddenly, hard at the shore. And there was great excitement that everything had worked out so well. And Henry's parents are waiting ashore, and we go home together."

The suggestion of a meadow has stimulated the subject's fantasy to create an atmospheric image of nature. It is a harmonious setting, a walk with familiar people, although with a few, scattered tense moments: there are nettles and obstructing stones, and plants grow that first devour their victims and then release them. The fantasy's structure includes several bizarre elements: the bamboo forest represents a surprising scenery, and the thought that one might get lost in it seems odd. The exotic plant is not only unusual, but its symbolic empowerment seems to evoke a particular fascination.

The dream is characterized by a dynamic event, with the dreamer fully involved. She has taken control of a ship, which she is actually unable to steer, rushes much too rapidly into port, and avoids an accident only with the captain's help. The dream is bizarre in several ways. The port, which might be a house, provides an unreal setting. The captain acts oddly as she leaves the totally inexperienced dreamer in control during the peculiar speed-up of the ship, equipped with two clutches, and only comes to her rescue at the last moment.

If we compare the two reports, actually only differences really stand out. While the fantasy created an idyllic setting, albeit a rather fragile one, the dream offers a dramatic event. Both reports contain bizarre elements, but these differ in impact. During the fantasy, the bizarre seems imposed and not harmoniously integrated into events; within the dream, the bizarre is interwoven with the events and dictates their startling progress. Fantasy and dream differ further because of two opposite pairs. The loose association of images stands in contrast to a dramatic succession of events; the Fantasy Self's passive-contemplative attitude differs from the heavily involved position of the Dream Self. These polarities contribute to the impression that the dream is somehow more serious, more immediate and unaffected, while the fantasy appears more restrained, controlled and non-committal.

There is no single answer to the question of how independent or how closely linked dreams actually are: on the one hand, dreams are often related to individual waking experiences, to the ways in which people live and think. On the other hand, their manner of appearance displays unique characteristics, and they are always capable of turning the familiar into something novel.

11

In Search of Dreams:
A Summing Up

While experimental dream research is still in its early stages, drawing a balance does not seem premature. Extensive collection and evaluation of dreams in sleep laboratories has substantially expanded our knowledge of dream processes, and the time has come to revise certain popular views concerning the dream.

Physiological sleep measurement, a major methodological achievement, now enables us to elicit dreams under carefully controlled conditions. The continuous recording of nightly brainwave activity has made it possible to awaken subjects from their sleep at appropriate times, in order to question them about their dreams. Until this significant advance in method, we were limited to purely visual observation of a sleeping individual, unable to determine whether the subject was asleep, in a state between wakefulness and sleep, or simply in a relaxed waking state. Even the subjects' own claims concerning their state of consciousness, prior to awakening, do not necessarily correspond to their actual physiological condition. Dreamers may assert that they were awake, although the EEG indicated a sleeping state; they may feel that they were asleep, although the EEG clearly showed alpha rhythms.

In addition to pinpointing sleep states, recordings of brainwaves, eye movement and muscle tension provide a frame of reference that enables us to perform awakenings at specific points in time. The physiological signals show from which stage we awaken a sleeper, how long a given sleep period has lasted, whether there was prior short-term activation and how the awakening process occurs. This information permits us to integrate dream experiences into the cyclical pattern of sleep and to connect the dreams' occurrence and manner of appearance with each accompanying physiological state.

Physiological measurements are absolutely essential to achieve controlled dream elicitation. Still, their importance should not be exaggerated, as would be the case if one were to regard them as 'objective' dream indicators. Such an assumption would be erroneous, because dreams are not defined by brainwave patterns, rapid eye movements or other bodily functions; rather, dreams represent psychological experiences that belong to an alternate dimension of living. Although body and mind are complementarily related, they do not explain themselves either unilaterally or reciprocally.

Sleep measurements permit controlled dream elicitations, but dream researchers remain dependent on dreamers' self-observations, as they provide the only direct access to their dreams. We are able to awaken a sleeping subject under the most favorable conditions, but we cannot predict whether our sleeper will recall a dream, and we certainly cannot anticipate the dream's content.

Dream recall is particularly significant to research, being the only key capable of opening the gate to the world of dreams. Until now, however, it has remained unclear why recalling dreams is quite so incalculable and elusive and why it does not occur in the same way with everyone.

Among the many physiological and psychological variables that facilitate or hamper access to dreams, the specific sleep stage is of considerable importance. Awakenings in the sleep laboratory have shown unequivocally that REM sleep results more often in dream recall than does NREM sleep. On the average, we receive dream reports after nine out of ten REM awakenings, while only about every second awakening from NREM sleep is successful.

That dreams are more easily recalled from REM sleep could be explained by the fact that dreamers, in this case, are awakened from a particularly activated, close-to-waking stage of sleep. That dream recall is often lacking from the waking-remote NREM stages reflects, in our view, a difficult access to the sleep experience, rather than a sporadically occurring 'dreamlessness.' We refer to the plausible assumption that the psychological activity of a living organism never ceases completely, but, at most, adopts different qualities. Still, as we can comprehend a dream only by remembering, we are ultimately unable to answer the question whether dreams accompany sleep continually.

REM awakenings yield ample dream material, which is why we awaken our subjects from REM sleep. But, as recall fails even here on occasion, and with some people quite frequently, the specific sleep stage cannot, by itself, represent a sufficient condition for dream recall.

Of equal importance is the transition from sleep to the waking state. Just how someone awakens depends not only on whether the subject is awakened from a deep or a light sleep stage, but equally on the sleeper's immediate reaction to this change in the state of consciousness. If, following awakening, we do not abruptly abandon the dream world, but try to retain contact with it, there is a greater likelihood to recall a dream. If, conversely, our attention focuses immediately on the waking world, such distraction may hamper dream recollection, because new impressions tend to overshadow the dream.

Dream quality also has an influence on whether, on awakening, we place greater emphasis on the just-experienced dream or on our first impressions while awake. Dramatic and intensive dreams would seem to be most readily remembered, as their impact produces a stronger after-effect and they are therefore more easily seized than routine dreams. This statement cannot, however, be proven, as we do not know the nature of dreams that elude our memory. Still, this view gains support from the observation that striking waking experiences are more easily remembered than unimpressive events. Night terrors, with their archaic character, are further proof that even experiences in deep sleep will spontaneously penetrate our waking consciousness, as long as they are particularly intense.

A dream's nature not only contributes to its greater or lesser transference into the waking stage, but also determines how detailed and how accurate a dream report is. Each recollection of a dream represents an effort to reconstruct a holistic experience and to transform it into language. There are dreams that make it difficult for us to comprehend and remember all their nuances. This may be the case with dreams that are undetermined in structure and vague in content, but also with dreams whose elements are interwoven in unexpected and unusual ways. Memory of a dream is usually not very lasting, as is clearly expressed in repeated narrations of a night's dreams. This is partly due to the dream's very nature: dreams do not repeat firmly entrenched experience patterns from our memory, but create novel situations from known building blocks.

The specific sleep stage, the situation on awakening and the quality of sleep experience create significant conditions for dream recall, but are joined by the dreamer's attitude and motivation. A positive evaluation of dreams and fantasy, and the conviction that they contribute meaning to one's life, encourage vivid dream recall in that they favor unrestricted attention to all of a dream's facets.

Links between dream memory and these physiological and psychological factors are well documented. Still, we are unable to predict individual dream recalls, because we know too little about the impact of different factors or about the manner in which they support, supplement or even cancel-out each other.

Our laboratory procedure seeks to awaken subjects from a sleep stage that facilitates dream recall. Our subjects know that they will be awakened in a personalized way, addressed by name. We try to limit distractions and do not enter the bedroom while eliciting dreams. We allow for the motivation factor: as a rule, we select subjects who are good at recalling dreams and who have clearly indicated a positive attitude toward dreams by volunteering their participation in our experiments. Thus we are able to create a setting that encourages dream recall, but unable to influence the vividness of dreams, as we cannot write their dramatic scenario.

The collection of dreams within a sleep laboratory creates the most favorable conditions for eliciting dreams that we would miss at home. A frequent objection that the laboratory situation might create somewhat artificial dreams, which fail to reflect the 'true' dream world, has been disproven by several studies: comparisons of laboratory dreams with dream diaries, and not with incidentally remembered dreams, have failed to discern any marked differences in content.

Even when we collect several dreams in the laboratory during the course of one night, we can, of course, only capture a segment of dream activity. Still, such insights into the dream experience are more representative than spontaneous dream recall. Dreams elicited under laboratory conditions form, therefore, an appropriate basis for a comprehensive depiction of the structure and appearance of the dream world.

Dreams impress as integrated experiences: dreamers encounter a perceptual world that evokes their reflections and triggers their emotions. Dreams should not simply be regarded as a succession of images: the dream experience encompasses all our senses in the same order as the waking stage. While visual images dominate the hallucinated dream world, these are frequently supplemented by speech and listening, by tactile and bodily sensations, as well as, however rarely, by smell and taste.

Dreamers create a dream world in which they are personally included. But they are not just carried along by dream events: they participate, they think about the dream event, and they occasionally activate their knowledge or co-determine dream events by word and deed.

Thought processes during dreaming are doubly unlike those of the waking state: they are simpler, do not persist, and dreamers do not command the full extent of their knowledge. While dreaming, we deal predominantly with events of the moment. These demand our total attention. We do not ask, at the same time, what has gone before, what will happen later, or whether the roles we assume correspond to our self-image.

Emotions that occur in dreams cover the full range known from the waking state. Specific emotions, such as joy, fear or anger, appear in every second dream, while other dreams are only associated with a single mood state or lack emotional reaction altogether. Although emotions in dreams may be quite intense, they do not always accompany a dream. Emotions, like thoughts, apparently are not a necessary condition to experience a dream as if it were real. Quite a few dreams embroil dreamers in eventful happenings, but fail to arouse specific feelings or mood states.

In view of the many dreams that are emotionally neutral, the concept that dreams are constantly accompanied by emotions cannot be maintained. The additional assumption, that dreams are mainly subject to negative feelings, should also be revised. The ratio of positive to negative dreams is, on the whole, in balance; only where specific feelings are involved do negative affects predominate.

The sporadic appearance of dream feelings and the discontinuous awareness of emotional impressions are comparable to the waking experience—there, too, we are not continuously aware of intensive feelings and lasting moods. Feelings of self-evaluation in the social context, such as guilt and shame, appear only rarely in dreams. This may be due to the fact that the dreamer usually does not judge herself or himself against a background of a lifetime's fears and hopes.

Dreams create eventful and action-oriented life situations that manifest themselves through varying arrangements and changing décor. The staging of dream plays brings forth many familiar settings, occasionally alienated by individually substituted elements, but, more frequently, fresh sets are constructed. Of course, the dream stage is not always designed and illuminated in complete detail. It frequently lacks a geographically fixed locale, and it often merely provides the background for the dream event.

It is certainly not surprising that dreams occur in varying landscapes or at different places. If this were not the case, dreams would not be experienced in realistic terms. The inclusion of familiar, unknown, or not quite specific sceneries seems to depend on whether they fit the dream event and can be integrated into the overall dream pattern. Viewed this way, dream environments are of rather secondary importance, unless they come to occupy a central position through sudden change, as when a landscape turns into a theatrical scenery, or when they come to convey meanings that force the dreamer to switch activity, as when the sleep laboratory is transformed into a bathroom.

The most varied people and creatures appear on the dream stage. As dramatic producer, the dreaming subject may prefer a cast of familiar and well-known figures, but the dreamer also assigns leading parts to strangers, fills the stage with extras and, if it fits the scenario, adds professionals and animals. The manifold characters that make their appearance in dreams reflect the dreamer's horizon of experience, which is not only concerned with close acquaintances but seeks novel encounters as well.

The large part played by strange dream figures is actually not surprising, as we constantly encounter unknown persons in waking life as well. It is notable, however, that dreamers deal exclusively with strangers in nearly every third dream. Furthermore, unfamiliar dream figures often remain strangers, even though the dreamer engages them in a joint undertaking. This points to a particular feature of dream experience, whereby we tolerate the strange apparently more readily or unconcernedly than in our waking existence, where we seek to become familiar with a strange counterpart.

In most dreams, dreamers are actively engaged in events, although they are able to create dream situations in which they are merely observers, or in which they do not participate at all. The Dream Self is active in multiple ways,

mainly of a social nature. Communications with dream figures predominate, largely in the form of conversations. It is
notable how few dreams deal in purely superficial chatter
and conventional ritual. When dream persons meet, they
do not usually ask, "How are you?" and they do not spend
time with talk about the weather. They do not bore each
other, but quickly get down to cases. Dreams are characterized particularly by linear and event-oriented scenarios.
Dreamers do not constantly wonder who they are, how they
impress others and what results their actions might have.
Still, they rarely act out of character, but usually participate, quite unsophisticated and involved, in dream events.

The high degree of self-participation in dreams is not
particularly surprising. After all, why should dreamers create events, night after night, that do not involve them? This
may also explain why dreams deal largely in everyday
events, rather than in especially spectacular happenings:
dreams concern us, at the outset, because we play a crucial
role, move actively within the dream world and constantly
experience something new.

Dreams create ever-changing units of experience,
where the familiar is constantly transformed into new, integrated designs. If we judge dream designs by standards of
the real world, comparing them to our experiences within it,
we are primarily struck by their inventive realism. Dreams
appear most often as realistic-fictional when they create situations that originate in reality, but do not correspond to it,
incorporating unexpected and quite unlikely events. Such
bizarre touches may apply to all kinds of dream building
blocks and surface at different points of the dream. It is,
however, notable that bizarre phenomena are usually scattered within a dream event in a manner that does not question our basic relation to reality.

Frequently, dreams resemble reality entirely, but even
such realistic dreams do not totally repeat previous experiences in detail. A dream's link to reality most certainly does
not imply that, either while being experienced or reviewed,
it becomes boring or monotonous. In this respect, dreams

never give a banal impression, because they simulate a reality that involves us, in which we can find our way around, and which presents us with novel experiences.

It may seem surprising how rarely dreams expand into the dimension of the fantastic. Such dreams do occur occasionally, but are not characteristic of the dream experience. In fact, they are exceptions that leave strong impressions and thus encourage hasty generalizations. The limited number of reality-remote dreams may have a special reason: if dreams were to abduct us, night after night, into a totally fantastic and alien world, we would have to reestablish our identity each morning and make sure of the daily world's solidity. The moderately bizarre nature of dreams permits us to be neither frightened by our nightly fantasies, nor to turn away from them in boredom.

Experimental dream research has undertaken numerous studies designed to relate dreams to accompanying body processes. Discovery of REM sleep, and its relation to the recall of vivid dreams, initially led to the one-sided assumption that dreams were restricted to cyclically-occurring REM stages. This seemed evident, as particular activation features of REM sleep appeared to correspond to the dreamer's psychological activity, and rapid eye movements to the visuality of dreams.

Eventually, when it could no longer be ignored that dreams occur even after awakenings from sleep stages that showed no significant activation features, the equation of REM sleep with dream sleep had to be abandoned. As this shortcut had been so convincing, many researchers continued to find it difficult to view dreams during other sleep stages as equally relevant and to incorporate them into their considerations regarding the generation and function of dreaming.

As dreams accompany all stages of sleep, the question arises whether there exist correspondingly different categories of sleep experiences. Available results have, so far, resulted in no definitive delimitation of dreams during different stages of sleep. NREM dreams can be just as perceptual, vivid and impressive as REM dreams. We are, therefore, not readily able to tell on the basis of a report from which sleep stage it originates. NREM dreams are, however, as a rule shorter than REM dreams, and this difference causes NREM dreams to be less elaborate in content and structure.

Ultimately, it cannot be determined whether dreams during NREM sleep are, in fact, more fragmentary and less dramatic or whether it is just not possible to recall this experience completely. If NREM dreams are viewed as more thoughtlike, we have to allow that a hampered recall process may cause impressions to fade or disappear. By comparison, a more fluid transition from dream to waking state permits different aspects of the dream experience to enter our consciousness more vividly and with a more lasting effect.

Dreams during NREM sleep have not been as thoroughly researched as REM dreams, and most studies have emphasized the features that prompt them to lag behind REM dreams. NREM dreams tended to be described as 'incomplete dreams.' We need to examine in greater depth whether they might represent a unique category of experience, employing patterns that draw on different memory storages and utilize other structural materials.

On the one hand, the sources from which dreams gain their elements may be traced easily, as all dream building blocks are taken from our memory, our knowledge of the world and our personal experiences. On the other hand, we know very little about the origin of individual dreams and about the matter in which they are combined into new situations. Dreams show a preference for day residues, selecting material much less from a memory bank that is inaccessible to a waking grasp. This illustrates a close relationship between memory traces of waking and sleep, as nearness in time is an important precondition for the selection of dream elements. It is additionally notable that dreams prefer building blocks that fit into a dream's narrative and that contribute to the development of situations which resemble reality. These elements are frequently so appropriately selected that they may make a dream uniquely meaningful to the dreamer.

It remains unclear, however, what rules prompt specific day residues or impressions to enter dreams during sleep. Attempts to influence dreams experimentally have shown clearly that the dream follows its own game plans. It keeps its own counsel on whether to respond to a suggestion or signal, and if it does take them into account, it remodels them in unpredictable ways and places them into a different frame of reference.

Dreams incorporate waking experiences and reveal how we deal with our images of the world during an altered state of consciousness. This finding is significantly documented during the developmental stages of dreaming among children and youths. The dream world of children changes in accordance with the development of their thinking and of the power of their imagination. Once children are able to think up stories while awake, they are also capable of creating action-oriented dream events. Only when they have developed a self-image are they ready to occupy an active role in their dreams. Children's dreams reflect self-development and demonstrate how the horizon of their experience expands.

While different stages of personal development are accompanied by striking changes in dream activity, dreams of women and men differ only in degrees of emphasis among individual dream features. Men generally interact more frequently with male dream figures. The structure of their dreams is more reality-oriented and they claim more positive dream emotions. Nevertheless, the dream world of both sexes does not differ basically. This is not particularly surprising, as their waking experiences demonstrate more commonalities than differences.

Dreams exhibit many parallels in structure and content with our waking fantasies. They utilize the same creative devices and their building blocks originate with the same waking experiences. Dreams and waking fantasies call upon related creative potentials: they construct new worlds, with an ever-changing population. The observation that memory data are creatively transformed does not only apply to the dream, but is an expression of the human mind's basic ability to rearrange experiences. Still, although the structure and progress of dreams nearly always give the impression of being genuine and immediate, waking fantasies occasionally appear as deliberate and detached.

Dream and fantasy also share common ground in the broad scope of their scenarios, which range from reality-oriented situations to fantastic happenings. Dreams as well as fantasies may narrate ordinary plots, just as extraordinary events may occur in dreams and fantasies. At this point, the two areas of experience overlap, dreams may appear wake-like, while fantasies may seem dreamlike. Bizarre designs may stand out among fantasies because of their extreme manner. But dreams, being generally imbued by a moderate degree of the bizarre, are ultimately more bizarre.

Actually, dreams differ from waking fantasies in only one distinctive aspect: they cannot be consciously controlled, and they transport us into a virtual reality, where we act as if unaware that we are in a world of our own creation. This particular nature of the dream possibly exists only because, while dreaming, we are just not aware that we are dreaming. But it is also feasible that we do not question the reality of our dreams, because they mainly create reality-oriented situations.

Our attempt to describe experience during sleep has concentrated on dreams in general, designed to define the dream experience comprehensively and in its typical features. Inevitably, such efforts at classification lead from extensive concretization of individual dreams to abstract considerations. The manifold designs and wide thematic repertoire of dreams nevertheless also find expression within higher-level categories. Dreams move among different polarities: static-dynamic, fragmentary-coherent, thoughtlike-sensory, or, disconnected-integrated. Within a given dream, which may range from positions remote from reality to others close to reality, the Dream Self plays such different roles as the emotionally involved or detached, the event-oriented or reflective.

Dreams permit insight into psychological activity during sleep. Their manner of appearance has stimulated numerous theories concerning their origin and function, ranging from the largely physiological to the purely psychological. Our considerations concerning the function of dreams start with the supposition that the psyche of a living organism is active at all times. Even during sleep, our memory bank constantly emits images: internal signals are acknowledged and, within certain limitations, external information is registered, evaluated and absorbed. The manifold dream processes may primarily and quite generally serve the continuity of psychological activity—at a time when attention toward the outer world has been reduced, a world that stimulates our thoughts and images constantly while we are awake.

Still, psychological activity during sleep is not only continuous; dreams offer scenically structured experiences and arrange memory elements that are by no means selected accidentally. This coherent creative power of dreams shows that the human psyche utilizes sleep-time to transform memories and waking impressions into fresh experiences, thus giving them a new life. These meaningful dream elaborations may contribute to the comprehension of waking experiences and to attempts at problem-solving.

We also assume that psychological activity during sleep follows the principle of employing its energy continually, but of not to exhaust it, either. Following this assumption, dreams must inevitably be mundane, as the psyche uses its energies economically, creating a balance between the familiar and the novel, between activity and passivity, between stimulation and relaxation.

The significant gain from dreams in personal life may, however, be seen in their function of providing a setting, night after night, where we perceive ourselves as free of social duties, of critical self-evaluations, and are able to deal creatively with waking experience. Dreams permit us to enjoy a sort of second existence. While it is certainly not always rosy, it is forever new. And it is an existence that permits us to engage in novel experiences, but also to deal with the world quite playfully.

Bibliography

Antrobus, J. 1983. REM and NREM sleep reports: Comparison of word frequencies by cognitive classes. *Psychophysiology 20(5)*:562–568.

Aserinsky, E. and Kleitman, N. 1953. Regularly occurring periods of eye motility and concomitant phenomena during sleep. *Science 118*:273–274.

Berger, H. 1931. Ueber das Elektroenkephalogramm des Menschen. *Archiv für Psychiatrie und Nervenkrankheiten 94*:16–60.

Borbély, A. 1984. Schlafgewohnheiten, Schlafqualität und Schlafmittelkonsum der Schweizer Bevölkerung. Ergebnisse einer Repräsentativumfrage. *Schweizerische Aerztezeitung 65(34)*:1606–1613.

Bosinelli, M., Cicogna, P. and Cavallero, C. 1983. A model for dream modifications. *Sleep Research 12*:184.

Boss, M. 1953. *Der Traum und seine Auslegung.* Bern: Huber.

Calkins, M. W. 1893. Statistics of dreams. *American Journal of Psychology 5*:311–343.

Cartwright, R. D. 1974. The influence of a conscious wish on dreams: A methodological study of dream meaning and function. *Journal of Abnormal Psychology 83(4)*:387–393.

Cartwright, R D., Lloyd, S., Knight, S. and Trenholme, I. 1984. Broken dreams: A study of the effects of divorce and depression on dream content. *Psychiatry 47*:251–259.

Cavallero, C., Cicogna, P. and Bosinelli, M. 1988. Mnemonic activation in dream production. In W. P. Koella, F. Obál, H. Schulz & P. Visser (Eds.), *Sleep '86. Proceedings of the Eighth European Congress on Sleep Research. Szeged, September 1986*, pp. 91–94. Stuttgart: Gustav Fischer.

Dement, W. and Wolpert, E. A. 1958. Relationships in the manifest content of dreams occurring on the same night. *Journal of Nervous and Mental Disease 126*:568–578.

Domhoff, G. W. 1993. Do dreams have meaning? *A quantitative approach to an age-old question.* (in press)

Fisher, Ch., Byrne, J., Edwards, A. and Kahn, E. 1970. A psychophysiological study of nightmares. *Journal of the American Psychoanalytic Association 18(4)*: 747–782.

Foulkes, W. D. 1962. Dream reports from different stages of sleep. *Journal of Abnormal and Social Psychology 65(1)*: 14–25.

Foulkes, D. 1978. *A grammar of dreams*. New York: Basic Books.

Foulkes, D. 1982. *Children's dreams. Longitudinal studies.* New York: John Wiley & Sons.

Foulkes, D. and Schmidt, M. 1983. Temporal sequence and unit composition in dream reports from different stages of sleep. *Sleep 6(3)*:265–280.

Foulkes, D., Sullivan, B., Kerr, N. H. and Brown, L. 1988. Appropriateness of dream feelings to dreamed situations. *Cognition and Emotion 2(1)*:29–39.

French, T. M. 1954. *The integration of behavior*. Chicago: University of Chicago.

Freud, S. 1964. *The interpretation of dreams*. London: Hogarth. Original publication, 1900: Die Traumdeutung.

Gardner, R., Grossman, W. I., Roffwarg, H. P. and Weiner, H. 1975. The relationship of small limb movements during REM sleep to dreamed limb action. *Psychosomatic Medicine 37(2)*:147–159.

Gass, E., Gerne, M., Loepfe, M., Meier, B., Rothenfluh, Th. and Strauch, I. 1983. *Traumdatenbank (TDB). Manual für die standardisierte Gewinnung von Traumberichten im Labor und die Handhabung einer zugehörigen Datenbank auf dem Computer.* Unpublished Manual, Zurich University, Psychological Institute, Department of Clinical Psychology.

Haas, H., Guitar-Amsterdamer, H. and Strauch, I. 1988. Die Erfassung bizarrer Elemente im Traum. *Schweizerische Zeitschrift für Psychologie 47(4)*:237–247.

Hacker, F. 1911. Systematische Traumbeobachtungen mit besonderer Berücksichtigung der Gedanken. *Archiv für die Gesamte Psychologie 21*:1–131.

Hall, C. S. 1953. *The meaning of dreams.* New York: Harper.

Hall, C. S. 1984. "A ubiquitous sex difference in dreams" revisited. *Journal of Personality and Social Psychology 46(5)*:1109–1117.

Hall, C. S., Domhoff, G. W., Blick, K. A. and Weesner, K. E. 1982. The dreams of college men and women in 1950 and 1980: A comparison of dream contents and sex differences. *Sleep 5(2)*:188–194.

Hall, C. S. and Van de Castle, R. L. 1966. *The content analysis of dreams.* New York: Appleton-Century-Crofts.

Hartmann, E. 1984. *The nightmare. The psychology and biology of terrifying dreams.* New York: Basic Books.

Hervey de Saint-Denys. 1964. *Les rêves et les moyens de les diriger.* Paris: Claude Tschou. Original publication, 1867.

Hobson, J. A. 1988. *The dreaming brain.* New York: Basic Books.

Hobson, J. A. and McCarley, R. W. 1977. The brain as a dream state generator: An activation-synthesis hypothesis of the dream process. *American Journal of Psychiatry 134(12)*:1335–1348.

Jacobson, E. 1938. *You can sleep well. The ABC's of restful sleep for the average person.* New York: Whittlesey House.

Jung, C. G. 1928. *Über die Energetik der Seele. Psychologische Abhandlungen, Bd.II.* Zürich: Rascher.

Köhler, P. 1912. Beiträge zur systematischen Traumbeobachtung. *Archiv für die Gesamte Psychologie 22*:415–483.

Koukkou, M. and Lehmann, D. 1983. Dreaming: The functional state-shift hypothesis. A neuropsychophysiological model. *British Journal of Psychiatry 142*:221–231.

Koulack, D. and Goodenough, D. R. 1976. Dream recall and dream recall failure: An arousal-retrieval model. *Psychological Bulletin 83(5)*:975–984.

Kramer, M., Hlasny, R., Jacobs, G. and Roth, T. 1976. Do dreams have meaning? An empirical inquiry. *American Journal of Psychiatry 133(7)*:778–781.

Kramer, M., Roth, T. and Palmer, T. 1976. The psychological nature of the "Rem" dream. I. A comparison of the Rem dream report and T.A.T. stories. *The Psychiatric Journal of the University of Ottawa 1(3)*:128–135.

Kramer, M., Whitman, R. M., Baldridge, B. J. and Lansky, L. M. 1964. Patterns of dreaming: The interrelationship of the dreams of a night. *Journal of Nervous and Mental Disease 139(5)*:426–439.

Kuhlo, W. and Lehmann, D. 1964. Das Einschlaferleben und seine neurophysiologischen Korrelate. *Archiv für Psychiatrie und Zeitschrift für die gesamte Neurologie 205*:687–716.

Ladd, G. T. 1892. Contribution to the psychology of visual dreams. *Mind 1*:299–304.

Maury, A. 1865. *Le sommeil et les rêves*. Paris: Librairie Académique.

Meier Faber, B. 1988. *Psychophysiologische Faktoren der REM-Traumerinnerung*. Dissertation, Philosophical Faculty I, Zurich University.

Monroe, L. J., Rechtschaffen, A., Foulkes, D. and Jensen, J. 1965. Discriminability of REM and NREM reports. *Journal of Personality and Social Psychology 2(3)*:456–460.

Moser, U., Pfeifer, R., Schneider, W. and von Zeppelin, I. 1980. *Computersimulation of dream processes*. Report No. 6 of the Interdisciplinary Center for Conflict Research, Sociological Institute, Psychological Institute, Zurich University.

Purcell, S., Mullington, J., Moffitt, A., Hoffmann, R. and Pigeau, R. 1986. Dream self-reflectiveness as a learned cognitive skill. *Sleep 9(3)*:423–437.

Rechtschaffen, A. 1978. The single-mindedness and isolation of dreams. *Sleep 1*:97–109.

Rechtschaffen, A. and Buchignani, C. 1983. Visual dimensions and correlates of dream images. *Sleep Research 12*:189.

Rechtschaffen, A. and Kales, A. 1968 (Eds.). *A manual of standardized terminology, techniques and scoring system for sleep stages of human subjects*. Washington, D.C.: Public Health Service, U.S. Government.

Riemann, D., Löw, H., Schredl, M., Wiegand, M., Dippel, B. and Berger, M. 1990. Traum und Depression. Experimentelle Untersuchungen zu Traumerinnerung und Trauminhalt depressiv erkrankter Patienten. *TW Neurologie und Psychiatrie 4*:531–543.

Roffwarg, H. P., Dement, W. C., Muzio, J. N. and Fisher, C. 1962. Dream imagery: Relationship to rapid eye movements of sleep. *Archives of General Psychiatry 7*:235–258.

Roffwarg, H. P., Herman, J. H., Bowe-Anders, C. and Tauber, E. S. 1978. The effects of sustained alterations of waking visual input on dream content. A preliminary report. In A. M. Arkin, J. S. Antrobus and S. J. Ellman (Eds.), *The mind in sleep: Psychology and psychophysiology*, pp. 295–349. Hillsdale, New Jersey: Lawrence Erlbaum.

Shimizu, A. and Inoue, T. 1986. Dreamed speech and speech muscle activity. *Psychophysiology 23(2)*:210–214.

Silberer, H. 1919. *Der Traum*. Stuttgart: Enke.

Snyder, F. 1970. The phenomenology of dreaming. In H. Madow and C. Snow (Eds.), *The psychodynamic implication of the physiological studies on dreams*, pp. 124–151. Springfield, Illinois: Charles C. Thomas.

Strauch, I. and Meier, B. 1989. Das emotionale Erleben im REM-Traum. *Schweizerische Zeitschrift für Psychologie 48(4)*:233–240.

Uslar, D. von 1964. *Der Traum als Welt: Untersuchungen zur Ontologie und Phänomenologie des Traums*. Pfullingen: Neske. Third revised edition, 1990, Stuttgart: Hirzel.

Vogel, G., Foulkes, D. and Trosman, H. 1966. Ego functions and dreaming during sleep onset. *Archives of General Psychiatry 14*:238–248.

Winget, C. and Kramer, M. 1979. *Dimensions of dreams*. Gainesville: University Presses.

Index